Legitimate Opposition

Legitimate Opposition

ALEXANDER S. KIRSHNER

Yale UNIVERSITY PRESS

New Haven and London

Yale University Press books may be purchased in quantity for
educational, business, or promotional use. For information, please
e-mail sales.press@yale.edu (U.S. office) or sales@yaleup.co.uk
(U.K. office).

Set in Minion type by IDS Infotech Ltd., Chandigarh, India.
Printed in the United States of America.

Library of Congress Control Number: 2021952516
ISBN 978-0-300-24346-8 (paperback : alk. paper)

A catalogue record for this book is available from the British
Library.

This paper meets the requirements of ANSI/NISO Z39.48-1992
(Permanence of Paper).

10 9 8 7 6 5 4 3 2 1

For Hélène

Contents

Acknowledgments

This book was written in Durham, North Carolina. I am so appreciative of the colleagues, staff, and administrators, too many to list, who have contributed to making this a fruitful environment in which to research, write, and teach. Duke Political Science is a vibrant intellectual community. And I am glad to be a part of it.

I am especially grateful to Michael Gillespie, Ruth Grant, Jack Knight, and Tom Spragens, the pillars of Duke's theory community—a community sustained through their hard work over many years. I have profited personally and intellectually from my ongoing conversations with Michael, Ruth, Jack, and Tom (as well as from their direct feedback on my work). Geneviève Rousselière arrived on campus more recently, and I have gained enormously from being her colleague. Jed Atkins and Ian MacMullen, members of our group, also contributed to this project, saving me from many errors. Graduate students have made Duke an exciting place to undertake this project. Thanks to Sam Bagg, Lucy Britt, Judah Buckner, Eric Cheng, Colin Devine, Mike Hawley, Jihyun Jeong, Chris Kennedy, Jacob Little, Antong Liu, Charlie Nathan, Alex Oprea, Wan Ning Seah, Brian Spisiak, Isak Tranvik, Will Wittels, and Somia Youssef. Special acknowledgment is owed to Jeff Spinner-Halev. I rely on him as a political theorist and as a friend.

Significant progress on this project was made while I was a fellow at Princeton's University Center of Human Values. My year in Princeton was a thrill. The UCHV's intellectual community is remarkable and inspiring. My work benefited from my interactions with the faculty and fellows. I am indebted to Chuck Beitz, Melissa Lane, Kim Lane Scheppele, Steve Macedo, Alan Patton, Philip Pettit, and Annie Stilz, all of whom made time to discuss this project. Special thanks to Jan-Werner Müller for his intellectual generosity and support. I am obliged to Maureen Killeen for enriching my experience at the UCHV. Thanks are due to the other fellows and especially Nicholas Vrousalis and Claudio López-Guerra. They are impressive political philosophers. I am grateful for their friendship.

Many scholars have given me feedback, advice, and encouragement through this process. I am indebted to Corey Brettschneider, Turku Isiksel, Anthoula Malkopoulou, Russ Muirhead, Shmulik Nili, Andrea Pozas-Loyo, Melissa Schwartzberg, and Ian Shapiro. Thanks also to the Yale University Press and particularly Bill Frucht for guiding this project to completion. I am also grateful to the anonymous reviewers whose suggestions and questions improved the final draft.

In the acknowledgments for my first book, I noted that my family had been growing. Happily, it is even larger now. Thanks to my parents, Judith and Jules, as well as to Françoise and Jean-Raymond. I am grateful to Jessica, Dan, Rebecca, and Evan. My children, Élodie and Jules, are magic—I am grateful for their silliness and smiles. And, finally, thanks to my love, Hélène, to whom this book is dedicated.

Some material from chapter 4 was previously published in "Legitimate Opposition, Ostracism, and the Law of Democracy in Ancient Athens," *Journal of Politics* 78, no. 4 (2016): 1094–1106. © 2021 Southern Political Science Association. All rights reserved.

1

Introduction

In political systems defined by legitimate opposition, those who hold power allow their rivals to peacefully challenge and displace them. And those who have lost power do not seek to sabotage the winners even as they pursue future victories.

Across the globe, legitimate opposition is under assault. Donald Trump, the former president of the United States, refused to acknowledge that he had been defeated by Joe Biden, pressuring state officials and the vice president to subvert the electoral process, stoking unjustified suspicion of his loss, and instigating the ransack of the US Capitol. Were these actions surprising? Not really. Prior to the election, Trump made his intentions evident, insisting he would not accept the outcome were he to lose. And four years earlier, he had famously threatened to imprison his electoral rival, Hillary Clinton. Trump epitomizes the rejection of legitimate opposition. And the threat to the United States' system of legitimate opposition may not have subsided. But Trump is hardly a singular example. The governing party of Hungary has deployed the legal and institutional resources of the state to cut the legs from beneath its challengers. Populist parties hostile to practices allowing their opponents to win power are gaining strength all over the world. And the military in Myanmar has just demolished its country's experiment with competitive elections.

Challenges to the play of legitimate opposition have generated dismay, political conflict, and not a few books about threats to democracy (Snyder 2017; Mounk 2018; Przeworski 2019). At the same time, the imperiled political systems are shockingly imperfect, far distant from our democratic ideals. Consider the United States. In an electorally important district—Florida— former felons who have completed their sentence are only allowed to vote if they pay a fine. Yet many have no path to ascertaining how much they owe. It is a preposterous, Kafkaesque spin on the practice of electoral democracy.[1] This is not a lonely example with limited implications beyond Florida. Recent years have witnessed successful efforts to make it more difficult for certain citizens to vote, to remove some voters from the voting rolls, to barricade officeholders in power, and to undo the impact of lost elections and referenda (A. Sullivan 2019; Smith 2020; Timm 2019; Maguire 2016; Smith and Davey 2018; Gardner and Rozsa 2020). Mechanisms for distributing political power at the federal and state levels allow minorities to more easily control the course of affairs than majorities (Wasserman 2017; Bronner and Rakich 2021). The infirmity here is not merely institutional. American politicians evidently do not fear that their constituents will punish them for taking the actions just described; their constituents evidently do not prioritize the achievement and maintenance of democracy. And the United States is not unique in this regard.

This is an unsettling moment, one generating discordant responses: reasonable fear that electoral regimes will be undermined; grave dissatisfaction with the undemocratic flaws of the systems under assault. Scholarly and popular works often tackle these issues individually. Some works extol the value of democracy and call for its defense. Others outline all the ways our existing regimes fall short (Levitsky and Ziblatt 2018; Klarman 2020). As I hope to persuade you, this bifurcated approach leads us to misperceive and misunderstand our current moment. Accordingly, I follow a different course. In this book, I try to get my hands around a practice that is fundamental to modern representative government—legitimate opposition—and, in doing so, make sense of *both* our fears and our dissatisfactions.

A simple idea powers my argument: legitimate opposition should be distinguished from democracy. Doing so will help us to reevaluate and reappraise legitimate opposition, to look at it with fresh eyes. Following this path, I believe, will help us come to grips with whether opposition warrants active, even militant defense (Kirshner 2014; López-Guerra and Kirshner 2020). It will help us understand why it is wrong for political actors to reject the practice. And it will help us appreciate why we should fear the collapse of the United States' competitive system even while we acknowledge its long distance from our ideals.

On my view, legitimate opposition *can* be a crucial element of a democratic political system. It can also be crucial element of a system that is well short of democracy. By implication, we need an independent account of opposition's value, an account that does not depend solely on its relation to egalitarian self-rule. There are obviously many definitions of democracy. I treat it as a political system that instantiates individuals' political equality, including their capacity to rule (e.g., by voting) and their equal interest in being ruled well. Building on the initial sentences of this book, by "legitimate opposition" I mean the regular, rule-based, nonviolent competition for power. I spell out this minimal definition shortly, but in systems of opposition, political losers cede their place to winners, and winners do not keep losers from challenging them in the future. Nancy Rosenblum has coined a term neatly capturing the practice: "regulated rivalry" (2008, 123).

The attack on the US Capitol in early January 2021 elicited widespread recognition that legitimate opposition is precious. There is something of the uncanny at work when political actors, individuals whose lives revolve around the pursuit of influence, willingly give up their positions, encourage their supporters to accept a loss, and work with those who have defeated them. In the months after the 2020 presidential election, Americans were exposed to the dread and bitter anxiety of an unsuccessful political transition, of the failure of legitimate opposition.

No doubt, those instinctive responses capture something critical. Yet in this work, I drive beyond that deep sense of unease, answering the following interrelated questions: What is lost when a flawed, real-world polity undermines legitimate opposition? And does opposition warrant deference and defense from leading political actors and everyday citizens alike?

Traditionally, normative explorations of legitimate opposition consider opposition as an element in a scheme of democratic government, or they explore the personal ethics of democratic opposition and political partisanship (Christiano 1996; Shapiro 1999; Goodin 2008; Muirhead 2014; White and Ypi 2016; Schedler 2020). I concede that as a practical matter, there is a good reason to follow those paths. It may be difficult for nonscholars to embrace a practice like legitimate opposition if they do not associate it, mechanically, with democracy. Still, if one's theory of opposition's value rests on conditions unmet in most societies, we will still face the question of whether to value the practice in those societies. Similarly, one's ethical admonitions will inevitably be blunted if the theory relies on practices and attitudes characteristic of an exemplary and therefore distant democracy. Approaching opposition with a bit more skepticism and a bit more realism will help us elude these theoretical obstacles. For that reason, distinguishing opposition from democracy is a bullet worth the bite.

Outlining what I call the *adversarial conception of legitimate opposition*, I explore the value of opposition as it is. Systems of opposition are manned by individuals who often treat each other as adversaries, not just as partners. These systems are often unfair and infuriatingly unequal. Why might they merit costly protection? Because opposition instantiates a valuable form of respect for the agency of those who can participate. Even if people are not treated as equals, even if some individuals' votes count more than others, even if the wealthy are able to exercise outlandish influence, even if citizens do not view each other as partners and are riven by partisan loyalties, competitive systems of opposition still allow opponents of the government to peacefully challenge those who hold power. They allow large groups to influence the course of political affairs without fear of violent reprisal and bloody conflict. Opposition is, I conclude, an essentially liberal practice. It is not necessarily an egalitarian one. Of course, opposition is often unruly, nasty, and uninspiring. It does not guarantee a liberal society, liberal outcomes, or even its own stability. But opposition's procedures necessarily treat people as actors, as coauthors of political life. Given the difficult conditions of political life, legitimate opposition is an achievement.

The real-world rivals to opposition, such as electoral autocracy, are disrespectful of individuals' capacity to play a constructive role in politics. They manipulate and subvert citizens' agency. They demean and debase. Garry Kasparov, the great Russian chess champion, put his finger on this dynamic when Vladimir Putin announced his intention to run for reelection in 2018: "Did he also announce the results? Would save everyone a lot time and effort" (Kasparov 2017). Russia is an easy fit for my argument. The nature of its electoral system is only one of many reasons to find that regime objectionable. But, as I will show, even in ostensibly liberal Singapore—the ideal liberal autocracy—the electoral system is designed so that no matter how a participant votes, for or against the regime, she will advance the regime's ends (Gandhi and Lust-Okar 2009; Simpser 2013). Singapore's political system does not treat citizens as actors. It treats them as pawns.

The adversarial conception of legitimate opposition turns on the value of political agency. That normative argument is complemented by a revisionist reconstruction of opposition's history, a reconsideration freed from two common assumptions: that opposition is modern and that it must have emerged with political parties or representative democracy. Reevaluating opposition's past in this light generates a series of insights into its character and its value:

- Opposition clearly marked the political life of the ancient polities of Athens and Republican Rome.
- The Roman experience illustrates an underappreciated virtue of opposition: it is robust. It facilitates the valuable exercise of agency under an array of conditions, from those that are highly attractive to those that are very far from democratic. This flexibility is a distinctive feature of opposition. And it allows us to regard opposition as an achievement even under circumstances bearing little resemblance to our political ideals.
- When critiquing opposition and advocating for alternatives, political theorists often assume the validity of *clockwork constitutionalism*—a view that political actors will act like figures in a clock, moving in accordance with the desires of institutional designers. As I argue, works that make this assumption are flawed, leading to gross underestimations of adversarial opposition's value.
- Contra the arguments of justly esteemed scholars like Richard Hofstadter (1969), nonpartisan, regular, rule-based opposition was already accepted in Britain *before*

the emergence of political parties. Were this not the case, it would be impossible to make sense of the vigorous electoral contests of that period.

- The emergence of a distinctively *partisan* or *organized* mode of opposition was driven by the perceived failure of a widely accepted constitutional principle: the separation of powers. In modern regimes, with executives wielding the resources to bully past institutional boundaries, organized oppositions do the grunt work of limiting the government's power and safeguarding opportunities to exercise agency. Normative defenses of parties that presume a linkage between democracy and parties overlook this critical role and therefore underrate systematically the value of parties.

- Efforts to establish a democracy without opposition during the French Revolution failed and illustrate the difficulty facing people searching for alternatives to legitimate opposition.

One might reasonably ask, Why do we need an adversarial conception of legitimate opposition? Throughout this book, I refer to the dominant, traditional approach as the *democratic conception of legitimate opposition*. On the orthodox view, the answer to the motivating question of this book is plain. What is lost when opposition is undermined? Democracy. Indeed, it would be shocking to hear anything else. Why? Because proponents of this approach, scholars and political commentators alike, treat legitimate opposition as intrinsically democratic. It is a testament to the democratic conception that it is espoused and understood as a given by influential democratic theorists of almost every possible stripe—from agonist theorists such as Chantal Mouffe to liberals such as Nancy Rosenblum, from deliberative theorists like Robert Goodin to the political theorists and empirically minded political scientists who embrace a Schumpeterian, bare-bones conception of democracy, like Ian Shapiro and Adam Przeworski (Mouffe 2000; Rosenblum 2008; Goodin 2008; Shapiro 1999).[2]

The democratic conception of legitimate opposition shapes key debates in political theory. For instance, the emergence of populism has triggered an avalanche of political theorizing describing its causes, consequences, and meaning (Mudde and Rovira Kaltwasser 2012; Urbinati 2014; Rovira Kaltwasser et al. 2017). Populists often pillory systems of opposition because they empower "enemies of the people." Once in power, populists may graduate from rhetorical assaults, sabotaging the institutions and practices associated with legitimate opposition (Müller 2016). Undemocratic inequality and elitism are sometimes identified as potential drivers of support for populist forces (Arditi 2004). But the vast majority of theoretical works on the topic take the democratic conception of legitimate opposition for granted. If populists pose a threat to opposition, they pose a threat to democracy (Rummens 2017).

The democratic conception also propels debates about the value of political parties and the nature of ethical partisanship (debates to which I hope this book contributes). Parties are, of course, key players in the modern practice of legitimate opposition. And contributors to this debate have shown how partisan contestation, appropriately focused on the public weal, appropriately limited and appropriately institutionalized, can be consistent with the strict demands of democratic legitimacy. Some participants in these debates focus on the role parties and partisans might play in deliberation and the justification of legitimate government action (White and Ypi 2016; Bonotti 2017; Wolkenstein 2019). Others have focused on how parties link diverse peoples to their government, instantiating in government the pluralism of modern polities while, at the same time, making effective government possible (Rosenblum 2008; Muirhead 2014; Herman 2017; Muirhead and Rosenblum 2020; Herman and Muirhead 2020). The debate about partisanship is rich. These diverse works, however, are bound by one common assumption: partisan forms of legitimate opposition are democratic. As two of the leading voices in this conversation have observed, contributors to this debate seek to offer "a defense of parties for democracy and democratic practices broadly" (Muirhead and Rosenblum 2020, 99).

The democratic conception drives efforts to comprehend our political situation. Its cogency matters. But proponents of the democratic conception often fail to give proper weight to, or even acknowledge, the important conceptual and practical distinction between legitimate opposition and egalitarian self-rule.

Here are two different ways to think about this distinction. As numerous recent commentators have been at pains to highlight, we often overlook the democratic credentials of random procedures, like sortition or lot, to make decisions or select officeholders (Estlund 2008; López-Guerra 2014; Guerrero 2014). Such egalitarian systems are arguably democratic. And they do not feature legitimate opposition—since they do not feature regulated rivalry. These arguments have changed the way I think about democracy and about the distinctive value of legitimate opposition—for example, many astute scholars rightly link opposition and pluralism, but sortition-based systems can also foster pluralism. I hope my work contributes to the debate about the merits of legitimate opposition relative to systems that rely on random selection (Lafont 2019; Landa and Pevnick 2021). Here I want to emphasize the following: the possibility of random democratic procedures should prompt us to reevaluate the relation of democracy to opposition and to reconsider opposition's value.

Here is a second, starker way to spot the divide between democracy and legitimate opposition. Imagine a regime that excluded women from voting. It features political parties and all the other trappings of electoral politics. In such a system, power would change hands peacefully. It would feature legitimate opposition. A massive part of the population, however, would be blocked unjustifiably from participating. The regime in question is highly unequal and undemocratic. And theories that defend opposition by tying it to democracy may trip over a case of this sort. Is opposition still democratic, though women cannot participate? If so, what does this say about your conception of democracy? If this regime is not democratic, do we still have any reason to value opposition in this case? Note, this is hardly some madcap scenario. Regimes defined by legitimate opposition, like the United States and the United Kingdom, disenfranchised women for much of their history.

As I noted earlier, opposition *can* surely be democratic. It is not hard to envisage a system of fair elections that would fit this bill. And those who embrace the democratic conception of legitimate opposition could, of course, acknowledge the opposition/democracy gap. Jeremy Waldron, for instance, maintains that experience with opposition can be a prerequisite of democracy, a view that logically depends on the distinction between opposition and democracy (2016, 106). And one might reasonably argue that in existing regimes, when opposition fails, democracy fails too.[3] Yet merely acknowledging this distinction does not mean one has fully grappled with its implications or that one's perspective on opposition does not still revolve around self-rule. In *Polyarchy: Participation and Opposition*, Robert Dahl draws lines between opposition and ideal democracy and between ideal democracy and polyarchy—that is, a minimal democracy. Nonetheless, his account of opposition's value still pivots entirely on its relation to democracy and the likelihood that it will lead to democracy (Dahl 1971).

Theories that embrace the democratic conception of legitimate opposition offer dependent accounts of the practice. They compose images of opposition refracted through prior understandings of democracy. As I discuss at greater length shortly, dependent accounts systematically impede our perception of the essence of opposition. And, I believe, they lead us to underestimate the achievement that opposition actually is—that is, how fortunate we are to have even flawed systems of opposition given the unjust and unequal conditions in which they were forged.

In sharp contrast to the traditional approach, the adversarial conception of legitimate opposition is an independent account of opposition: an account that does not turn on democracy. It sidesteps many of the conceptual difficulties generated by the democratic conception. It allows us to rethink both the virtues and the limitations of the practice. Recent efforts to compromise legitimate opposition become much less puzzling if we follow this course. We are better positioned to recognize how flawed these regimes were before the recent crises. We are better positioned to identify how weak the commitment to democratic norms has been during this age of polarization. We are better positioned to see how great an influence opponents of opposition wielded before their projects yielded such dramatic fruit. And we are better positioned to understand precisely what is lost when these systems are brought to their knees.

As I write, people are contributing their effort, time, and money trying to protect the United States' imperfect political system. And outside the United States, individuals are risking their freedom to establish political systems like the one here, a system in which oppositions are regularly afforded a real shot at winning. Should they succeed, they will not have defended or established ideal democracies or even plausibly egalitarian political systems. We can be clear-eyed about this while still seeing their actions as justified and inspiring. In a world in which many people are not committed to the equality of their fellow citizens, a system that treats people as capable of shaping the terrain of political life is worth committed defense.

Defining Legitimate Opposition

A polity features a system of legitimate opposition when opponents of the political status quo can seek and make changes to the current government or policy via a regularized form of political competition. By "government," I do not mean the entire constitutional setup. Instead, I am referring to the individuals who exercise power within the regime at any given time. By "regularized form of competition," I mean repeated, rule-based, nonviolent forms of political contestation. When legitimate opposition defines the political life of a community, those who are in power allow their rivals to seek to displace them, and in defeat, they peacefully relinquish their position, refraining from unjustified efforts to undo their losses or destroy their opponents.

There are many ways of opposing power holders, of engaging in political contestation. Posting online, taking part in a public debate, voting, and protesting in the streets are just a few examples. I assume that the practice of "legitimate opposition" refers to a specific subset of oppositional activity: the pursuit of official power via regularized processes. By implication, though dissident activity in contemporary China may be legitimate, it is not evidence of legitimate opposition. Similarly, it is not difficult to imagine a regime that allows its citizens to speak freely, to dissent and even to vote, without abiding real competition for influence.

The heart of opposition is the possibility of alternations in power and policy. But a basic feature of the practice is that political losers need not fold up shop. After a loss, they are allowed to critique those who are in power, hold them to account, and even hamper their efforts. There is no credible normative justification, I think, for the claim that a single election resolves all matters of political dispute, rendering further resistance to the government illegitimate. Certainly, in any flawed, inegalitarian, real-world polity, electoral outcomes do not reflect a popular will, they do not finally settle questions debated during the course of an election, and they do not address all the matters dividing the various groups in society (Arrow 1963; Habermas 1998; Markovits 2004; Lefkowitz 2007). Losers are under no obligation to surrender their causes even as they acknowledge their defeat. Competitive systems would have only the shortest of lives if government opponents were not afforded the liberty to oppose and gather support for their projects after an election. Where opposition was only allowed during a formal competition phase, officeholders would surely use this advantage to cement their position. The capacity to displace the people in power is inextricably tethered to the ability to oppose power holders between periods of contestation, for example after an election. By implication, if I am able to demonstrate the value of allowing groups to challenge and unseat those who are in power, I assume my argument extends to the ability to oppose more generally.

Following Robert Dahl, I treat legitimate opposition as an *institutional system* or *practice* (Dahl 1966). Legitimate opposition is sometimes connected or identified with a set of *norms*. The foundational norms are that (1) those who are out of government should oppose the government but not the political system itself and (2) those who are in government should recognize that opposition to the government is normal and valuable, that it is legitimate. Historians of political thought have traced the origins of these norms, while normative theorists have pondered their implications for political actors—namely, do they require compromise, responsible action on the part of the government, steadfastness on the part of the opposition, or the need to express loyalty to the state, the constitution, or something else? (Hofstadter 1969; Shapiro 1999; Leonard 2002; Engel 2011; Muirhead 2014; J. Selinger 2016; Waldron 2016; Rosenbluth and Shapiro 2018; Skjönsberg 2021).

I focus on *systems* rather than *norms* for three related reasons (though questions about norms come up inevitably). First, in my estimation, the question of *why* we should value legitimate opposition is upstream from the question of *how* to oppose well. For adherents of the democratic conception, the former question does not warrant much concern. Their focus is on what actions are consistent with democracy. If legitimate opposition is democratic and if democracy is valuable, then we ought to follow the norms sustaining systems of opposition. This logic applies neatly to high-functioning democracies. And I think there is much to recommend the constrained, fundamentally collegial forms of partisan activity defended by these works. The kinds of regimes in which opposition is vulnerable, however, are not high-functioning democracies. And it is worth asking why we should support those systems of opposition. That is the task I have set myself.

Here is a second reason I focus on systems rather than norms. The normative and theoretical puzzles I am concerned with simply vanish once we imagine that rivals will act well, for instance by treating their opponents as colleagues or partners, as individuals self-evidently committed to the well-being of each other and the community as a whole. Ronald Dworkin often contemplated the institutions and principles of a community defined by common causes, shared values, and mutual confidence. He sometimes called this ideal a "partnership democracy" (Dworkin 2006a). Among partners, the handover of power will be low stakes, even unremarkable, its uncanny character stripped away. That form of legitimate opposition would be very far from our own. And it is unlikely that it would ever be waylaid by populists. Just as scarcity is a circumstance of justice, the presumption of a certain level of disagreement, distrust, and dislike are, I think, necessary for a practical theory of legitimate opposition.

Finally, many political actors do not follow the various norms thought to define legitimate opposition. They do not seek compromise, behave responsibly, act loyally, pursue the common good, or even accept the prospect that they could be legitimately defeated. Again, this is especially true of the systems that are actually in danger. Therefore, understanding whether systems of opposition warrant defense requires an account of opposition's value that does not assume compliance with those norms. We need to grapple with the actual practice's crude defects as well as its virtues. Moreover, as I argue in chapter 2, many of the idealistic norms advanced by scholars of democracy and political partisanship should not be followed when only one side is committed to them.

My focus is *legitimate* opposition, not *loyal* opposition. The underlying concepts are quite similar, I think. The term "legitimate" stands for the idea that the practice can be justified or explained to individuals subject to it. And the goal of this book is to provide such an explanation. By contrast, the attraction of the term "loyal" opposition is largely vestigial. Originally coined as a joke in the British Parliament, it was formulated at a moment when opposition to the government could, in principle, be described as opposition to the Crown itself (Anastaplo 2003). In other words, the practice of loyal opposition was meant to be acceptable to the monarch, not those who were subject to the monarchy.

Prominent scholars like Jeremy Waldron have explored the potential force of "loyal" opposition for contemporary politics. As he rightly concludes, there is little justification for requiring those who challenge the government to be loyal to a specific constitutional system (or to a monarch) (Waldron 2016, 122). Members and supporters of the Scottish National Party want to break free from the United Kingdom, plausibly threatening that polity's constitution. They are disloyal. Yet they are using legal means, and their actions are not obviously illegitimate. Of course, one might claim that political actors should be loyal to democracy. This may be true. But the regimes I am primarily concerned with are not fully democratic. For those cases, we still need at hand an explanation of why a commitment to democracy entails respect for opposition. Ultimately, a political theory of legitimate opposition must not simply *assume* that loyalty to something is warranted. Instead, that theory should *explain* whether it is. Understanding the *legitimacy* of opposition, then, precedes consideration of *loyalty*.

My definition of legitimate opposition is stripped down and minimalist, singling out the fundamental features of the practice. For instance, I do not treat the existence of an "official opposition" as a necessary element of the practice. Moreover, I have not insisted that legitimate opposition requires giving members of the opposition formal avenues for influencing policy. In the United States, federalism is the most obvious example of this practice. One party might lose the presidency and majorities in both houses of Congress and still exercise substantial executive control over various states.[4] Some parliamentary regimes allow members of the opposition to chair critical committees. These practices, according to Waldron, manifest a powerful commitment to opposition. Critics of the government are not only allowed to pursue influence at the next election but are actually granted a role in governance (Waldron

2016, 111). This position captures something important. Yet, as Dahl found when he studied opposition in the 1960s, polities take a confoundingly diverse set of approaches to fostering and managing political competition (Dahl 1966, xviii). My stripped-down definition will surely strike some readers as too spare. But my goal is to develop an account that applies as broadly as possible. And given the diversity of these systems, an overloaded definition would thwart productive inquiry. That is why I focus on competitive processes, the nerve of legitimate opposition.

My definition even omits elections and political parties. Partisan electoral competition is *the* paradigmatic contemporary form of opposition. Still, it is quite easy to imagine nonelectoral rivalry. Imagine a regime that shunned elections, relying on referendums instead. And imagine that regime featured parties campaigning for their preferred policy—the parties would compete over policy outcomes, not offices. This system would raise many of the challenges we associate with opposition, and it could advance the same ends. Similarly, it requires little work to imagine nonpartisan opposition. In the eighteenth century, both Britain and the United States featured competitive elections without parties, elections that significantly shaped the course and contours of policy and government power.

By not assuming that parties are a defining feature of legitimate opposition, I can reconsider their relation to opposition. As I lay out in chapter 6, those who govern modern states have massive resources at their disposal, resources that can be deployed to tilt elections in their favor. Under these conditions, parties have an indispensable role in maintaining the ability of political outsiders to effectively contest for office, a role essential to preserving opposition. Given that role, partisans have a distinctive duty to support and defend legitimate opposition. Because defenders of political parties take the connection between parties and opposition for granted, even the most ardent of them underestimate their value and arguably do not fully apprehend the special duties associated with partisanship.

Why We Cannot Rely on the Democratic Conception of Legitimate Opposition: Ideal Theories

The orthodox democratic conception makes it difficult to persuasively describe what is lost when opposition is undermined and why citizens and political elites should defend the practice. To demonstrate this, I consider two paradigmatic strains of the democratic conception—one ideal and one minimal and deflationary.

In *Considerations on Representative Government*, John Stuart Mill provides democratic theory's most influential brief for vigorous competition. Indeed, throughout this work, I refer to Mill's approach, and those of his many followers, as *Millian collegial rivalry*. When political philosophers flesh out appealing, streamlined forms of contestation, they are working within this Millian tradition. These modes of competition are strictly limited, highly schematized, and fundamentally intellectual. Though my argument focuses on Mill, I believe it applies more broadly.

Opposition, on the Millian view, amounts to a contest of ideas about the best way to advance the commonweal. He conceived a body of elected representatives that would "be at once the nation's Committee of Grievances, and its Congress of Opinions" (Mill 2008a, 282). The Victorian polymath was famously optimistic about the power of such deliberative contests to generate salutary policies and to benefit the participants themselves (Thompson 1976).

Showing that competition could be compatible with "real democracy," a democracy in which the interests and views of all received due consideration, required two important moves (Mill 2008a, 305). First was the elaboration of a public-minded system of legitimate opposition. Mill stipulated that discursive combat be almost apolitical in character. Representatives would have no hand in policy. They would debate with one another so that "every person in the country may count upon finding somebody who speaks his mind, as well or better than he could speak it himself—not to friends and partisans exclusively, but in the face of opponents, to be tested by adverse controversy; where those whose opinion is overruled, feel satisfied that it is heard, and set aside not by a mere act of will, but for what are thought superior reasons" (Mill 2008a, 282). The victor in this sketch is not an individual or a party. The victor is an idea about how to advance the commonwealth's well-being.

Mill's second move was to imagine a set of political institutions reflecting a deep commitment to the interests of all. He defended proportional representation and granting additional votes to the educated—with the aim of ensuring that those who were concerned with the public interest could wield real influence. His arguments hinged on the following idea: the beneficiaries of these schemes would use their power to advance the commonweal, and their public-minded ambitions would be common knowledge, allowing the wise to wield intellectual authority over others (Mill 2008a, 317). In this context, participants might not think of themselves as adversaries but as collaborators or partners. This is contestation of the friendly sort. It is some distance from the world in which peaceful transitions can be rightly regarded as achievements, as something remarkable. The paradoxical phrase "team of rivals" perfectly captures the peculiar conception of adversarialism informing Mill's view (Goodwin 2005). It is this now-familiar combination of intellectual competition within the tight bounds of collaboration that exemplifies collegial rivalry.

There is much to be learned from Mill's account of legitimate opposition and from scholarship in the Millian tradition. Still, we cannot rely on works of this sort, including Mill's own, to tell us why we should regret the fall of opposition in flawed contemporary regimes. This is so for many reasons. Here are four that apply broadly.

The first reason is straightforward: the institutions and dispositions defining the political life of contemporary competitive regimes, the regimes currently under threat, do not closely resemble Mill's vision. In most modern representative systems, political representatives do not just debate but try to directly influence policy. The mechanisms for choosing representatives and the large role played by parties eclipse the voices of many citizens, effectively keeping them from informing public debate. Competition in these regimes is bruising. Many political actors do not pursue the common good, and many have entirely reasonable doubts about whether their rivals are motivated by the welfare of others.

My claim is not that it would be unfeasible or unrealistic for a regime to be Millian (though that may be true). My claim is that the regimes currently under threat lack Millian practices and institutions (or other ideal practices and institutions). Accordingly, when legitimate opposition is felled, we cannot conclude that this is regrettable because the regimes no longer feature Millian practices and institutions.

This conclusion leads to a second reason we cannot rely on Millian theories: there are little grounds to assume that oppositional regimes are more likely to develop into Millian regimes than are regimes that do not feature opposition. To me, it seems reasonably unlikely in both cases. Consider the German example. The Nazi regime obviously did not approximate Mill's democracy. But its failure and military defeat fostered the creation of a relatively admirable regime. The new German regime may be even more admirable than regimes that have not experienced interruptions of opposition, like the United Kingdom. We simply lack strong evidence about which kinds of regimes are more likely to become Millian. By implication, we should not regret the loss of opposition because it makes less likely the speculative achievement of a very far-distant ideal.

Of course, one might think that oppositional regimes are *closer* to Millian democracy than are their real-world, autocratic rivals. As a result, we should fear the destruction of these regimes and stand ready to defend them. This train of thought depends on the import of approximation when assessing political institutions. Approximation is a bearing wall of a familiar argument for legitimate opposition: regimes featuring the practice are *more* democratic. And many contemporary efforts to assess the quality of political regimes depend on this logic (Freedom House 2017; Marshall, Gurr, and Jaggers 2017). Similarly, in *A Preface to Democratic Theory* (1956), Robert Dahl proposed distinguishing polyarchies—that is, representative regimes—from autocracies on the basis of the degree to which they approximated individual characteristics of an ideal democracy.

Notwithstanding our intuitions about the import of approximation, it does not provide advantageous terrain from which to mount a defense of opposition. In truth, actually determining which real-world regimes more closely approximate our ideals is more complicated than simply tallying up institutions and practices. This is a third reason to turn away from Millian-type ideal theories.

Take Mill's twin standards for assessing political institutions: their capacity to generate good policy and their educative effect. Neither the real-world regime featuring legitimate opposition nor the real-world regime stifling the practice will generate well-formulated policy in the sense Mill hoped for. Contra Mill's recommendations, lawmaking and law application are influenced and controlled by political forces in both kinds of regimes. Similarly, the political system of neither real-world regime will have the educative effect on the citizenry that Mill hoped for. The kind of competition we observe in these regimes is not institutionalized in the way Mill imagined. If one were feeling particularly contrary, one could even argue that real-world regimes *lacking* opposition are actually closer to Mill's ideal, for those who govern are given greater protection from comprehensively partisan and adversarial processes, and the political system does not encourage everyday citizens to intentionally set back the interests of others (Hussain 2020).

The preceding claim is an exaggeration. Nonetheless, it carries us toward the underlying issue. Both Mill's regime and real-world oppositional regimes feature legitimate opposition. But these forms of legitimate opposition are unalike. As a result, we err if we assume that the ideal and nonideal regime resemble each other just because they feature some form of competition. Accordingly, it is not obvious that the real-world regime marked by legitimate opposition will actually more closely approximate Mill's ideal.

I know full well that some readers will find the preceding argument tendentious. Imagine I conceded the point. Even if we assume that real-world oppositional regimes *did* more closely approximate Mill's ideal, we could not reasonably conclude that they would be preferable for that reason. Approximation-based defenses of legitimate opposition, like Dahl's discussion of polyarchy, are a fundamentally flawed, fundamentally broken way of thinking about political institutions (Lipsey and Lancaster 1956–57).[5] These issues are captured by the idea of the second best. And it is the fourth and most important reason why Millian, ideal accounts of democratic opposition give us so little grip on our present circumstance.

Consider the following. Imagine I want to travel from Durham, North Carolina, to Paris, France. I hope to visit my wife's family there. Nonetheless, I would certainly prefer to stay in Durham than to get halfway to Paris—that is, the middle of the Atlantic Ocean. My chances of ever seeing my wife's family are greater if I stay in Durham. Approximation does not systematically imply an improvement in one's situation (Margalit 1983, 79).

Here is an institutional example.[6] Suppose I really value free speech. I also think that specific forms of hate speech should be restricted. Suppose, further, that I happen to live in a society in which political officials consistently act in a wise and disinterested manner. In that society, I might conclude that restrictions on hate speech could be justified. Those restrictions would be enforced judiciously (Matsuda 1989; Lawrence 1990; Waldron 2012). But in a society where political officials cannot be trusted, I might reasonably determine that they would use hate-speech laws to restrict excessively other forms of speech. In that society, I would generally prefer an institutional rule permitting no restrictions on speech. In this familiar set of circumstances, I would prefer not to approximate my institutional ideal. Approximation would make the situation worse.

Similarly, in choosing between two flawed but otherwise similar regimes, it is possible that I might reasonably prefer the regime that does not approximate Mill's—that is, the regime without opposition, a regime like Singapore. Of course, it is not the case that any movement toward an ideal will be worse than the status quo. We just cannot *assume* that approximation implies improvement. And without an independent account of opposition's value, an account that does not depend merely on its proximity to a democratic ideal, we simply cannot know whether it is an institution worthy of defense.

In sum, Mill's idealistic defense of intellectual competition throws only inconstant light on the normative character of the real-world practice. It therefore provides relatively little visibility on what is lost when that practice is curtailed. The reasons for this are general, not turning on the specifics of Mill's account. Any overly idealistic account of legitimate opposition will suffer in the same ways. To understand whether opposition merits protection, we need an account of its value that takes it as it is.

Why We Cannot Rely on the Democratic Conception of Legitimate Opposition: Minimalist Theories

This section evaluates a sharply different version of the democratic conception, one that simply boils democracy down to flawed, real-world legitimate opposition, treating them as equivalent. This approach is most closely associated with Joseph Schumpeter and other theorists of elite democracy (Schumpeter 1943).[7] Minimalism about democracy is *the* dominant view among political scientists. This intellectual phenomenon is not, I think, ultimately rooted in well-formed normative arguments. It is driven primarily by the fact that opposition is observable, usefully facilitating empirical research.

The best-known contemporary version of minimalism has been developed by Adam Przeworski. Przeworski has written insightfully and prolifically about democracy. Because it helps illustrate my argument, I focus on his most influential, early articulation of minimalism.[8] On that account, democracy is not best thought of as a "battle" of ideas waged by a team of rivals, an egalitarian system of self-rule, or an idealistic system of deliberation. Democracy just *is* a nonideal system of legitimate opposition. According to Przeworski, a regime is democratic when competitive elections determine who holds high office regardless of whether citizens' votes are weighted equally or whether they can even all vote. Przeworski is hardly the only one to emphasize the connection between political turnover and democracy. Samuel Huntington famously argued that a democracy ought to be regarded as stable or consolidated after power had turned over two times. "Selecting rulers through elections is the heart of democracy, and democracy is real only if rulers are willing to give up power as a result of elections," Huntington observed (1991, 33).[9]

In stark contrast to idealized, Millian conceptions, minimalist accounts provide a plain answer to why regimes that undermine opposition are less democratic. They are less democratic precisely because they have threatened the play of opposition (see, for instance, Rummens 2017). On the other hand, these theories may misfire as accounts of why we should mourn the loss of opposition and, by implication, democracy too.

For Przeworski, competitive political systems allow for "conflicting forces to advance their interests within the institutional framework" (1999, 50). But on his view, the mere fact that groups can achieve their ends is not a reason to value opposition and democracy. Przeworski has little patience for the ideal of popular sovereignty or the idea I defend in this work: that systems of opposition provide citizens opportunities to exercise their agency together in valuable ways (Przeworski 1999; 2010, 110–11). For Przeworski, crediting either of these arguments requires faith in polities that are too large, too unequal, and too riven by disagreement.

Moreover, Przeworski is doubtful that competing groups' efforts to achieve their ends will reliably generate egalitarian outcomes. And he is also skeptical that groups' competitive pursuit of their interests will consistently allow citizens to hold their politicians accountable—a position with considerable, if not uniform, support among political scientists (Przeworski 1999, 2010). Instead, minimal democracy decreases the relative value and attractiveness of violent conflict by giving rival groups opportunities to seek their ends peacefully. Competition, or democracy, reduces the incentive to engage in political violence.

Przeworski's argument leaves gaps. Consider a regime that limited group struggle by resorting to sortition to fill political office. Imagine further that this regime would be as good as any feasible oppositional regime at keeping citizens from thinking of their fellow citizens as antagonists. This regime might also decrease the relative likelihood for conflict. Why would we prefer the oppositional regime? The potentially divisive effects of competitive opposition are well known (Posner 2004). Sortition might well do a better job of reducing conflict. In such cases, Przeworski's rendering of opposition does not offer a satisfying sense of what distinguishes the practice.

Setting aside imaginary sortition-based regimes, the minimalist argument may also leave us wanting when we compare oppositional regimes to Singapore and China. While those polities have many manifest faults, they are not currently marked by violence between competing political groups. Hong Kong's democratic system has been crushed by the Chinese state. It seems unlikely that these moves will lead to widespread political violence; the state will prevent that. Does that mean we have no reason to regret the demolition of Hong Kong's distinctive political system? No doubt, concerns about civil liberties and rights to free speech loom large. But there must be more to say about what happened to Hong Kong's system of opposition.

As will become abundantly clear, especially in chapter 5, Przeworski's career-long investigation of democracy fundamentally informs my argument. That competitive systems allow groups to pursue their ends without engaging in battle makes them a valuable achievement. That they are able to achieve this against backgrounds of inequality and injustice makes them more valuable still. Yet the reduction of violent conflict cannot be the main reason to value legitimate opposition or minimalist democracy. Why? Because many regimes without such institutions, perhaps not all, can achieve the same end. In different terms, if the argument for legitimate opposition depends solely on the lack of political violence, then opposition may not be especially valuable in many cases. In those cases, Przeworski's approach leaves us in the awkward position of valuing opposition solely because we have decided to use the loaded term "democracy" to refer to it.

Conceptions of democracy that sever it from robust political equality end up generating confusion about whether democracy and opposition are actually worth defending. Steven Levitsky and Daniel Ziblatt's recent book *How Democracies Die* dramatically illustrates this problem. Written to inform citizens about the United States' vulnerability to populism, the authors identify four signs that a political figure threatens democracy: "1) rejects, in words or action, the democratic rules of the game, 2) denies the legitimacy of opponents, 3) tolerates or encourages violence, or 4) indicates a willingness to curtail the civil liberties of opponents, including the media" (2018, 21–22). Among the essential, democratic rules are "basic civil [and] political rights" (8). But opposition occupies the core of their minimalist conception of democracy. This allows Levitsky and Ziblatt to embrace the United States' democratic identity and to sound the alarm about its future.

Describing the acceptance of legitimate opposition or "mutual tolerance" in the United States, Levitsky and Ziblatt claim that "the Civil War broke American democracy" (2018,

122). Presumably, they treat the slavery-era United States as a democracy because political opponents tolerated one another and incumbent governments yielded power when they lost (Przeworski 2015). The regime featured opposition. Yet antebellum representative institutions were comprehensively corrupted by the practice of slavery. By 1860, in states like Alabama, Florida, Georgia, and Louisiana, slaves accounted for more than 40 percent of the population. In Mississippi and South Carolina, they were the majority (J. Kennedy 1864, 594–95). Slaves were counted for the purposes of congressional districting. As a result, slave states sent extra representatives to Congress. And this, in turn, gave those states greater weight in the presidential Electoral College.

Suppose we accept the claim that the United States was a democracy before the Civil War.[10] It would imply that a regime can be a democracy when many individuals not only own other human beings, violating their basic civil and political liberties, but actually exercise *extra* formal influence because they own others. Moreover, as the term "antebellum" indicates, the political system of that United States did not keep the country from falling into violence—the main value that minimalist accounts assign to democracy.

This is how the democratic conception of legitimate opposition and the reflexive elision of democracy and opposition obscure what is at stake in our present political moment. *How Democracies Die* offers readers a timely and erudite account of why citizens should be concerned about the state of the United States' politics. It depends on the democratic conception. It is not a work of political theory. It does not scrutinize democracy's value. It assumes that its readers know what democracy is. It assumes that they value it. And treating the slavery-era United States as a democracy may be consistent with common parlance and minimalist conceptions of democracy. But when one's definition of democracy applies to the pre-1863 United States, it has become so estranged from any ideal of political equality that it is not clear why we should value democracy or opposition at all. And it is not clear why we should raise the alarm when opposition comes under assault. Instead of grappling with the morally complicated character of the practices under attack, conflating opposition and democracy allows us to ground our arguments for legitimate opposition on the weakest foundations: the positive rhetorical connotations of the term "democracy."

Discussing two paradigmatic representatives of the democratic conception, I have illustrated why approaching opposition from the perspective of democracy will not generate a satisfying answer to our question: Just what is lost when opposition is undermined? More importantly, this analysis indicates what a successful account would look like. That account should not be parasitic on the potential normative value of an ideal system. Nor should it place its weight on the vague but positive semantic connotations assigned to the word "democracy"—minimal or otherwise.

We need an independent account of the practice. That account should take the practice as it is without assuming that it is democratic. Such an account would allow us to reckon with the value of legitimate opposition. And it would allow us to weigh the predictable costs it entails. Providing that account is this book's work.

Tracking Opposition

My account relies on two kinds of analysis: normative and genealogical.[11] That choice is shaped by its twin ends: dislodging a long-held view of an institution and offering, in its place, a persuasive and realistic account of opposition's value. These

modes of inquiry are not discretely employed. Chapters focusing on opposition's history elaborate and embellish my normative claims.

Chapter 2 develops an independent account of opposition's value—that is, the adversarial conception of legitimate
opposition. Along the way, I critically discuss rival perspectives
developed by Ronald Dworkin, Robert Goodin, and Ian Shapiro. I use the word "value" advisedly. The aim of the chapter is
not to justify why the practice would be a necessary or intrinsic
feature of a fully legitimate regime. Instead, I describe why we
ought to abide by the practice and what is lost when it is not
institutionalized. Individuals have a number of interests that
might be advanced by a system featuring opposition. But my
argument focuses on individual and collective agency.

I assume that individuals have an important interest in
the opportunity to impact laws and policies to which they are
subject. Opposition not only creates chances for participants
to work together to advance causes they care about but also
gives them a chance to block or ameliorate projects they find
disagreeable. And it does this across a remarkably diverse array
of settings, both enviable and unenviable. To put it inelegantly,
legitimate opposition is a practical, robust, and scalable technique for simultaneously advancing citizens' valuable interest
in political agency under less-than-ideal conditions.

Developing these arguments, chapter 2 considers and
rejects two traditional strategies for defending opposition's
value, strategies focused on how opposition can facilitate Rousseauean society-wide forms of democratic agency and on how
opposition provides a republican check on the purview of
power holders.

Building off my initial account of the adversarial conception,
chapter 3 reconsiders recent challenges to opposition, like populism and autocracy. The orthodox, democratic conception, I have

claimed, leads to the systematic misdiagnosis of those challenges. My account puts us in a better position to identify the malady in question: real-world regimes that undermine opposition curtail the most effective limit on their influence and block the institutional paths that citizens can use to exercise their agency. What is more, they build institutions that persistently exploit and subvert their citizens' agency, encouraging them to participate in fraudulent political activity like elections whose outcome is forgone. This is what is lost when regimes undermine opposition.

Chapter 4 begins the historical section of the book, demonstrating that opposition is not exclusively modern. Legitimate opposition made a recognizable mark on fifth-century, democratic Athens. Corroborating this argument, I illustrate how the Athenian practice of ostracism and the rules governing its political system were used to distinguish, in practice, between acceptable and unacceptable forms of competition. These institutions were not focused on participants' commitment to popular rule, their loyalty. They were focused on their clout. Maintaining a lively space for competition, Athenian institutions and practices were antimonopolistic. They raised the cost of wielding excessive political power, forms of power that plausibly constituted a threat to that system. In other words, the Athenians distinguished between legitimate and illegitimate forms of opposition. Their approach has critically important implications for our understanding of where the boundaries of opposition should be drawn.

Have I just unwittingly undercut my central claim? Does the Athenian experience suggest that opposition *is* quintessentially democratic? When I originally conceived this project, I had full faith in the democracy-opposition connection. It was the reason I believed Athenian opposition merited investigation. The history of the Roman Republic, treated in chapter 5, renders that faith insupportable, severing the conceptual tendons fixing opposition to democracy.

Republican Rome was not a democracy. And it did not feature parties. But it was clearly marked by an adversarial system of legitimate opposition. The politically ambitious had a variety of offices to pursue through regular forms of political competition. Rome's elaborate systems of regulated rivalry allowed a multitude of nonofficeholders to exercise political agency together, and the Republic featured a portfolio of institutions limiting the predictable costs of the practice.

Earlier in this introduction, I critiqued minimalist accounts of democracy. But as Adam Przeworski has long argued, we should expect systems of opposition to limit the violent pursuit of power. Using the Roman case, chapter 5 draws out the important theoretical implications of this function. To be effective, systems of opposition must reflect, in a rough manner, the violent capacities of different groups. This may seem a commonplace, even obvious. Many students of politics less readily acknowledge what this commonplace observation implies: oppositional systems will rarely be truly egalitarian and truly democratic because they will reflect groups' unequal capacities for violence. Exceptions to this rule will be restricted to a small set of cases where de facto political power is distributed equally *before* systems of opposition are established.

In Athens, for instance, the establishment of opposition was preceded by a rarity: a successful popular revolution. Though the Athenian experience remains a touchstone for institutional imagineers, few pay sufficient heed to the peculiar preconditions of its institutional forms. Democratic theory offers many egalitarian alternatives to opposition, notably deliberative-based institutions and sortition-based systems for filling offices. When outlining the relative benefits of these alternatives, their defenders engage in clockwork constitutionalism. But these proposals typically suffer once we explicitly account for the possibility that political actors can resort to violence instead of following institutional rules. Practically, establishing those egalitarian systems would require the successful use of violence, as occurred in the Athenian case. Or it would require the existence of the very same egalitarian conditions that the institutions promise to instantiate and promote.

Chapters 4 and 5 develop a wholesale reinterpretation of opposition's history. If my account is correct, the orthodox view that opposition is the product of the eighteenth century is false. We might reasonably expect to see evidence for my claims in the writings of figures like Henry Bolingbroke, David Hume, and Edmund Burke, the key protagonists in the intellectual development of the party-focused form of legitimate opposition. Chapter 6 lays out that evidence. Those authors' writings are consistent with the view that opposition was not an eighteenth-century invention. Their arguments depend on their readers' acceptance of opposition. What was not accepted, what required justification, was *formed* or *partisan* opposition. This shift in perspective allows us to see the acceptance of organized opposition in a new light.

The embrace of formed or organized contention was not driven by a new appreciation for opposition, I argue. It was driven by a spectacular failure, the failure of separation-of-powers theories to predict how government would work. Such theories did not anticipate a modern executive's ability to coordinate legislative collective action. That reality rendered unorganized opposition ineffective. It is impossible to correctly construe the shape and demands of modern opposition unless one takes this institutional fact as a starting point.

Richard Hofstadter, Harvey Mansfield, and Nancy Rosenblum have carefully mapped the distinctive intellectual contributions of figures like Bolingbroke, Hume, and Burke to debates about the legitimacy of partisanship (Mansfield 1965; Hofstadter 1969; Rosenblum 2008). However, these eighteenth-century authors' arguments are bound together by a common premise: if opposition was legitimate, then in a modern state organized opposition was legitimate too.

Chapter 6 also reconsiders Mill's proposal for a representative, democratic government. Crafting his totemic brief for intellectual, collegial rivalry, Mill engages in clockwork constitutionalism, explicitly sidestepping the problem of executive advantage. That limits, radically, the applicability of his ideals. And if modern theories in the Millian mold intentionally or unintentionally adopt the same approach, their arguments will suffer the same flaw.

Chapter 7 burnishes the relative standing of competitive institutions by investigating the reception of legitimate opposition during France's Revolutionary era. In particular, I draw on this history to weigh noncompetitive alternatives to opposition. The dream of a popular regime innocent of political competition or opposition marked the writing of the Abbé Sieyès and the Marquis de Condorcet. Both theorists are influential forerunners of fundamental developments in contemporary democratic theory—such as the embrace of deliberative and epistemic approaches to self-government. Both thinkers recognized a distinction between an ideal democracy and an oppositional regime. They recognized that securing one might mean forgoing the other, that these were arguably rival visions of political life. And they both explicitly rejected brute oppositional politics.

Unlike more recent theoretical critics of opposition, Sieyès and Condorcet had the opportunity to participate in a sustained attempt to fashion an oppositionless form of popular rule, or what became France's early Revolutionary regime (1789–91). That experience provides an extraordinarily valuable opportunity for assessing the still common belief that competitive action could be controlled if only institutions were established that did not encourage it.

In fact, Revolutionary institutions that aimed to facilitate popular rule while blocking competition were breathtakingly misjudged. Competitive collective action inflected Revolutionary politics from the moment popular institutions were formed. Moreover, because competition was not anticipated, it was not planned for. Few measures were created to limit the predictable costs of adversarial one-upmanship. The Revolution birthed an irregular, disorganized, sometimes violent system of opposition. Sieyès's and Condorcet's proposals depended on the possibility that competitive impulses could be contained. The Revolutionary experience illustrates that where we have reason to doubt that assumption—that is, almost anywhere—we should prefer systems defined by opposition.

Conclusion

Watching the news or reading Twitter, it feels like we are living in an unprecedented political moment. Legitimate opposition is under siege. But more than two centuries ago, the First Consul of France, Napoleon Bonaparte, questioned whether it was "possible to conceive of such a thing as an opposition to the sovereign people" (Rosanvallon 2008, 99). He would soon name himself emperor. Challenges to opposition are not novel.

Reconsidering the traditional, timeworn understanding of opposition's value and history, this book provides a novel and clearer perspective on the challenges we face today and a better grip on the institutions in need of fortification.

Legitimate opposition can be democratic. But the existence of the practice does not imply widespread acceptance of democracy or of the legitimacy of one's opponents. Competitive regimes tend to be flawed. Defending them requires defending inegalitarian political systems. This is how such systems can simultaneously allow mass political agency without consistently generating violence. As a result, efforts to improve and sustain the practice may never be complete. And a credible theory of opposition should not ignore that fact. To do so would leave us with a one-eyed account, one that ignores its quite evident limits and misunderstands why it merits vigorous defense.

2

Opposition's Value

The Adversarial Conception of Legitimate Opposition

I t is one of the minor ironies of democratic theory that Joseph Schumpeter, the person most closely associated with linking democracy to political competition, was, at one point in his life, an unabashed admirer of monarchy and aristocracy (Schumpeter 1943; Medearis 2009, 70). This might be too hasty. Many political theorists probably do not find this fact ironic. It is unsurprising, they might think, that someone who favored rule by inheritance fashioned a political theory in which democracy is reduced to one grandee competing to step into the other's shoes.

Outcomes determined via a competitive process are often criticized as failing to approximate standards of collective reason or public good. And competition's compelled search for political advantage is associated with a variety of costly side effects such as the intensification of antagonism. As the prominent democratic theorist Jane Mansbridge once contended, giving a warm embrace to a competition-based definition of democracy "verges on moral bankruptcy" (1980, 18). Conclusions of this variety have driven political theorists to develop richer, more demanding accounts of self-rule.

These are legitimate concerns. Yet understanding the current political moment still requires that we develop an independent, direct account of legitimate opposition, an account that does not depend on our view of democracy or an ideal system of opposition, only indirectly related to the systems we actually observe. This chapter begins to outline and develop such an account: the adversarial conception of legitimate opposition.

Making my argument, I outline the limitations of two rival ways of thinking about opposition's value—both of which are embraced by prominent advocates of the democratic conception of legitimate opposition. First, political theorists like Ronald Dworkin and Robert Goodin have developed agency-based defenses of opposition's role in a democracy. They argue that systems of opposition might allow citizens to see decisions they disagree with as their own, as products of their own actions and commitments. Like J. S. Mill, these theorists draw optimistic, rosy pictures of opposition, accounts necessarily providing only indirect, dependent justifications of flawed, actually existing competitive systems. And like Mill's own proposals, the oppositional systems elaborated in these accounts are competitive in the thinnest possible sense—they are competitive, yet opponents in these accounts might better be described as partners rather than rivals. In actual regimes, political conflicts are won, and they are lost. Opposition is rivalrous. As a result, the dependent, indirect method advanced by Dworkin and Goodin can only take us so far in understanding the agency value of existing oppositional systems and what is lost when such systems are felled.

Political theories focused on the value of nondomination may seem a more natural way of connecting democracy and opposition and of grasping the value of legitimate opposition as it appears in the real world. These theories, like the one developed by Ian Shapiro, emphasize the negative potential of opposition, the value of popular accountability and control that even flawed systems of political competition allow. Yet these theories often fail to acknowledge the oversight mechanisms employed by nonoppositional regimes. And they underplay the valuable opportunities to positively impact political outcomes that competitive regimes can provide. That is, they underplay opportunities for agency. As a result, they provide a partial account of opposition's value, an account that might not even apply to many of the regimes in which opposition is under assault.

The adversarial conception of legitimate opposition takes opposition as it is. Real-world oppositional regimes are imperfect, inegalitarian, and frequently unjust. Relative to going alternatives, these competitive regimes still generate valuable opportunities for citizens to act as agents. This is the upshot of the adversarial conception. Citizens in polities marked by opposition *cannot* justifiably understand all laws as products of their own agency—as Dworkin and Goodin suggest might be possible. Those citizens *can* peacefully pursue their political projects in ways that matter, impacting issues of basic import.

Agency in oppositional systems is Janus-faced. Citizens have opportunities to join together to positively advance ends they care about. And they have opportunities to block or alter projects they oppose. In many cases, exercises of agency will be small and partial rather than grand and final—instead of a bill being passed, perhaps one only succeeds at persuading one's neighbors. Many efforts to seize these opportunities will end in failure and distressing loss. And those opportunities necessarily allow citizens to participate unthoughtfully, self-interestedly, and vituperatively. But by cultivating these opportunities, both large and small, competitive regimes nonetheless instantiate a valuable respect for citizens' agency. By "respect," I mean that the institutions and practices of those regimes are liberal, reflecting citizens' status as moral and political actors. Because individuals have an important interest in the opportunity to exercise this form of agency, regimes that instantiate this respect will be more attractive as a result.

My claim is not that opposition is a necessary feature of a legitimate regime, a regime in which political leaders have the right to rule. Nor is my claim that opposition is necessary for a regime to possess democratic authority, a regime in which citizens have an obligation to obey laws and decisions because they were promulgated by democratic procedures (Buchanan 2002). Instead, I am picking out what would be lost, with respect to citizens' morally important interests, just in case a real-world regime, like Hungary, undermines legitimate opposition. In a nutshell, I provide a defensible account of opposition that avoids both Schumpeterian minimalism and Rousseauean collaborative maximalism.

Many readers will judge my account too minimal and undemanding. Is a respectful orientation toward individuals' agency all that can be said for the opposition? Opposition may often yield instrumental benefits. And compared with accounts of just or egalitarian institutions, my account *is* spare. That is hardly a shortcoming. Rather than offering an elaborate defense of ideal institutions, my goal is to assess, as accurately as I am able, the value of institutions as they are. If my account appears spare, that is because I have found the moral value of these institutions to be sparer, or less weighty, than many people suppose.

Still, my argument has force. To show this, it is worth pulling back the curtain and offering a glimpse of an argument to come. In chapter 3, I consider the threat posed by efforts to undermine opposition—whether by populists, as in Poland, or by nonpopulists. After opposition is undermined, elections are still held, rallies take place, inaugurations are organized, representative bodies are called into session. Popular political life does not come to a halt. But over and above any bad outcomes that might follow when regimes kneecap their opponents, those regimes wrong their citizens by subverting and manipulating their political agency. The wronged include opponents of the government *and* those who support it. Real-world regimes that lack opposition simultaneously encourage citizens to act as if they are agents, to perform the part of individuals who are choosing leaders and impacting policy, while directing that activity toward a distinctly different end: firming up the foundations of the ruling regime.

Rigged elections are not problematic fundamentally because they are deceptive. Participants may know that the outcome has been determined in advance. Rather, these institutions demean citizens by usurping their agency. Participants are not treated as actors who can heed their desires, commitments, and principles. They are forced to be actors in an elaborate play that they have not written, have little part in directing, and cannot quit. Rather than instantiating respect, those political systems demean and demoralize. I hope this brief description of the real-world alternative to opposition is suggestive, illustrating why we have reason to value adversarial regimes that are positively oriented toward their citizens' agency. But I aim here at more than a suggestion, so a fuller argument follows.

This chapter unfolds over several sections. The next two outline why we might value opportunities to exercise our agency and why it is appropriate to assess the value of opposition from the perspective of agency. I then critically consider the argument that opposition allows citizens to justifiably recognize laws as their own, as products of their agency. Building off my critique of that Rousseauean approach, the fourth section outlines the grounds for the adversarial conception of legitimate opposition. The following sections weigh potential objections to the adversarial conception, in particular whether it overlooks the value of popular control of political officials.

Evaluating Opposition: Relational Equality and Instrumental Benefits

For the purposes of this book, I assume that we can evaluate legitimate opposition from the perspective of three related interests: an interest in good outcomes broadly defined, an interest in achieving or maintaining egalitarian relationships, and an interest in the opportunity to shape the institutions, laws, and decisions to which we are subject. The first of these relates to citizens' role as subjects of political decisions; the latter relates to their role as a maker or participant.[1] Our interest in egalitarian relationships spans both roles. It can be advanced or retarded by what decisions are made *and* how they are made.

Of these three interests, I believe our interest in egalitarian relationships has only an oblique connection with rivalrous, legitimate opposition. In other words, this interest is not necessarily advanced or retarded by the practice. Why bother pointing this out?[2] Because I suspect that most political theorists and most non-political theorists assume that egalitarian concerns will figure centrally in a defense of legitimate opposition. And I want to underline the fact that they do not occupy that place in this account. I take for granted that individuals have an interest in procedures and outcomes that do not undermine their relations as equals. I am worse off, on this view, just in case there are some members of my community who are treated as my social superiors, if, for instance, I have to kowtow to others (Anderson 1999). Recent discussions of the moral character of democracy have turned on this interest (Kolodny 2014b; Viehoff 2014). And it is easy to imagine an egalitarian competition: a competition in which individuals possess equal formal and informal influence over the outcome. It is just as easy to conjure a satisfyingly egalitarian, if imaginary, political process that is wholly uncompetitive. What if, instead of having candidates compete for political office, officeholders were selected via a lottery-based system giving citizens an equal chance of holding office. That system would be egalitarian: no one would have a greater chance of holding office than anyone else. But that system evidently does not feature the practice of legitimate opposition.

More importantly, a brief consideration of contemporary regimes demonstrates that competitive systems are defined by formal and informal political inequalities. The United States is exemplary in this regard. And it is not hard to think of even less egalitarian political systems in which office is attained via peaceful, regular, rule-based, competitive elections. Imagine a polity in which only white men could vote. That inegalitarian system would feature legitimate opposition. Whatever value the system possessed would not be grounded in the instantiation of egalitarian relationships. By implication, those who are narrowly focused on relational equality may recognize little intrinsic value in opposition. And we must, therefore, look elsewhere if we are to understand the practice's value.

Our interest in good outcomes, outcomes that advance our well-being and the cause of justice, is reasonably straightforward (though the nature and identity of this interest is subject to considerable debate). There is a strong case to be made that generally speaking, competitive political systems better advance the well-being of their citizens than going alternatives do (Acemoglu and Robinson 2012). And many of the traditional benefits of legitimate opposition fall into this category—for example, the competitive process keeps a polity nimble, limits corruption, generates new ideas, and so on. But the evidence here is far from incontestable. And in a particular case, a regime lacking opposition might credibly claim that it advances the well-being of citizens at least as well as many existing oppositional regimes do, while remaining open to the best ideas with respect to governance.

This is precisely how ostensibly decent regimes like Singapore defend limits on political competition. In an ethnically diverse polity, like Singapore, the typical by-products of competition, like partisan enmity, make the practice too much of a risk to a reasonable form of government, some people say (Yew 2005). What if these self-serving claims were valid? Would we still have grounds to think that something is lost just because Singapore does not feature opposition? To answer this question, we require an intrinsic account of the practice's value, one that does not solely depend on the outcomes it generates. As later chapters will illustrate, I do not deny the weight of instrumental considerations or the potential instrumental value of opposition.[3] The attractiveness of opposition relative to other ways of organizing political life depends, for instance, on its capacity to reduce the attractiveness of violent political conflict. Of course, even if I successfully provide an intrinsic account, we may still have reasons to reject opposition in any given case. If competition will predictably generate unattractive outcomes, for instance, the moral cost of those outcomes might outweigh competition's intrinsic value. Still, all else equal, an intrinsic account will allow us to understand what, if anything, is lost just in case a regime blocks opposition.

Evaluating Opposition: The Import of Adversarial Agency

Agency is hardy. Individuals can exercise their agency in valuable ways even under difficult and nonideal circumstances. And that is why it is at the heart of my argument. Our interest in exercising agency is our interest in seeing ourselves as authors or makers of our lives (Raz 1986, 369; Stilz 2016).[4] In a political context, satisfying our interest in agency requires that citizens have the opportunity to, in Ronald Dworkin's terms, "treat politics as an extension of [their] moral life" (2000, 204). Dworkin's conception is highly moralized, but it is evidently a concern with agency. Amartya Sen famously pinpoints the intuitive import of agency by noting our distinct responses to someone is who starving and someone who is fasting (1992, 52). Sen's example conveys the value of impacting the world as a result of decisions we reasonably recognize as our own. The outcomes here are equivalent: someone does not eat. In one case, the individual sees her hunger as, at least in part, the product of her own choice. Fasting is a decision. The choice not to eat is in a familiar sense "hers." Someone who starves cannot eat. The outcome is imposed on her. And that impacts our evaluation of these cases. Sen's example *suggests* why we might value institutions making *greater* space for our agency even when such institutions produce a comparative worsening in the outcomes generated—that is, because we might justifiably recognize the state of affairs as, in part, of our own making.[5]

Providing a complete description of agency's character or a full justification of political agency's value would take its own book (or books). And my fundamental interest is the practice of opposition and its history. Accordingly, here I provide a mere sketch, one that is ecumenical among the major attempts to grasp agency's character. As I understand it, agency refers to a bundle of important capacities. To exercise agency, one must be capable of forming desires, judgments, principles, or commitments that one has good reason to see as one's own. In turn, one must be able to assess choices, form intentions, and carry out choices on the basis of those desires, judgments, principles, or commitments. Finally, agency requires the capacity to reflect on those choices, assessing whether they are, in fact, consistent with one's desires, judgments, or commitments (Bandura 2006, 2018). The basic thought is that agents do not merely act on desires but are able to assess and regulate which desires to act on, allowing them to recognize certain actions as theirs.[6] Fasting might be a product of someone's agency because she holds certain religious beliefs or is committed to a particular cause. That individual can then see fasting as a way to make good on those commitments.

This sketch implies that some of our choices may be inconsistent with our agency. If I were addicted to heroin and felt compelled to take the drug, I might see the desire to do so as foreign. "Heroin is terrible for me," I might tell myself. But I cannot keep myself from wanting it or keep myself from acting on that desire. If I actually go forward, injecting the drug into my vein, I may retrospectively regard that decision as foreign to me, as inconsistent with my agency. On this view, we exercise our capacity for agency when we make choices that we can reasonably view as our own and when we can identify the outcomes thereby generated as, perhaps only in part, of our own making. To return to the political domain, if we, along with others, act to advance a particular cause through the political process, we might reflect on the achievement of that end as a product of our (and others') agency.

There are many reasons to value opportunities for agency. For instance, we may be more likely to advance our well-being when we can choose for ourselves (i.e., we might be more likely to obtain better outcomes for ourselves). There may also be a significant psychological benefit to understanding ourselves as the authors, in part, of our own lives. Certain valuable social activities, like the giving of gifts or the exchanging of vows, depend on the possibility that the choices involved are *our* choices. Moreover, being kept from exercising our agency can signal unwarranted disrespect—for example, if I block you from making a choice because I hold some invidious view about you and it is known that that is why I acted. I believe these reasons for valuing agency hold in many cases. In an individual case, however, any one or all of these reasons may lapse. I may exercise my agency in ways that are harmful (e.g., making a bad investment). I may face choices that I would prefer not to face (I would prefer not to see myself in the outcome). And I may predictably make choices that violate the rights of others (Scanlon 1986).

The central reason to value opportunities to exercise agency is, I believe, largely resistant to concerns about the disutility of any individual opportunity to choose. And it is a fundamentally liberal reason: among the features that distinguish humans from the other kinds of beings whose welfare is a matter of moral concern is our capacity to make decisions that cohere with our life plans, beliefs, principles, and commitments to ourselves and others. Being able to exercise judgment about choices and being able to identify certain courses of action as consistent with our commitments is central (if not essential) to the kinds of beings we are; it is central to our capacity to act morally, to our ability to cooperate on a massive scale, to the way we can recognize ourselves in our world, and it is central to why we value freedom—that is, the ability to determine our own course. So if Person A were to systematically deny Person B the opportunity to exercise her agency in a crucial domain or domains, A would be blocking B from exercising a function that is emblematic of her humanity. A's effort would therefore be inconsistent with B's dignity, even if that effort was aimed at advancing B's well-being. That is, at a minimum, the sense in which A's actions would be illiberal and disrespectful when A systematically denies B opportunities to exercise her agency. By "disrespectful," I do not mean to imply

that negative or disrespectful judgment is necessarily commu-
nicated by A's actions. I mean instead that A's actions do not
appropriately reflect the import or value of B having an
opportunity to act as an agent—of having good reason to understand oneself as, in part, the author of one's own life. Taken
together, I take this concern and those described earlier to
ground an interest in individuals having opportunities to exercise their agency. And these concerns also ground individuals'
interest in not having their agency unjustifiably manipulated,
exploited, subverted, or blocked. If this is correct, then we have
pro tanto reasons to value states of affairs allowing us to make
decisions in ways that reflect our agency.

Does this analysis extend to the world of politics? I think
so. The value of agency is clearest with respect to self-regarding
decisions—for example, Should I dedicate my life to painting
or plumbing? In the political domain, our decisions impact
others, obviously. And it is not clear that others are obligated
to provide us with valuable opportunities to exercise our
agency if those opportunities may fundamentally impact their
own well-being, as political decisions have a tendency to do
(Kolodny 2014a). This is the crucial reason why some scholars
have turned from agency-based arguments when exploring the
authority of democratic procedures, whether those procedures
can generate decisions that citizens have an obligation to obey.
But equally important, from my perspective, is that the value
of oppositional systems need not turn on whether they are
authoritative. To see this distinction, consider the following. My
wife was under no obligation to marry me. I had no right to
her hand. Still, both I and others might acknowledge the value
of our marriage and the value of our ability to get married,
relative to a state of affairs in which we could not marry. Value
and obligation may not be in sync. It is in light of this reality
that I couch my argument in terms of the "value" of political

systems that allow individuals the opportunity to exercise their agency, not individuals' "right" to such opportunities.

Even if this seems plausible enough, there remains a potential disanalogy between opportunities to exercise agency personally and opportunities to exercise agency in, say, a competitive political system, a disanalogy between largely self-regarding actions and largely other-regarding actions. I might accept that those opportunities are valuable in the former and reject the idea that they are valuable in the latter.

I think our reasons for valuing agency will extend to the political domain under the following reasonably familiar conditions.[7] Individuals inhabit a common world with others and are subject to a political system or political rule. Such systems generate coercive outcomes shaping one's life, one's welfare, and one's projects. And they are costly to exit. Assuming that individuals have an interest in contributing to decisions that impact them, in being able to see their life as, in part, of their own making, these features of the political landscape give individuals a special interest in opportunities to exercise agency within it, in the chance to shape that system and its outputs. In sum, when these conditions exist, all else equal, we will have a reason to value political systems that offer more and better opportunities for citizens to exercise their agency over systems that offer fewer and worse such opportunities.

Comparing states of affairs from the perspective of opportunities to exercise agency is likely to be a complicated affair. And I will not offer a mechanical approach for doing so, stipulating, for instance, that six opportunities are always better than five. Any attempt will have to consider both the quantity of opportunities to exercise agency and their quality—that is, whether the choices cover decisions of subjective and objective import.

Our interest in the opportunity to exercise agency is not, I think, in the opportunity to have outcomes *directly and fully*

conform to our wishes as a result of our choices (in the way
outcomes conform to wishes when one orders a dish in a res-
taurant). It is not self-evident that we can consistently attain
what we most desire in the personal domain. And *it is* self-
evident that we *cannot* all attain what we most desire in any
large-scale social situation. Moreover, securing this end for
any single individual would be morally unattractive when many
individuals have a variety of distinct and incompatible wishes.
The agency claim we have is shared with others. And that claim
is limited by the claims of others. The conception of agency we
are concerned with here turns on our ability to pursue our
valuable projects in the world in such a way that we can *reasonably* recognize that world, at least in part, as of our own making
(Sen 1992; Dworkin 2000, 203; Tuck 2008, 55; Christiano 2008;
J. Cohen 2009, 300; Stilz 2016).

Three features of our agency interest will gain import
downstream. First, even if we accept that, generally speaking,
opportunities to exercise agency allow individuals to see
their choices and their lives as their own, the normative weight
of that conclusion relative to other considerations will depend
on the broader circumstances of those opportunities—not just
their quantity and quality. The more felicitous the conditions,
the greater the weight it is reasonable to assign to the fact that
individuals can exercise agency. Under highly felicitous conditions, we can say that individuals have opportunities to exercise
their agency autonomously or freely (i.e., when individuals are
not subject to coercion or manipulation, have many valuable
options to choose between, and possess a great deal of information about those options and the capacity and willingness to
weigh that information). This is the root of the fundamental
connection between agency and freedom. And when a decision
is freely made, we will be apt to assign greater weight to agents'
choices and to their responsibility for those choices.

As conditions become less felicitous, as decisions are no longer rightfully treated as autonomous, our judgments should change. For instance, we may be less apt to regard decisions that individuals recognize as their own as autonomous. We may therefore think that their responsibility for those decisions is mitigated. This month, I have been reading William Goldman's novel *The Princess Bride* (2007) to my daughter and son, Élodie and Jules. At one point in the story, the protagonists, Buttercup and Wesley, are captured by the evil Prince Humperdinck. Buttercup and Wesley share a great love, probably the greatest ever recorded. But Buttercup offers to marry evil Prince Humperdinck if he agrees to let Wesley go. The Prince accepts. Buttercup's decision is not freely made—the Prince has captured her and Wesley, limiting their options unjustifiably. As a result, Buttercup is not responsible for this decision. That responsibility surely falls on the Prince's shoulders. Here is the upshot: assessing the agency value of political systems, we have to consider not only whether they offer opportunities for citizens to exercise their agency but also the background conditions of those opportunities. A system that allows citizens to make free or autonomous choices will surely be more attractive than one that does not.

This raises a crucial question. Do we have reason to value opportunities to act as agents under less-than-ideal conditions? I think we do. Let us return to the *Princess Bride*. Even under the constrained circumstances Buttercup faces, she might still see her choice as her own: it evidently reflects her love for Wesley and her willingness to sacrifice for him. It is *her* choice. And it is easy to see why the author has a character whom we are intended to root for make this choice. Committing to this course demonstrates the depth of her commitment, her character, and her dignity. Moreover, there is little reason to think that Buttercup's situation is unique. People frequently make choices that cohere with their life plans even when such choices cannot be fully autonomous. One might insist that choices like this are devoid of value. But why take this course? Certain opportunities to exercise agency clearly lack value—that is, a Sophie's choice situation. And Buttercup's circumstances are far from ideal. But the chance to exercise her agency generates the possibility of a more desirable outcome (Wesley lives) and allows her to justifiably see her life as one oriented around the greatest love in the history of literature (the malign Prince Humperdink secretly plans to kill Wesley, but his schemes are not relevant to my analysis). In other words, even in infelicitous or less-than-ideal conditions, our reasons for valuing the opportunity to exercise agency will typically apply. This conclusion makes sense of the common view that one can exercise agency even when one is unfree—for example, hunger strikers in prisons. By implication, all else equal, there is reason to see those opportunities as valuable (even if not as valuable as opportunities under better conditions).

Critically, advancing our interest in agency does not require that we have equal opportunities to exercise influence (Dworkin 2000, 203). I can regard myself as contributing to an outcome even if I am less influential than others are. A surge of philosophical work has clarified the intentional structures of group agency—of the way activities can reasonably be understood as something done by and attributable to a group, rather than a collection of individuals (Gilbert 1990; Kutz 2000; Bratman 2014). The details distinguishing these theories will not detain us; but none require equal influence. Consider a common example: an orchestra performing a symphony. It makes sense to treat this as an act of joint or collective agency: the orchestra can play a symphony; a single violinist cannot. Typically, the conductor has a greater influence on the final product than the third violinist does. But the third violinist may still listen to a recording of the orchestra's efforts and recognize it as, in part, his or her own work. By implication, we might all have an equal claim to advance our interest in agency, and that interest may underwrite a claim to participate for eligible individuals. But a separate argument would be required to sustain the claim that individuals ought to have precisely equal formal opportunities to exercise their agency. And as the preceding example illustrates, formal political equality is not likely to be required to advance our interest in agency.

Finally, whether and how our "maker interest" should be recognized institutionally cannot be, I believe, determined a priori. Among a very small group of people who share a common perspective and preferences, one could probably advance one's agency without a formal mechanism for doing so. As societies grow larger and more diverse, however, formal mechanisms may serve important functions, coordinating the advancement of this interest as well as limiting any costly by-products thereby generated. Competitive opposition surely is not the only way of creating opportunities to advance this interest. But this book's historical chapters help define the conditions in which competitive opposition is an appropriate or fitting mechanism. And they illustrate why it is a practical and scalable technique for doing so under less-than-ideal conditions. By "scalable," I mean that competitive institutions allow citizens to exercise agency in polities of different scales, both small and large (Heath 2016).

Does Opposition Allow Citizens to View All Decisions as Their Own?

Vigorously competitive processes offer citizens valuable opportunities to act as political agents. Before defending this assertion, I will illustrate the limitations of a more familiar way of connecting

mass agency and political competition. In these accounts, competing parties or politicians offer citizens distinct, well-reasoned
policies. Ideally, on Ronald Dworkin's view, for example, citizens
engage in a collective process to choose among those policies. At
the end of the process, participants can reasonably see the ultimate
outcome, even an outcome they disagree with, as their own (just
as the third violinist may disagree with a conductor's interpretation of a piece of music and still see the final outcome as the
product of her agency). Elements of opposition are embedded in
these accounts. But as I show, they fall squarely within the tradition
of Millian collegial rivalry. Again, by "collegial rivalry," I mean a
largely intellectual *competition*, one that turns on who has the best
plan for advancing the commonweal. I italicize "competition"
because Dworkin's parties and politicians compete in the most
constrained sense: they advance different ideas, but they think of
themselves as part of a joint enterprise, they are motivated by joint
interests, and they know this to be true of their ostensible competitors. Notwithstanding the attractions of these accounts of
collective agency, there remains a fundamental breach separating
the dispositions and institutional practices required for us to
justifiably recognize political decisions we disagree with as our
own and the dispositions and practices typical of non-Millian
competition.

In *Freedom's Law: The Moral Reading of the Constitution*,
Dworkin describes an idealized relation between an individual
and the acts of her community. He labels this ideal, "[the] constitutional conception of democracy" (1997, 17). Dworkin later
rebranded his vision as "partnership democracy" (2006a, 131).
It is helpful, I think, to keep the word "partnership" in mind
when assessing the form of competition he embraces. On
Dworkin's view, participants should treat the impact of a decision on others as "equally significant a reason for or against that
decision" as its impact on themselves (1997, 25). Once this and

other conditions were met, citizens would justifiably regard laws and decisions as their own, as expressions of their own agency, even laws or decisions they thought were unwise. "If I am a genuine member of a political community," Dworkin argued, "its act is in some pertinent sense my act, even when I argued and voted against it, just as the victory of my team of which I am a member is my victory or defeat even if my own contribution made no difference either way" (1997, 22). In contrast to the minimalist account of competition that I defend, this take on political agency reveals a Rousseauean level of ambition. Dworkin's is an account of when we would be *justified* in viewing outcomes as our own. That means these decisions might be (or might not be) products of our agency even if we fail to recognize that this is the case.

Consider the Jewish citizens of the Weimar Republic. German Jews, Dworkin contends, were not moral members of Weimar Germany even though they could vote. Why? Because non-Jewish Germans did not treat Jewish interests with the same consideration they gave their own interests. As a result, German Jews who objected to a political outcome would reasonably see the law as foreign to them, imposed and shaped by a desire to harm and shortchange. Of course, Weimar Jews might nonetheless view a law as their own, even if they worked to defeat it. But on Dworkin's account, the value or moral weight of this identification would differ from the value of this identification under conditions of equal concern. The Weimar Jews' identification is normatively defective, like the felt agency of someone who is fasting even when there is no food to eat.

Dworkin provides an all-or-nothing view of political agency. He contrasts his treatment of communal agency with a merely "statistical" agency, in which agency is not collective but individual. The statistical approach to political agency was normatively "barren" (Dworkin 1997, 24). Taken individually,

the vast majority of people exercise little formal or informal
influence over decisions. It would be senseless, on this view, to
treat their individual contributions and the opportunities to
make those contributions as valuable. A voter in a regime not
imbued by the reciprocal attitudes that mark a partnership
democracy might *feel* that her choice contributed to the election
of her favored candidate. But there would be little reason for
others to treat this infinitesimal exercise of agency with much
respect (though there might be nonagency reasons to do so).

Is this all-or-nothing vision of political agency compatible
with legitimate opposition? One might think so. In *Innovating
Democracy: Democratic Theory and Practice after the Deliberative
Turn* (2008), Robert Goodin develops an account of party competition that would advance the cause of collective agency of
the sort described by Dworkin. For Goodin, like Dworkin, democracy is an egalitarian political system allowing individuals
to treat a law or decision as their own. Like Dworkin, Goodin
does not provide an account of the value of seeing a law as one's
own but of the conditions required for individuals to do so
justifiably. Crucially, citizens must know the justification, ratio-
nale, or grounds of a law, what Goodin calls its "*ratio*" (213–14).
In polities of any size, parties advance citizens' interest in collective, rational agency by offering them clear choices between
well-defined options, presented with clear justifications. Accordingly, Goodin contends that a two-party democracy, with
ideationally unified parties, is preferable to multiparty (+2)
democracy.[8] "Democracy," Goodin contends, "requires multiple
competing parties" (218).

Goodin's idealistic vision of partisan activity illustrates
how democracy and a certain form of competition can be
meshed. But the argument does not actually imply that real-
world oppositional systems will be democratic in the sense he
describes. The form of politics embraced by Goodin, the form

of politics necessary to allow citizens to think of most laws and decisions as products of their collective agency, is essentially cooperative. Goodin's theory is, in other words, a particularly impressive example of collegial rivalry.

Consider a dilemma that a party leader would regularly confront in Goodin's democratic regime. Let us assume, following Goodin, that there are two parties: Red and Blue. Imagine that the Blue Party proposes policy B, a proposal with clear majority support. Leaders of the Red Party now face a dilemma. They can offer and defend a rival policy, policy R, giving voters a clear, coherent choice. But given policy B's popularity, that course may come at the cost of political success. Alternatively, the leaders of the Red Party can offer policy B+, which is very similar to policy B. Offering policy B+ will increase the Red Party's chance of success while reducing the quality of the choice provided to voters. It should be clear, I think, that in Goodin's (or Dworkin's or Mill's) ideal democracy, party leaders ought to choose the policy that best advances citizens' interests, including their interest in collective agency. In other words, those leaders should choose policy R, a choice that will set back their own cause. Doing so will advance the commonweal. Indeed, even in the wake of political defeat, it might not make sense for a party to shift policies. Such a shift might leave voters with a less diverse choice set.

On Goodin's account, party leaders would actually go further than this. Presumably, they would publicize information about their proposed policies' shortcomings. It would be wrong and inconsistent with this agency-based view of democracy for political officials to shortchange the deliberative process by hiding this information.

It is clear, I think, that this notion of collective self-rule requires parties that do not act as adversaries or competitors— groups that are set against their opponents. It requires different parties to act as partners, offering distinct options but not really seeking to win. In this respect, what Goodin describes is a highly idealized, even exotic system of opposition—a system in which no one loses. Partners will not regard the victory of another as a setback at all; they will trust that the competitive system reliably advances the common good. This allows participants in oppositional systems to see results they disagree with as their own. By contrast, adversaries may be motivated by the commonweal. But they will regard a victory by their opponent as a setback for themselves and the polity. And they may reasonably resist the idea that outcomes they have opposed are products of their own agency.

Collective political agency, for Dworkin, requires equal concern for others' interests. I think this reciprocal set of attitudes powers Goodin's institutional proposal as well. Under what circumstances would the Red Party be justified in offering policy R, undercutting its own electoral prospects? When it was confident that the Blue Party would bite the same bullet. Similarly, the Red Party ought to provide negative information about its own preferred policy when it is confident that the Blue Party would do the same. But this is just what it means to be a partner, not a competitor.

Unfortunately, these arguments are not especially robust. All institutional proposals are sensitive to *some* shifts in our assumptions about the way individuals will behave. These proposals are *very* sensitive to shifts in those assumptions. As a result, they probably do not provide us with a defensible conception of opposition's value. For instance, like James Madison, we might believe that some of our fellow citizens will not be committed to the common good—that is, that there will be factions (Madison 1961a). Or we might have strong evidence that our fellow citizens are so committed to their own understanding of the common good that they will resist reciprocal activity. Those citizens' intentions are not malign. Still, they are not our partners. What follows if we imagine that some of our fellow citizens will not behave as our partners?

Suppose you were the leader of the Red Party. You have a warranted belief that your policies and leadership would better serve the commonweal than would those of the Blue Party. In that case, it is not clear that the best way to advance your fellow citizens' interests would be to publicize all the deficiencies of your proposals. It is not clear that you should offer proposals that will predictably undermine your electoral success. When citizens cannot be confident that their fellow citizens are treating them as they should, when they view others as rivals, parties will be unlikely to engage in the self-abnegating behavior required to achieve the collective agency that Goodin describes. Under those familiar conditions, it would be imprudent to make that form of agency a goal. Doing so would be self-defeating.

The preceding conclusion is hardly groundbreaking. But it illustrates the somewhat limited application of partnership-centric, all-or-nothing accounts of political agency. If Dworkin and Goodin are correct about the conditions of justified collective agency, then real-world competition probably does not allow citizens to regard political decisions that they disagree with as their own. Indeed, given the high requirements described by Dworkin, even in cases where our preferred policy is adopted, if that policy reflects the need to compromise with or maneuver around those who do not have our interests at heart, we will not have a valid reason to regard the outcomes as ours. The implication here is stark. In real-world oppositional regimes of any size, only politicians and other select members of the elite will possess opportunities to exercise agency of anything more than the "statistical" sort.

Is that really it? Is mere statistical agency all that is possible in oppositional regimes? If so, my own agency-based argument will be unlikely to persuade you. As you might expect, I do not accept that conclusion. The next section spells out why.

Adversarial Agency

According to all-or-nothing accounts, political agency is either advanced collectively, at the level of a society, or it is individual, a merely "statistical" kind of agency, causally and morally barren. These accounts are naturally viewed with skepticism by political observers who assume that political agency cannot be exercised en masse, that it can only be exercised by individuals taken one by one (Przeworski 2010, 110).[9] Yet all-or-nothing accounts like Dworkin's actually take on board the agency skeptic's view in some respects. They deny the possibility or value of collective agency at a level below that of the polity as a whole—that is, in cases where it would be unreasonable to consider decisions as having been made by the citizenry, collectively. All-or-nothing accounts actually imply that political systems defined by *real*, non-Millian, adversarial rivalry cannot regularly and effectively provide valuable opportunities for individuals to act as political agents.

The all-or-nothing view of collective agency is untenable. Accepting it requires that one of two claims would have to be correct. First, the only alternative to polity-level group agency would actually have to be individual agency. Second, the only kind of group agency that we have reason to value is polity-level agency—the kind of group agency that allows individuals to recognize almost any political decision as their own. Illustrating why neither of these claims is plausible will go some way toward showing how competitive systems advance individuals' agency interest and the way in which such systems instantiate respect for members of that polity.

It should be readily apparent, I think, that the first claim just mentioned is incorrect. There is little reason to think that collective agency is possible at the level of a polity but not at the level of a party, a social movement, a secondary association, a civic group, and so forth. The institutional and motivational requirements for group agency—the idea that "we" are doing something—will be easier to satisfy within the groups just canvassed than within a polity. All of these groups actually exist in adversarial political systems. And the rule-based character of political competition provides these groups formal and informal opportunities to influence political outcomes of various sorts—for example, the nomination of someone for office, an alteration in a single element of proposed legislation, an increase in the level of public awareness about an important problem, and so on. On reflection, the Manichean contrast that Dworkin draws between full democratic agency and statistical agency is not especially compelling.

The second claim—that we only have reason to value polity-level agency—has greater plausibility. In a large-scale competitive political system, group agency at the level of a party or a social organization will necessarily be partial and intermittent, combining moments of felt influence with moments of dispiriting impuissance. Sometimes you and others will achieve some important end—you will have stopped an offensive piece of legislation. Sometimes you and others will fail to achieve some important end—offensive legislation will pass, and you will regard the outcome as misguided and misinformed. Dworkin's polity-level notion of group agency is effectively persistent, allowing an individual to view all outcomes as consistent with her agency, as something we have done together. All else equal, I might prefer a system that allowed me to experience all political outcomes as an "extension of [my] moral life" (Dworkin 2000, 203). But this contrast does not imply that group activity in a system of opposition will be morally weightless. Surely, outcomes generated by a group can be justifiably understood as extensions of the moral life of some segment of the population.

Political theorists' millennia-long effort to comprehend popular sovereignty, to comprehend the moral weight of democratically made law, may explain the focus on polity-level agency (Aristotle 1996b; Waldron 1999). And that focus may explain why some theorists assume that individuals can justifiably see themselves as agents only when their activities have contributed, however minimally, to a specific element of law. Concentrating on legislation, however, we limit ourselves to exercises of political agency that are positive and, in some sense, final. By "positive," I mean that the activity in question results in a change to the status quo. By "final," I mean that the object of our agency is the ultimate outcome or end we are aiming for. Focusing exclusively on positive and final outcomes might be entailed by theoretical inquiries into the authority of law and the legitimacy of constitutional courts. Yet there is little reason to think we only exercise our agency meaningfully when we achieve positive and final ends.

Here is an instance of negative agency. Imagine that I engage in a large-scale effort to block the passage of a law. In coordination with thousands of others, I call my legislative representative registering my complaints. Suppose the legislation is not passed. In that case, I might reasonably see the outcome as being, in some very small part, mine. I joined with many others to achieve this end, an end that could only be achieved via large-scale collective action. Would the value of the agency I exercised in this case be of less moral weight than if I had favored the legislation and acted to advance it and it was passed? I do not see why that would be so.

Here is an instance of a more provisional kind of agency. Imagine that I favor the legalization of gay marriage and that I support a political candidate who is unlikely to win. Nonetheless, the candidate's participation in the campaign makes legalization more salient and allows us to change the views of our fellow citizens. These efforts might plausibly lead to future policy shifts. But I might see increased salience and support for legalization as extensions of my political agency. And there is no inherent reason to value a contribution of this sort less than a contribution to a successful effort to change a law. Imagine that I contribute to a shift in the legal speed limit from fifty miles per hour to fifty-one miles per hour. Is this achievement a more valuable exercise of my agency than the partial ends I have just described? I cannot think why this would be so. The bifurcated, all-or-nothing view of political agency is inaccurate. There is a range of ways to advance one's interest in agency short of seeing all legislation as one's own.

Having rejected the all-or-nothing conception of political agency, we can see how political systems defined by opposition instantiate a certain kind of respect for potential participants: they provide citizens opportunities to exercise collective agency competitively. And in contrast to the all-or-nothing conceptions of agency that I have discussed, this account is robust across a variety of political conditions; it does not require that citizens treat each other as partners or even as equals. This is a conception of political agency fit for adversarial politics.

Drilling down further, six features of oppositional systems allow the advancement of political agency:

1. Some outcomes are not foreclosed—including both changes to the status quo and the maintenance of the status quo.
2. Those outcomes are determined, in significant part, via formal, competitive activity.
3. Competitive activity is generated by participants' choices and judgments.
4. The differences between nonforeclosed outcomes are material and important.

5. More than one outcome can be pursued without
   being subject to coercion.
6. Rule-based, competitive systems coordinate and
   facilitate informal exercises of political agency.

In competitive systems, some outcomes are not foreclosed. The import of this is clear. If outcomes are foreclosed, if one cannot choose, one cannot exercise one's agency. Openness to different outcomes is frequently conflated with political uncertainty.[10] Uncertainty about what will happen in a contest implies that some outcomes are not foreclosed. But we can easily imagine a competitive system in which there is little uncertainty about the outcome but in which different alternatives could occur. Imagine that Country A featured the ideal competitive political system. It is liberal, egalitarian, uncorrupted, fair, and so forth. And imagine that the Socialist Party of Country A is extremely popular. The socialists are so good at governing and so esteemed for that reason that everyone knows that they will win a parliamentary majority at the next election. We are certain about the outcome of this election. But because the outcome is not foreclosed, because, say, the Liberal Party could win if popular opinion shifted, the system would still be competitive and would still offer opportunities for individuals to exercise their agency.

Second, oppositional systems allow citizens to exercise agency because outcomes are determined via a competitive process, a process that coordinates the activity of many actors. Competitive actions, in other words, can determine the course of a competitive process. Critically, I have not stipulated that this competition be electoral. Why not? Elections, of course, allow for mass participation in a competitive process. Not everyone will typically participate as a candidate, but voters can still play a role. Other rule-based forms of competition, like a debate or a game of poker, might also be used to determine political outcomes. Presumably, they would offer fewer chances to participate, but participants could nonetheless influence the outcome. From an agency-based perspective, one would naturally prefer a political system that offers more people more opportunities to exercise agency than a poker game (and surely there are other reasons to object to a poker-based system). Still, that poker-centric political system would feature legitimate opposition. It would still be defined by the fundamental feature of oppositional systems: those who are in power would have to allow their competitors to impact fundamental policy matters.

This relates to the third feature described earlier. In systems defined by opposition, outcomes turn, at least in part, on participants' choices, choices related to the ends of that competition. Consider a foot race that will decide some matter of political import. There are two runners, and they are evenly matched. Imagine that the two runners are forced to run. They will be killed if they do not run as fast as they are able. Even though an outcome is determined via a competitive process, the participants do not exercise their agency by participating. The winner will not be able to recognize the outcome as her own, because she cannot exercise judgment about whether to run.

Similarly, if a competitive process is used to select a political official but that official's role is entirely ceremonial, the opportunity to participate in that process will not be of value. It will not allow participants to justifiably see themselves as shaping their own lives. This explains the fourth feature of truly competitive political systems. They allow individuals to make choices about matters of some import.

The fifth feature, that participants can choose between different options without being subject to coercion, guards against systems that offer only Hobson's choices—that is, "vote for the incumbent or face some dire penalty." For instance, a

massive work stoppage might impact the policy of an autocratic government. But in autocracies, effective efforts to impact
important policies are often conducted under the threat of
punishment. Elections are frequently held in those regimes, yet
sanctions may be attached to voting for anyone who does not
support the rulers. Systems requiring participants to endure
threats of punishment as the cost for making political choices
cannot be considered respectful of citizens' agency.

There is a sixth and final way that rule-based, regular
competitive systems allow citizens to exercise their agency.
Formal competitions make it clear how organized informal
activity and mobilization can impact political outcomes that
matter. If I talk to my neighbors about candidate X, for example, they may vote for candidate X. Moreover, the organizational mechanisms used to engage in competition—like parties,
most obviously—can also be used as mechanisms to influence
political outcomes in moments when formal competition is not
occurring, that is, between elections (Disch 2011).

Oppositional systems feature these attributes. They therefore allow participants to engage in political action in ways that
permit them to justifiably view some outcomes as, in part, of
their own doing. These systems therefore provide opportunities
to exercise agency collectively. If a political system lacks one of
the first five features described earlier and no alternative
mechanism is provided, then the political system will not instantiate respect for participants' agency.

This is a minimalist account of the conditions necessary
to advance our agency. Weighing the value of choice in a competitive political system, Adam Przeworski has pondered the
weighty constraints on citizens' electoral choices. Przeworski
concludes that these constraints are inconsistent with the classical ideal of collective self-government. Real-world regimes
cannot be justified via a simple analogy with individual self-rule,

he concludes. Moreover, he finds little analogical power in Sen's famous distinction between fasting and starving. In oppositional systems, the main options for political engagement may not be to our liking. Choosing among undesirable options may not carry the independent agency-value that Sen identifies (Przeworski 2010, 106–7).

Przeworski's worries about agency misunderstand the force of Sen's analysis. Przeworski conflates the demanding conditions of self-rule with the less demanding conditions of valuable choice. Following Przeworski, I will assume that the set of options necessary to allow for political self-rule must be reasonably broad. And I will further assume, *arguendo*, that this condition is not fulfilled in many regimes featuring legitimate opposition. In many oppositional regimes, some citizens will not be able to identify a party that is committed to their full range of policy preferences. And even if such a party existed, it might have little influence on political life. Yet valuable agency is robust. It can be employed in circumstances that do not approximate a democratic ideal. Suppose you are an American socialist. You might find both major parties, Democratic and Republican, dissatisfying, perhaps even immoral. Nonetheless, you might still be able to acknowledge the gulf separating these parties. And in choosing to support or alter one of them, you would have the opportunity to exercise your agency in ways that are valuable. It matters, in other words, that I have a choice to contribute to a project of import. And competitive systems provide formal opportunities to engage in such projects. Accordingly, competitive systems instantiate respect for citizens' agency even when they do not secure the restrictive conditions of self-rule.

To sum up this section, it makes sense to recall Robert Goodin's treatment of "competitive" agency. In that system, individuals act together as a single collective agent, exercising their agency by choosing between political parties during elections.

Goodin develops an insightful model of the way a large group might come to view a narrow but important set of political decisions as their own. Unfortunately, the system that Goodin describes can only loosely be described as competitive. Its connection to the actual practice of legitimate opposition is faint and indirect. As a result, it cannot provide an accurate picture of what is lost when real-world systems of opposition are undermined.

On my account of adversarial agency, individuals acting in groups exercise their agency by contributing to formal and informal efforts to enact political change they favor and to block change they disfavor. Here, opposition facilitates agency in multiple ways, not just via elections and legislation. An obvious flaw mars my model: in a real-world regime marked by opposition, individuals will not be able to recognize their agency in many, if not most, political decisions. By implication, a relatively respectful orientation toward political agency may not be sufficiently weighty to ground an agency-based, all-things-considered justification of competitive political systems. My account has an obvious advantage too: it suggests why we might have reason to value the kinds of competitive systems we actually observe—the space they provide for individuals to advance an interest of import. It therefore identifies what is lost just in case opposition is undermined.

Is Opposition's Value a Matter of Control?

In this section and the ones that follow, I treat some foreseeable objections. Does my account of adversarial agency overlook the most important reason to value competition: because it allows the people to control political officials? Defenders of opposition and contestation sometimes cede the ground of collective political agency, choosing to defend opposition from more favorable theoretical heights. John Wilkes, perhaps the most controversial eighteenth-century member of the British Parliament, championed opposition to a French interlocutor in the following way. "The freest of nations is never sure enough of its liberty, which is a fortress constantly under siege," Wilkes contended. "The ramparts must be manned, even when the firing has stopped" (qtd. in Baker 1990, 197). Wilkes's claim is a familiar one. Put anachronistically, he argued that competitive opposition was not primarily valuable because it allowed individuals to exercise their agency via an adversarial political process. It was valuable because it outlined a regular path for groups to check one another, to man the ramparts, to exercise a measure of control over those in power.

The idea that competition can be justified principally as a check on the powerful, as a mechanism for avoiding political domination, finds significant support in contemporary democratic theory (Pettit 1997; Shapiro 1999). I do not doubt the moral import of control. Accounts that focus on it, however, may overlook and fail to capture the positive, active, creative face of opposition.[11] They do not identify why we might struggle to achieve institutions allowing individuals to undertake their political projects, not just check the projects of others.

For Ian Shapiro, a prominent defender of political competition, opposition is a key element of a just regime. Shapiro defines justice as nondomination, and domination as "the avoidable and illegitimate exercise of power that compromises people's basic interests" (2016, 5). On this view, the virtue of competition, its "distinctive center of gravity," is "accountability of government to voters" (79).

Shapiro's down-to-earth account is explicitly Schumpeterian. He does not imagine that participants will treat one another as partners. He assumes that they will not. Systems of opposition, on his view, block the formation of political

monopolies. But they also force leaders to attend to voters' basic
interests, to determine what most voters want to do. If politicians
fail to care for voters, they will be removed from office. Despite
the manifest virtues of Shapiro's account, it and others in the
same tradition conflate the import of choosing among rivals for
political power—a feature of competitive opposition—and the
import of being able to throw the bums out, which can be a
feature of noncompetitive political systems.

The preceding distinction is obscure. So consider the following example of noncompetitive accountability: Imagine a
political system in which leaders are selected via lottery from a
pool of *qualified* candidates—that is, the candidates would meet
certain prespecified criteria set out by reliable public institutions. At appropriately regular intervals, voters have the opportunity to remove leaders from office via a majority vote.
Removed leaders would then be replaced via the lottery mechanism. This noncompetitive system is legitimate. Its leaders are
chosen by a fair process. It provides citizens a measure of control over political officials. It blocks political monopolies, encourages politicians to attend to constituents' basic interests,
and pushes officeholders to consider attractive new policies. It
is evidently consistent with Shapiro's definition of nondomination.

Compared to a system marked by legitimate opposition,
this noncompetitive system makes less room for individuals to
make positive change, to try to see their political plans realized
via political activity. Why? As a general rule, the system will be
less responsive to that activity. To be sure, citizens can join
together to remove officials from office. That *is* an opportunity to exercise agency collectively. The newly selected representative will, presumably, be wary of engaging in the activities
that resulted in her predecessor's removal. Still, voters will not
have the chance to select a new candidate. The winning candi-

date will not have made any commitments about the kinds of policies she supports. She will not have justified or explained those positions. And she will, therefore, be freer to exercise her own will than an elected counterpart would be. As a result, constituents will have less reason to see any ensuing political outcomes as their own (either because they find those outcomes pernicious or because they had less of a role in generating them). All else equal, citizens will have less valuable opportunities to exercise their agency. The uncompetitive system is less attractive for that reason.

I suspect that Shapiro would accept the claim that the system of noncompetitive accountability is less attractive than a competitive system is. He acknowledges the import of voters choosing their leaders. And he has argued against institutions that weaken incentives for politicians to offer policies that voters support. Moreover, the system of uncompetitive accountability would be less likely to generate a productive battle of ideas (Shapiro 2016, 80).[12] As you might imagine, I believe this rejoinder has considerable force. But the reasons for preferring the competitive system are not closely related to nondomination—which requires that political actors be accountable to citizens and, as a result, heed their interests. From the perspective of Shapiro's conception of nondomination, the competitive system is largely equivalent to a political system in which citizens can merely remove offending officials from office.

It is possible that there are *not* persuasive theoretical reasons to systematically prefer competition to my imaginary system of noncompetitive control or accountability. Contingent conditions in specific cases may be a reason to rate one over the other. But I believe the systems are not equivalent. Vindicating that claim, however, requires more than understanding opposition's negative face—the way it facilitates control over political officials. In competitive systems, systems marked by legitimate opposition, political change occurs via the political activity and mobilization of coordinated groups. And that activity should have a place in our theory of the practice. Considering opposition by focusing narrowly on control, or nondomination, is likely to miss out on potentially valuable features of the practice.

Let us tighten our grip on the theoretical mismatch between Shapiro's approach and the value of legitimate opposition. Imagine that Polity A is defined by opposition. And in A, the majority persistently reelects majorities from a party that serves its basic interests inconsistently, at best. Now imagine that there is a similar country, Polity B. Polity B is an autocracy, but its leaders are absolutely terrified of the possibility of unrest and rebellion. Accordingly, they have established elaborate mechanisms to help ensure, to the degree possible, that members of the ruling party act in ways that track citizens' interests— higher-ups, for instance, punish local officials for corruption. Political officials in Polity B attend to citizens' interests. But they are not accountable to citizens. Note that Polity B is not fantastic—it is the end to which some autocracies aspire. Recall that Shapiro's theory turns on whether citizens' basic interests are compromised. Consistently applying Shapiro's account would, I think, lead one to prefer Polity B, to prefer the attentive autocracy.[13] The example reveals that neorepublican defenses of legitimate opposition may depend on an unjustifiably simple view of the institutional alternatives to competitive opposition. But that is not the deepest issue here.

Shapiro's theory does not actually give us weighty reasons to value the oppositional systems in which citizens do not exercise their control consistently and well. For Shapiro, the mere fact that the ruling party in Polity A could be removed has no value if people are not inclined to remove that party, if they are not inclined "to man the ramparts." By implication, his theory would struggle to show us what would be lost if opposition were undermined in these cases. This is a significant hole for a theory that is meant to apply to a world in which citizens regularly fail to man the ramparts, electing figures who may well threaten their interests. A real-world account of opposition's value should be able to reckon with the existence of Polity As. The adversarial conception of legitimate opposition does so.

The Relative Value of Agency

What is the relative value or weight of adversarial agency? Defenders of relational theories of political equality, for example, would presumably question the value of institutions marked by formal and informal inequality even when they instantiate respect for individual agency (Kolodny 2014a, 217). This is a reasonable concern. Still, even if we accept the import of social equality, we cannot easily dismiss the import of agency (and I believe most social egalitarians do not dismiss it).

Why is that? Social egalitarians argue that a situation in which one person exercises unequal power over another instantiates an objectionable relation of inequality. The use (or perhaps even the consideration) of unequal power radically transforms the status of the affected individuals. That is why not being able to exercise the same power as others is morally objectionable.

Suppose that one thinks that the exercise of power *can* have that transformative moral effect on our status. It would then be odd to rule out the moral weight of the opportunity to exercise political agency. Both views turn on the import of the opportunity to exercise power. Both views see that opportunity as connected in some fundamental way to our moral status. Social egalitarians focus on one facet of that connection: its relation to equality. But if one sees the force of such arguments, there is no abstract reason to reject other facets, such as the relation between one's capacity to act politically and one's status as an agent.

Scholars who think that political systems are primarily valuable because of their instrumental benefits are even more likely to express doubt about the value of adversarial agency (Arneson 1993, 2004). Would a system positively oriented around citizens' agency really be preferable to one that more reliably advances the cause of justice? Perhaps not. As I stated earlier, opposition's value cannot be disentangled from instrumental considerations. Agency is a by-product of instrumentally driven activity. One exercises agency by making a choice intended to generate some effect. And we use systems of opposition to minimize political violence and maintain peace, a clear instrumental benefit and a condition for the valuable exercise of agency. It would be foolish to claim that all oppositional systems generating unjust outcomes would be preferable to all autocratic regimes predictably generating just outcomes. Still, if the argument I have been advancing is correct, something would be lost with the establishment of autocracy even in this scenario.

Of course, in nonideal conditions, many people will exercise their agency in ways that are not aimed at advancing the commonweal. What reason do others have for valuing such efforts? Not much, presumably. And my account therefore allows for various familiar restrictions, like legally entrenched rights, that aim to limit obvious efforts to wrong others or violate their rights. More importantly, my goal is not to vindicate efforts to undermine the public good. Instead, I have outlined the case for a political *system* that offers individuals valuable opportunities to exercise agency, whether or not they take up those opportunities. And I believe that even those who may not see all of their preferences reflected in policy have a reason to value systems of that sort. One way of seeing this value, of course, is to compare it to alternatives. *Any* system that allows many individuals to exercise political influence, *formal or informal*, will allow some participants to use those opportunities unwisely. Systems of legitimate opposition are not unique in this respect. Moreover, as I argue in chapter 3, most realistic alternatives to opposition do not merely limit opportunities for agency but actively pervert and manipulate citizens' agency. And even those who are skeptical about the import of the opportunity to exercise agency might nonetheless recognize the wrong in its perversion.

Cooperation within a Group versus Cooperation within a Polity

A distinct concern runs as follows: my argument depends on conflicting assumptions about the possibility of cooperation. On the one hand, I am skeptical about the modes of cooperation sufficient to undergird all-or-nothing accounts of political agency and collegial rivalry, more generally. On the other hand, I have suggested that in truly adversarial settings, individuals will be able to combine together to compete with one another, collectively exercising their political agency. These positions seem to be inconsistent. If cooperation is feasible at the level of the group, why is it not feasible at the level of a polity?

This concern fails to reflect how real-world competition may foster certain kinds of cooperation at the level of groups or parties. We can divide the possible mechanisms into two categories: psychological and interest based. The psychological argument is apparent enough. Competition between groups can spur individuals to identify with and trust members of their own group and party (Simmel, Wolff, and Bendix 1955; Sherif 1967). These forms of identification can motivate cooperation on their own, or they can be used by others to encourage cooperation

(Posner 2004). Applying social pressure, for instance, will be more effective when the target's failure to comply generates disapproval from a group. This means that cooperation, of a sort, is likely to flourish with competition. Of course, one might identify with one's polity writ large and feel some pressure to contribute to it. But the question here is not whether cooperation at the level of a polity is possible but whether it will be sufficiently pervasive and consistent to support a fundamentally cooperative approach to politics. I doubt that it is. And where it is not, theories embracing a form of Millian collegial rivalry will have little grip.

Beyond the psychological, competition for power and resources can create incentives for individuals to cooperate. This occurs when competition generates selective benefits for some or all of a group's members (Aldrich 1995). I use the word "competition" rather than "victory" here. Even if a group does not achieve its goals, if it merely mitigates the harm caused by rivals, its activities may generate selective benefits. Those benefits may be sufficient to induce some members of a group to cooperate. And those individuals can, in turn, distribute benefits to others, inducing them to cooperate. This is the basic logic of party mobilization. It is not surprising, in other words, that competitive systems sustain significant levels of cooperation within competing groups. Accordingly, there is no tension in thinking that competitive political systems might facilitate group-based forms of collective agency even in cases in which polity-wide forms of agency are unlikely.

Conclusion

What is lost just in case opposition is undermined? In this chapter, I have sketched an answer to that question: the adversarial conception of legitimate opposition. Political systems featuring opposition instantiate a certain kind of respect for participants' agency. This is true even if those systems are objectionably distant from our democratic ideals. And when they are pulled down, they are rarely replaced by systems instantiating the same forms of respect.

Chapter 3 goes further. It puts the adversarial conception of legitimate opposition to work, offering an alternative account of the threat posed by populist challengers to legitimate opposition and the normative toll when flawed, real-world systems of opposition are replaced by their most prominent real-world rival: electoral autocracy. Examining the electoral practices of nondemocratic regimes, I argue that those regimes go well beyond merely blocking opportunities to exercise agency. They deploy electoral institutions to subvert and manipulate their citizens.

3

Opposition under Attack
Democracy, Populism, and the
Specter of Electoral Autocracy

In 2020, Singapore's People's Action Party suffered a shocking electoral setback. The *Economist* (2000) took the measure of the electoral catastrophe in its famously restrained house style: "In Singapore, which has been ruled by the People's Action Party (PAP) since independence in 1965, this was the best performance by an opposition party ever in terms of seats won, and the worst by the PAP." The result was so bad for the ruling PAP that Lee Hsien Loong, the country's prime minister and the son of its previous prime minister Lee Kuan Yew, took it upon himself to bestow the title "Leader of the Opposition" on Pritam Singh, the leader of the Worker's Party.

Singapore experienced an electoral upheaval, but one illustrating its distance from an actual system of legitimate opposition. Despite the PAP's poor performance, the party still won eighty-three of the ninety-three seats up for contestation. The incumbent party's advantages are legion: they control the design of electoral districts, the rules around polling, the length of electoral campaigns, what kinds of campaigning are allowed, the number of votes needed to win a seat, and so on. The PAP also tightly controls how public funds are expended. As a result, even in areas in which the PAP has lost, its local officials remain the de facto representatives of the government—responsible for attending to constituents' concerns. Voting for an alternative to the PAP is largely symbolic. Indeed, the Worker's Party leader even conceded that his goal was not to replace the PAP but to improve its performance (perhaps tightening the PAP's grip on power) (Yang 2020).

No one would mistake the People's Action Party for a populist movement. It lacks populist style and bombast. But it has designed a political system in which one party uses the rules of the game and the resources of the state to bolster its political dominance. And that system is a model for movements that are currently assailing legitimate opposition. This chapter uses the resources of the adversarial conception of legitimate opposition to assess systems of this sort, taking seriously the normative character of autocratic institutional designs.

Regimes lacking opposition do not provide citizens adequate formal opportunities to impact political outcomes. As the Singaporean example illustrates, the government's freedom from adversarial opposition means that it can change the rules or bring extra resources to bear if it faces defeat. But nonoppositional governments go well beyond clamping down on those who might challenge their power. In fact, they force citizens to advance the interests of the government. To do so, they repurpose oppositional practices, such as elections and representative bodies. Even in nonoppositional polities, these institutions require a citizen to act like an agent—to vote for the government's candidate or boycott. But whatever a citizen chooses, she will serve the government's end. In the case of Singapore, for instance, voters looking to effectively oppose the government can choose between the PAP and the Worker's

Party, a party that aims to improve the performance of the PAP. In this way, citizens' capacity to act and make choices is perverted, turned against itself. These realities contort the political process. They fundamentally distinguish political life in Singapore from political life in Norway, for example.

Why Singapore? Because not every electoral autocracy is Russia. Autocratic regimes are diverse. And they take a diverse approach to individual rights. But in modern regimes lacking opposition, including both Singapore and Russia, popular political procedures, like elections, are attacks on citizens' dignity, on their ability to see their actions as their own.

Here is the intuition driving my argument. In the movie *Cool Hand Luke*, Paul Newman plays Luke, a rebellious character who drunkenly tries to steal several parking meters. For his trouble, he is sent to a prison camp. Even in prison, even without his freedom, Luke preserves his agency. He refuses to back down when challenged by a hulking inmate. He completes an assigned task as fast as he can, faster than the prison guards expect. Doing so, he carves out a few moments free from work. And he shows the other inmates that they can still exercise some measure of self-rule.

After an escape, Luke is brought back to the camp, beaten, and sent to the hole, that is, solitary confinement. He is then subjected to a series of punishments intended to break him. At one point, he is required to dig a deep pit. For no apparent reason, he is made to refill it, and then dig it again. Finally, he collapses. The guards could have kept Luke in the hole. They could have beaten him. But Luke's punishment is not merely to be dominated, subjected to the arbitrary power of others. His punishment targets his agency. His actions and choices advance no end but his own subjugation. If he slows down, he will have more work to do. If he speeds up, he will have more work to do. Forcing someone to contribute to their own subjection, subverting someone's agency in this way, is, I believe, especially alienating and demoralizing. This has been a commonly understood feature of our moral world at least since someone told the story of Sisyphus. In the film, Luke emerges from this punishment not merely unresisting but compliant, willing to act for his jailers.

I believe the disrespect entailed by this kind of punishment is a defining feature of real-world regimes lacking legitimate opposition. This is the basic nature of the political institutions established in contemporary Russia. It is the basic nature of the institutional framework under construction in Hungary. This orientation toward citizens distinguishes the political system of a model autocracy like Singapore from that of an unjust, unequal oppositional regime like the United States. The United States may feature a flawed political system, but citizens have the opportunity to impact political outcomes that matter through a competitive process. They can meaningfully pursue what they think is right. And that comes into question when a presidential candidate, like Donald Trump, threatens to jail his political rival. The freedom to seek office without fear of unjustified legal reprisal is, of course, necessary for electoral opposition. Without it, only those who are compromised by the government will seek office, transforming an election from an opportunity to take political action into an instrument of demoralization.

The Populist Threat and the Question of Democracy's Import

Jan-Werner Müller's *What Is Populism?* tries to pin down what populism means, as well as the threat populists pose. These are issues of pressing import. And the book has reset the terms for academic and public debate about this critical, if conceptually slippery, idea.[1] Müller's arguments are worth considering here because they help illustrate the analytical value of the adversarial conception.

Populists, Müller contends, consider themselves the sole representatives of *part* of the nation. And populists claim that that *part* of the nation is actually the "true" or "authentic" people (Müller 2016, 22–23). For Müller, democracy is an open-ended contest about who the "people" are and what they "want" (22–23). Populists have no time for this pluralist vision of democracy. And they have no great fondness for legitimate opposition either.[2] "For populists, there cannot be such a thing as legitimate competition when populists run for office," Müller argues. "When they are in power, there is likewise no such thing as a legitimate opposition" (27). Populists, on this view, act wrongly because they do not "try to find fair terms of sharing the same political space with others whom [they] respect as free and equal but also irreducibly different in their identities and interests" (82). And this manifests itself in how they pursue power and how they govern.

Müller's account of democracy is deflationary, not too demanding. And it is consistent with the democratic conception. Here, opposition is a democratic practice. This allows Müller to draw a bright line between flawed regimes where populists have not taken power (democracies) and those where they have (nondemocracies or regimes hurtling toward nondemocracy). Yet, like the minimalist approach to democracy that I discussed in the introduction, this maneuver has an unsatisfying side effect: Müller's notion of democracy does not do as much work as he might like.

Let us assume, following Müller, that democracy is an open-ended contest between those who claim to be the people's voice. Why should we value this process? Here is one thought. Systems in which almost everyone treats each other fairly, treats each other with the respect owed to free and equal citizens, are of great value. That seems correct to me. Yet there is a snag. The existence of populist movements suggests that many individuals do not accept this vision of democracy and do not intend to treat each other respectfully. Müller's democracies, the regimes we are worried about, like Hungary and even the United States, are not respectful regimes. Therefore, it will not be evident what is lost when democracy or opposition is compromised.

Here is a second stab at the question. Democracy's value lies precisely in its capacity to frustrate the ambitions of those who claim to represent the people exclusively, that is, populists (though precisely why that would be valuable is still not clear; Garsten 2010). Widespread mutual respect and acceptance of democracy are not required, on this view. There is a hitch here too. It is the blatant *vulnerability* of these institutions, their *incapacity* to frustrate populists, that Müller has so effectively and consistently brought to public attention (Müller 2018).

Here is a third take. Individuals are likely to suffer in some morally important respects when a process allowing political actors to claim to represent the people is demolished, even if the society in question is unequal and individuals do not regularly treat each other as free and equal. This looks more promising. Calling the process in question democratic, however, does not actually give us much insight into the way individuals will suffer when the process is endangered. Müller, of course, does not embrace or defend regimes boasting radical political inequality. Yet the issue remains: adopting a minimalist vision of democracy leaves the moral price of populism unclear.

Other scholars have raised concerns about the minimalist conceptions of democracy used to define the populist challenge. But those who raise this concern also embrace a version of the democratic conception. They see legitimate opposition as an essential feature of more egalitarian, less minimal democracies.

A leading scholar of populism, Cristóbal Rovira Kaltwasser, has argued, contra Müller, that "populism is something internal to democracy. Given that the core concepts of the populist ideology— the pure people, the corrupt elite and popular sovereignty—can be easily used to refer to the gap between democratic ideals and existing democracies, we should not be surprised at the rise of populist actors who seek to enact the redemptive side of politics, and re-politicize those that intentionally or unintentionally are not being addressed by the establishment" (2014, 484).

Kaltwasser's disagreement with Müller has little to do with their definitions of populism. It turns on their definitions of democracy. They agree that populists take aim at the elite, claim to represent the people, and pose a challenge to competitive institutions. For Kaltwasser, however, democracy is more than competition; it cannot be downgraded to a battle between groups claiming to represent the people. Democracy may entail that no one group can claim finally to represent the "people." Yet democracy worthy of the name requires egalitarian inclusion as well. A polity is less than fully democratic if only certain elite groups are able to make their partial claims heard. This is the situation in most competitive regimes. And the antidemocratic character of these regimes is, on this view, an accelerant for populist fury.

Kaltwasser embraces a more demanding definition of democracy than Müller does—one he draws from the writings of Robert Dahl. But this account carries the characteristic limitations of cashing out all important political questions in the currency of democracy. Following Dahl, Kaltwasser assumes that regimes more closely approximating a fully competitive, egalitarian democracy will be more attractive (Dahl 1971). At the cost of repeating an argument I developed in the introduction, that assumption is not warranted. Approximation may make things worse.

For instance, elections are held in regimes lacking opposition. Those elections are used to advance the ruling regime's ends. They seem to make those regimes more stable (Gandhi 2008; Schedler 2009; Simpser 2013). Institutionally, electoral autocracies more closely approximate ideal regimes than do regimes that completely lack elections. But are they more democratic or more attractive for that reason? I do not think so.

The same analytic difficulties plague Kaltwasser's assessment of the populist complaint. Are exclusions from power necessarily undemocratic? If conditions of full democracy are not met, we may not reasonably assume that something is gained with respect to citizens' interests just in case an excluded group gains influence. Imagine that the excluded group was only recently barred from political participation. Before, they wielded unjust dominion over a segment of the populace, amassing great riches. If allowed to participate, they will use their ill-gotten wealth to undercut unjustifiably the political influence of others. Would reenfranchising this group make things more democratic? Perhaps. Perhaps not. Surely untangling this conundrum requires careful argument, not mere assumptions about the import of approximation. The deep problem is that Dahl's notion of democracy (one he contrasts with polyarchy) is distant from contemporary political practices and relies on the faulty crutch of approximation. Approaches like this simply cannot generate defensible assessments of the costs involved when popular movements take aim at legitimate opposition.

The democratic conception of legitimate opposition impedes understanding of threats to opposition, including populism. What about an approach that directly considers the value of opposition, that is, the adversarial conception? Demonstrating that the adversarial conception provides leverage on threats to opposition is the next section's work.

Why Attacks on Opposition Are Attacks on Citizens' Agency

Democratic theorists sometimes contend that democracy's value, even of the most minimal sort, would not be questioned by subjects of autocratic regimes (Przeworski 1999; Shapiro 2016, 78). Only those cosseted by practices like opposition find their virtues negligible. Readers are usually asked to take the authors' word for it. Autocracy is bad news, trust me. And the wrong involved with autocratic government, the wrong brought by the destruction of opposition, is generally left to the readers' imagination. Here, I put conceptual meat on those argumentative bones.

I offer rough sketches of a regime where opposition remains intact, Oppositionlandia, and a similar regime where opposition has been undermined, Autocracia. Oppositionlandia does a relatively poor job advancing citizens' interest in political agency. This should make distinguishing it from Autocracia more difficult. On the other hand, if my argument succeeds, we can attribute our distinct assessments to the polities' treatment of opposition.

Oppositionlandia bears a close resemblance to the United States. It features similar levels of inequality and similar political rules—that is, first-past-the-post elections. Four features of Oppositionlandia's political landscape merit emphasis. First, it has a large population. One vote is unlikely to change the outcome of an election. Protesting may not keep a political official from implementing an objectionable policy. By implication, the type of political agency on offer is of a different character than the kind of the agency at stake when I choose laundry detergent. I might regard the electoral outcome as having major significance while acknowledging that my individual contribution is small.

Second, two major parties dominate the political scene. And the available mechanisms for sanctioning the parties are relatively limited. Political officials can be turned out of office, but there is little practical chance that a third party can exercise great power. Taken together, the dominant parties' influence is unchecked. Moreover, in a contest between the parties, there is little guarantee that individuals will think either party's candidate especially attractive. Many may vote. Yet that might be merely to avoid the lesser evil.

Third, opportunities to exercise political agency are not equally distributed. Political officials and officeholders have considerable power. And the wealthy and influential exert extra influence because they control resources that politicians want, including media coverage, money, organizational support, jobs, and so forth. I assume that the extra opportunities to exercise agency enjoyed by the influential cannot be justified.

Fourth, the political environment is pervaded by manipulation. Political actors and media sources regularly provide biased or untrustworthy accounts of the issues of the day, taking advantage of citizens' lack of information and playing on their biases. Manipulation might be justified in some cases (Wood 2014, 289–90). For the sake of argument, however, I will assume that it does *not* plausibly contribute to individuals' collective capacity to make wise judgments or even judgments that are consistent with their own values. This manipulation not only is allowed in Oppositionlandia but is fueled by the competitive nature of its politics. It is encouraged by the desire of the powerful to defend their own influence.

Oppositionlandia's political system instantiates a kind of disrespect for citizens' agency in at least four different ways. A typical citizen's opportunity to impact outcomes is limited. Voters rarely possess the opportunity to turn out the candidates of both major parties. They do not have the same opportunities to exercise their agency, and some of those inequalities are not justifiable. Finally, many are unjustifiably manipulated, and their actions are impacted, to some degree, by that manipulation.

Still, Oppositionlandia features legitimate opposition. Citizens therefore have opportunities to join together to impact outcomes that matter. The country may be dominated by two political parties, but the policy differences between the two parties are significant, even if citizens do not have an adequate set of choices (I leave "adequacy" undefined since my argument does not require it to be fleshed out). Moreover, if someone dislikes a policy or officeholder, Oppositionlandia offers institutional paths for changing that policy or unseating that officeholder. In this important way, Oppositionlandia's institutions instantiate a positive measure of respect for citizens' agency; citizens can look at their political institutions as reflecting their capacity to make decisions about issues that matter.

Now consider Autocracia. In many respects, it is similar to Oppositionlandia. People can assemble, and they can make their views known, though the main television channels and newspapers are owned by a small number of corporations. Elections are held, and representative bodies feature more than one party. Yet Autocracia does not feature legitimate opposition. There is, as a result, very little doubt about political outcomes. When there is doubt, the results in question will have no great impact on the course of public affairs. Real opposition parties may win seats in the legislature, but they are unlikely to take power. In Autocracia, electoral outcomes vary counterfactually with votes. The vote winner tends to be the person who takes office. But the electoral playing field is heavily tilted in favor of the government's candidates. To achieve this, the government employs a creative array of measures, including gerrymandering, media regulation, the effective political exclusion of some actors, the strategic use of social insurance programs, and support for Potemkin parties.

Why do regimes like Autocracia hold costly elections and fill representative bodies without allowing for meaningful opposition? Because electoral processes can build public and international support for the regime. They generate information about the citizenry and about the effectiveness of lower-level regime functionaries. Contests can demonstrate incumbents' great strength, and they can be effective in dividing and demoralizing the opposition. Sometimes candidates who are not members of a ruling party win office in Autocracia. But this is allowed because it serves the ends of the regime—helping its leaders identify and co-opt pliable rivals (Schedler 2009; Gandhi 2008; Simpser 2013).

Autocracia is less respectful of its citizens' agency than Oppositionlandia is. We have grounds to prefer Oppositionlandia's institutions for that reason. But making these claims stick requires meeting a challenge: there may be very little uncertainty about electoral outcomes in oppositional regimes. Imagine that one of Oppositionlandia's parties is very popular. It controls the government. Elections will take place in a month, and polls indicate strongly that the governing party will remain in power. For the sake of argument, we can assume that our confidence in the outcome depends, in part, on Oppositionlandia's electoral rules. The election, for instance, is conducted with territorial electoral districts, and that fact contributes to our confidence in the incumbent—that is, if Oppositionlandia was a single district, the incumbent's position might not be as strong. Moreover, members of the dominant party had a role in designing Oppositionlandia's political institutions. What distinguishes such an election from an otherwise similar election in Autocracia?

In both cases, the outcome of an electoral contest is effectively known in advance. In both cases, one party aims to dominate the others. In both cases, electoral rules contribute to one party's dominance. In both cases, expectations about the dominant party's victory will keep some potential challengers out of the race.

Now imagine that the tides of public opinion shift direction in both regimes. The governing parties looked sure to keep their places. Now they face defeat. In Oppositionlandia, the ruling party will lose as a result of this shift. Even if its members favored staying in power by any means necessary, the existence of alternative parties and their supporters in various institutions like the military or state governments would increase the costs of such efforts. Participants will now expect the incumbent to lose. Their activities will be guided by that expectation. In short, a political system defined by opposition will respond to regularized expressions of citizens' agency.

In Autocracia, by contrast, the incumbent government will not face resistance from an organized opposition. And it will predictably use the instruments of the state to maintain its position. Perhaps it will delay the vote or alter the rules of the contest (Casey 2018). Participants will organize their activities around the following fact: the incumbent will win, no matter how voters' preferences shift. The shadow of future interventions looms over Autocracia's political life. And the government's public commitment and capacity to get its way distinguish uncompetitive elections in Autocracia from those in Oppositionlandia. Voting and organizing take place in both regimes. Neither system is egalitarian. But political outcomes are not up for grabs in polities like Autocracia. Outcomes are determined, fundamentally, by the government itself. And because outcomes are determined by the government, citizens do not possess meaningful, formal opportunities to exercise agency competitively. This is the goal pursued by those who threaten legitimate opposition.

Opposition and the Perversion of Adversarial Agency

In fact, governments that undermine opposition go far beyond blocking opportunities to exercise agency. They subvert and pervert citizens' capacity to choose and act. How so? By coercing them to support the government. This includes citizens who oppose the government *and* those who support it. By "coercion," I mean that within the political arena, citizens are compelled to act in ways that advance the government's ends. Citizens' agency is not blocked. It is turned against itself. This notion of coercion differs from the use of conditional threats to change someone's actions—for example, if you do not show up to class, I will give you an F. That notion of coercion is a focus of the philosophical literature (Nozick 1969). Here coercion is institutional and more closely approximates physical constraint than threat.

Consider opponents of Autocracia's government. Imagine that there is an election in the offing. The opponents have three options. They can cast a ballot for a government-backed candidate. This, obviously, would serve the government. They can support a Potemkin candidate, a weak government opponent allowed to run to make the contest seem plausibly fair and generate information about the government's popularity. This too would further the government's ends. Or, finally, the opponents might simply decide not to vote, to boycott the procedure. But this choice also demonstrates the government's dominance and the fecklessness of the opposition. The opponents are forced to make a choice. No matter what they choose, they serve the government.

I began this chapter with an example drawn from a film— of a man forced to dig and refill a trench. Not acting is not an option. Yet no matter what he does, he will achieve nothing. Luke's capacity to act is turned against him, used as a means of punishment. Of course, *Cool Hand Luke* is fiction. But the political institutions I have described are not products of my imagination, fiendish devices concocted in my office. While writing the initial draft of this book, a debate raged within the Venezuelan opposition to President Nicolás Maduro about how they should approach a presidential election (Reuters 2018). The situation was typical. Leading candidates had been blocked from running, the date of the election was shifted to suit the incumbent, and previous election results were nullified. Many people in the opposition determined that their electoral participation would suit Maduro, lending public legitimacy to a fraudulent process. Others, like the former Hugo Chávez supporter Henri Falcón, claimed that the best strategy was for the opposition to contest an election designed so that it would lose (Falcón 2018). No matter what the opposition did, its actions would foreseeably strengthen the government. It faced an invidious choice, one that divided it.

This is what the subversion of political agency looks like. Nonoppositional regimes do not offer citizens a meaningful, if less than ideal, choice defined by a flawed, inegalitarian competitive system. They limit citizens' opportunities to make meaningful choices, forcing them to support the government. And by putting citizens in this position, drafting them to make choices that advantage those who hold power, they demonstrate and reinforce their dominance.

In *The Power of the Powerless* (1985), Václav Havel offers a famous analysis of this form of government. "Post-totalitarian" systems, Havel argues, specialize in perverting their citizens' capacity to act—forcing a greengrocer to choose between hanging propaganda in his shop window or outing himself as a rulebreaker, a subversive. "Farcical elections" and a Potemkin "legal code" provide political cover for tyranny (43, 73). They also attack citizens' dignity, their capacity to justifiably see their actions as their own. The fundamental aim is not to convince people to hang posters in their windows, any more than the aim of Autocracia is to get its citizens to vote. Instead, post-totalitarian systems corrupt their citizens' agency, making them "agents of the system," forcing them to "live within a lie" (31, 36). Citizens need not embrace these political institutions, need not regard them as fair or just. "It is enough for them to have accepted their life with it and in it. For by this very fact, individuals confirm the system, fulfill system, make the system, *are* the system" (31).

My focus has been on government opponents. What of those who support Autocracia's incumbent? What about those who embrace Nicolás Maduro (Venezuela), Vladimir Putin (Russia), or Lee Hsien Loong (Singapore)? Surely, they have opportunities to exercise their agency. They can understand their votes or other activities as efforts undertaken to support a government they value. And the promise of many populists is precisely that once the opposition is brought to heel, those who favor the government, "the people," will finally be able to see their will reflected in political outcomes.

Backers of Autocracia's government are mistaken. Their felt agency does not mean that they have opportunities to act as agents. Imagine dissidents who cast their ballots for a fake opposition candidate, a candidate who is running to lose (Mac-Farquhar 2017). As I argued in chapter 2, opportunities for agency must be rooted in some objective reality. To be of some value, that opportunity must allow the actor to contribute to an outcome that matters. For instance, the dissidents may believe they have exercised their agency, but nothing turns on their votes for the Potemkin candidate; they are mistaken. The government supporters are in the very same position. Government backers may believe that they are contributing to an outcome of import. Yet the political system is organized to deliver those specific outcomes regardless of their collective efforts. If those outcomes were not forthcoming, the system would be redesigned, the election postponed, additional inducements provided, the outcome voided, so that the appropriate end was achieved. In this respect, those who support the government are not protected from having their agency subverted.

My children like having pasta for dinner. Sometimes I begin to make it and only afterward ask want they want to eat. When they answer pasta and they get it, they feel like agents. But they are not. I already started cooking the meal. I would serve them pasta even if they had wanted something else. My children have been manipulated. And government supporters in nondemocracies are in much the same position. They get what they want, but not because they wanted it.

I have assumed that individuals have an interest in exercising political agency. But it is a truism that coercion can be justified, that there are cases in which I can be forced justifiably to act in ways that I object to. Modern states would, by definition, be illegitimate were this not the case. What, if anything, distinguishes justified acts of coercion from the forms of coercion engaged in by nonoppositional regimes? What makes the latter especially disrespectful?

I am required to pay income taxes, for example. Surely part of my taxes funds some projects I regard as unwise or unjust. If I do not pay my taxes, I will be subject to some onerous penalty. In this case, I am forced to act in ways that set back causes I care about. Here, coercion is used to fund some projects. Usurping my agency is a by-product of that effort. But, all else equal, if it were legal and more efficient for the government to simply remove money from my back account, I assume it would do so. Funding the project, not having *me* pay, is the heart of the policy.

By contrast, as Havel emphasizes, certain regimes take direct aim at citizens' agency. And in important ways, most regimes lacking opposition are focused on that objective. They flaunt their dominance by getting citizens—both supporters and opponents—to act as if they are making a choice (Wedeen 1999). This explains the ambivalent stance these regimes adopt when skewing political institutions. They do relatively little to hide their work. Yet they do not admit that the elections or other contests are a sham. Concealing their efforts to bias the system would signal weakness. Simply admitting that the elections were a sham would attenuate their agency-subverting potential, allowing citizens to give up on the lie. If the same goals could be satisfied without subverting citizens' agency, the regimes we are concerned with would still do so—that is, they would still hold fraudulent elections. This distinguishes the methods of coercion used in nonoppositional regimes from the forms of coercion common in flawed, oppositional regimes. Of course, fraudulent elections and similar practices serve other purposes, like gaining information about citizens' views and dividing the opposition. But the achievement of these purposes relies on the perversion of citizens' agency. No information would be obtained, no division would be sowed, if no one bothered to participate, if no one acted like an agent. In sum, nonoppositional regimes depend on getting citizens to act as if they are making choices even though they lack the opportunity to do so. These regimes induce citizens to act as agents even though they exercise no formal power.

Oppositionlandia's political institutions are imperfect, infuriatingly so. But Autocracia's political institutions corrupt and pervert their citizens' agency. And they do so in ways that ought to be regarded as illiberal. This is a reason to regret the collapse of legitimate opposition even in regimes that do not approximate our political ideals—countries like Oppositionlandia or the United States or Hungary or Poland.

It may be helpful to distinguish attacks on legitimate opposition from gerrymandering. Gerrymandering occurs when representative districts are drawn to advantage particular parties or officials. In principle, gerrymandering can be consistent with opposition, increasing the competitiveness of an election. Imagine that a party in power knows that it will be blown out at the next election. It redraws electoral districts, and this results in a more competitive election (without gerrymandering, the incumbent party would have been crushed). This maneuver might be problematic for a number of different reasons. Yet it does not deprive individuals of an opportunity to exercise their agency collectively. And that conclusion is entirely consistent with the distinctions I have drawn among democracy, equality, and opposition.

Gerrymandering can also surely be used to undermine opposition. This occurs when its effects are sufficiently extreme to foreclose political outcomes and when it contributes to a single party's or group's capacity to enact further changes to the rules. Debates about gerrymandering typically focus on a single map or single effort to swing an election. If my account is correct, the practice becomes especially problematic when it extends a shadow of political dominance beyond a single election—no matter what the voters do, the rules will be altered to advance the incumbent's ends. Like the lead character in *Cool Hand Luke*, when citizens seem likely to achieve some end, such as removing the incumbent, those who are in charge will simply revise the rules again, telling them that they have not achieved anything at all. In such cases, elections become exercises in the subversion of that agency.

There is another way that Autocracia's coercive apparatus can be distinguished from everyday coercive institutions. Coercion can be justified in many domains. But we might think that it is almost always illegitimate in others. The determination of one's religious faith comes to mind. In those domains, coercion is antithetical to the value of the practice involved. Opposition *might* be such a domain.

Opposition is a special domain, on this view, because it gives citizens the chance to make important decisions together. Regimes like Autocracia cannot reject this argument out of hand. Those regimes predictably claim that fraudulent elections reflect the will of the populace. "Thank you for the sincere support I received from the citizens of Russia at the presidential election," Vladimir Putin declared during his 2018 inauguration. "I view this support as a huge political asset and a reliable moral backing" (Putin 2018). Boasting like this, incumbents admit that elections really are about the opportunity to make choices. If this is correct, then individuals may have a special claim not to have their agency perverted in this domain. And those regimes may commit a special wrong when they use elections to manipulate and demean their constituents.

This argument supports my conclusion: undermining opposition leads to disrespectful and morally unattractive political systems. Yet I have not emphasized it. Why? Because it depends on a contestable view of opposition and its distinctiveness. We are apt to think that religious belief is especially critical to a person's identity, to her self-conception and life plan. That is why the domain of religious belief requires substantial deference. Is political agency of the same character? I am not sure. And I have greater confidence in the wrong involved with using coercion to corrupt and pervert someone's agency, whether or not that corruption occurs in an electoral context.

Assessing the Adversarial Conception

How does my argument compare with the treatments of populism considered at this chapter's start? Admittedly, my account lacks rhetorical oomph. If one's goal is to raise alarms about populism, it makes more sense to claim that populism spells the ruin of democracy. I do not honestly expect anyone to roll out the adversarial conception on the hustings.

Still, my account possesses several attractive features. It picks out an agency-based *pro tanto* reason to value opposition and to regret its demolition. It does not require a deflationary conception of democracy—one that papers over the limitations of contemporary regimes. This account sidesteps the debate about whether populist movements can be democratic. They may be. Yet all else equal, populist movements act wrongly when they undermine opposition even if the system they attack is less than fully democratic. Finally, this account boasts an attractive versatility: it applies to regimes dominated by populists and regimes in which nonpopulists thwart the play of opposition. This account illustrates why model autocracies, like Singapore, may rightly be thought illiberal even if they are not well-known fonts of populism.

Of course, I am emphasizing the relative merits of my approach. But my analysis also complements the rapidly developing research program on populist movements (Mudde and Rovira Kaltwasser 2012; Rovira Kaltwasser et al. 2017). If Müller is correct, populists are better positioned to undermine opposition because their ideology is inconsistent with the practice—he refers to this advantage as a "moral surplus" (2016, 83). And my account illustrates clearly why that moral surplus ought to be a source of concern.

Have I missed the forest for the trees? Opposition, one might think, is actually valuable for several reasons unrelated to political agency. Undermining the practice, governments infringe on various liberal rights, like free speech and free association. And when it is undermined, one group gains control of the state, allowing it to unjustifiably and unaccountably extract rents from others. Are these claims inconsistent with my argument? I do not think so. Again, agency-based arguments are not free from concerns about the instrumental value of opposition; they depend on them. For the opportunity to exercise agency to be of value, something important must be a stake in the process. And that process must be sufficiently free to allow individuals the opportunity to exercise their agency. Moreover, efforts to undercut citizens' interests and efforts to subvert citizens' agency are rooted in the same malign values and motivations.

Still, my argument has its own normative bite. There may be some cases—Singapore comes to mind—in which individuals can argue with a straight face that the populace's instrumental interests and their nonpolitical rights are cared for by a regime that does not allow opposition. And my argument identifies the wrong entailed when opposition is undermined, even if the regime appears to generate valuable outcomes for its citizenry.

Is it not possible that crushing oppositional institutions can be justified, all things considered? Sure. Imagine that my children are fighting. I might force them to dig and refill a hole in the backyard, keeping them busy, showing them who is in charge. The coercion may be justified because it avoids needless conflict. Singapore's rulers justify their power along just these lines (Yew 2005). Were it not for the country's uncompetitive electoral system, Singapore would descend into ethnic violence, they claim. And, all things considered, that form of rule may be justified. In both cases the subjects, my children and Singaporean citizens, are not treated like individuals capable of agency. And in both cases, the subjects' capacity for agency is used against them: every shovel of dirt removed from the ground will have to be put back. In this respect, these institutions demean even if they are warranted by the circumstances.

Conclusion

Legitimate opposition is under attack. But the normative questions raised by this political turn are not straightforward. Answering them requires a realistic assessment of flawed, real-world institutions and practices. The traditional approaches to the problem, I believe, make that effort more challenging. They inevitably lead us away from the practices and movements that generated our concern and toward the same, predictable questions: What is your definition of democracy? This chapter argues that the adversarial conception of legitimate opposition gives us a tighter grip on *one* critically important question: What wrong, if any, is done when opposition is undermined? Regimes lacking the practice do not treat their citizens as agents; they treat them as tools. And this is true whether those regimes are led by abrasive populists or suave, Oxford-educated autocrats.

Of course, there are many pressing normative questions not addressed by my account. In what circumstances are attacks on opposition justified, all things considered? What measures to defend opposition are warranted? What role, if any, do external countries and institutions have to play? The worth of my analysis depends on a wager. Focusing on one practice, legitimate opposition, and a narrower, simpler set of questions will provide insights that wider analyses cannot. Hopefully, those insights can inform the complicated, all-things-considered judgments required to respond to attacks on opposition. And, hopefully, those insights can also inform our response to the persistent and predictable limitations of legitimate opposition.

The preceding chapters developed a case for the adversarial conception of legitimate opposition. The following chapters elaborate these arguments via examinations of the history of the practice. Chapter 4 tackles the boundaries of legitimate opposition, the kinds of political participation that make an individual or group liable to have its participation restricted. Traditionally, debates over these matters have revolved around whether various ideological tests are consistent with a commitment to democratic values—for example, whether those who are disloyal to the constitution or democracy itself should be allowed to participate. Elsewhere I have argued against these standards (Kirshner 2014). But many people still regard this ideologically focused approach as the natural method for appraising the limits of legitimate political contestation.

Chapter 4 illustrates that this understanding is false. Investigating the history of fifth-century democratic Athens, I demonstrate that the Athenians defined an alternative boundary for opposition, one that is arguably better suited for our new gilded age: those who wielded outsized clout were subject to ostracism. Beyond a focus on the limits of legitimate opposition, chapter 4 undermines a central pillar of the democratic conception: that legitimate opposition is a wholly modern discovery.

4

Rethinking Opposition's Boundaries

Athens, Ostracism, and Monopolistic Power

Deliberation and sortition. Among democratic theorists, these, not autocracy, are the most prominent decision-making and office-filling alternatives to opposition. And the canonical instance in which they were deployed is, of course, classical, democratic Athens (Manin 1997; Elster 1998, 1; Fishkin 2009, 9). Treating Athens as the font of noncompetitive but resolutely democratic politics is consistent with the orthodoxy of the democratic conception, an approach to opposition that typically relies on the view that opposition was born with the development of modern, democratic parties. It may, therefore, come as a surprise that this chapter pries apart the democratic conception using the political practices of fifth-century, democratic Athens as a crowbar.

Athens lacked political parties—organized and relatively stable political associations formed to pursue political power.[1] But it was home to a vivid strain of competition, a strain of competition that clearly impacted key political decisions and facilitated the exercise of adversarial agency. Focusing on the institutional innovations of the fifth century, including ostracism and the rules governing Athens's political system, I show that the Athenians also distinguished, in practice, between acceptable and unacceptable forms of competition. Athenian institutions and practices raised the cost of wielding political power deemed excessive and therefore a threat to the regime. In other words, the Athenians distinguished between legitimate and illegitimate forms of opposition.

Reevaluating the origins of opposition offers valuable intellectual spoils. As I show, it can help us rethink the boundaries of legitimate opposition and, in particular, what boundaries are actually consistent with democracy. Richard Hofstadter argued in his canonical *The Idea of a Party System: The Rise of Legitimate Opposition in the United States, 1780–1840* that the acceptance of ongoing popular political contestation was yoked, practically and intellectually, to the realization that political parties were not synonymous with factions. Rather than posing an inherent threat to self-rule, parties were necessary to the effective functioning of representative government. According to Hofstadter, this discovery triggered a complete reconsideration of the character of acceptable political activity (Hofstadter 1969).[2] No longer would the test revolve around questions of organization—for example, Are individuals organized as a party? The test of unacceptability would now turn on a movement's ideas or ends—its ideology.[3] Groups deemed disloyal to the "constitutional consensus" or to the state itself were subject to penalties.

The conceptual and institutional revolution chronicled by Hofstadter helped fix the axis of modern debates about the boundaries of legitimate political contestation. The rise of populist parties unwilling to acknowledge the legitimacy of their political rivals has rekindled and stoked these arguments.

At one pole are those who embrace an ideological standard—according to which it is unacceptable for political competitors to question the legitimacy of their opponents or democracy (Waldron 1989; Quong 2004). At the other pole are those who are skeptical of any content-based or ideological restrictions on competition (Scanlon 1972; Dworkin 2006b, 2009). Skeptics fear that power holders will overreach, silencing people with a claim to speak. By implication, ideological restrictions on competition diminish the moral authority of representative regimes, undermining majorities' claim to create laws and policies that affect those who have been silenced. In *A Theory of Militant Democracy* (2014), I embraced the latter view, arguing that restrictions on competition could be justified on the basis of democratic principles but that they should aim to head off rights violations and should not turn on the views of participants.[4] This skeptical position is also open to a familiar criticism. It is too permissive, allowing defensive interventions in the political process only after individuals have been harmed or after a regime has already been seriously weakened (Loewenstein 1937). Hofstadter claimed that the practice of legitimate opposition was established just over two centuries ago. But anyone familiar with the debate over cases like *Citizens United v. Federal Election Commission* (558 U.S. 310 (2010)) knows that academic and legal debates about political regulation revolve, interminably, around the wisdom of restricting competition on the basis of participants' ideas.

The Athenian model of legitimate opposition highlights just how much political territory is occluded by traditional debates about the boundaries of legitimate opposition (including by my own contributions). The Athenians did not silence critics of democracy. Nor were they passive, allowing those who threatened the regime to act first. Maintaining room for citizens to exercise agency competitively, they established a chain of reinforcing institutional measures that increased the cost of wielding outsized clout—whether or not one wielded clout improperly.

Many Athenian political practices would be ill fitted to modern societies and unacceptable to modern democrats. "Ostracism in Athens," Benjamin Constant argued while giving his famous 1819 oration on liberty at the Athénée Royal in Paris, "rested upon the assumption that society had complete authority over its members" (1988, 321). The practice, he claimed, was essentially illiberal. And, evidently, it cannot be understood without invoking the particular challenges Athenian democracy faced and the particular background conditions of Athenian society, intellectual, political, and social.

Yet political stability and concentrations of power are perennial problems for popular regimes. Unconsolidated oppositional regimes must decide whether religious parties or extremist groups pose a threat. In countries like the United States, the exaggerated influence of figures like Donald Trump, Jeff Bezos, Michael Bloomberg, Robert Mercer, Charles Koch, Rupert Murdoch, George Soros, and Sheldon Adelson is now difficult to overstate, almost comically so.[5] These plutocrats are not beholden to political parties. And the challenges they pose are not reducible to bad ideas but to certain individuals' extraordinary, money-soaked influence. With respect to legitimate opposition, classical Athenian opposition may therefore hold more lessons than we might imagine. This chapter's final sections weigh that possibility.

There is another issue demanding attention before moving forward. On the definition I provided in the introduction, Athens would not qualify as a democracy. Citizens *were* treated to a significant degree as equals. The vast majority of the city-state's inhabitants, including slaves, however, were not citizens and thus did have the same status. Still, Athens is widely treated

as a canonical example of a democracy. And it serves as a critical repository of democratic practices. Aware of the this contradiction, I have concluded that it will not bias my account to
treat Athens as an instance of democratic self-rule. To that end,
in this chapter, I focus on the relations among Athens citizens.

An Ancient Model of Legitimate Opposition

It is generally allowed that the Athenian demos took power in 507
BC. The transition to democracy was preceded by a long history
of destabilizing, violent competition for power among aristocrats
(Forsdyke 2005, 26). Accordingly, the demos could not take the
durability of its new regime for granted. Its failure was not a
metaphorical possibility. And the array of institutional changes
marking Athens's transition to democracy understandably
reflected a concern that a sufficiently influential individual or
well-organized group of citizens could compromise the people's
regime. These reforms, often attributed to Kleisthenes, instantiated a peculiarly Athenian system of legitimate opposition. They
enabled individuals to engage in valuable forms of political competition, and they drew a line between acceptable and unacceptable activities. Perfect equality was not the aim or effect of these
reforms. The Kleisthenic institutional innovations, for example,
did not punish aristocrats by seizing their property or revoking
their special standing (Ober 1989, 241).[6] Instead, Athens's new law
of democracy raised the cost of translating aristocratic wealth
and standing into political power. Antimonopolistic in character,
the reforms marked the illegitimacy of wielding political influence
that was dangerously excessive and not based on the support of
the demos—that is, undemocratic.[7]

Consider the reorganization of Athens's most basic political units. Previously, the loci of political power had been the
four tribes of Attica, bodies dominated by aristocratic kinship

groups and families. The influence of these families sprang from their wealth, landownership, religious privilege, and ability to wield influence over a local domain (Ostwald 1988, 310). Leading families drew additional clout from sources that were external to the polis, including foreign regimes like Sparta. Perhaps most importantly, the dominant families' power within the tribes gave them a trump card over the rest of the polis's inhabitants: Athenian citizenship tracked membership in one of the four tribes. Excluded from a tribe, one was no longer a citizen of the polis. In sum, as Martin Ostwald argues, prior to 507, "these families, by commanding a following and by concluding alliances with other prominent families and their retainers, will have competed only with one another to secure the highest offices of state, to which they alone as members of the highest census-class were eligible" (1988, 309).

Under the Kleisthenic constitution, that mode of competition was curtailed. In its place, a new basic building block of political life was established: the deme. Each of the 139 demes, territorial subdivisions of Attica, had its own cults, shrines, assemblies, and political officers. Citizenship was now determined by membership within a deme. For the vast majority, that status was made hereditary, and membership in the deme could be extended by a vote of existing demesmen. Those who possessed the status gained a considerable measure of independence from their aristocratic betters. Beyond the deme, at a higher level, ten new tribes were established. The tribes were made up of three smaller units, trittyes, one each from the three main geographical regions of Attica. This remarkable bit of institutional engineering decreased the likelihood that the tribes would be dominated by citizens from any one locale or by the leading families from that locale. Shifting away from the four Attic tribes, the Athenians blocked an essential conduit for transmitting aristocratic status across the political system.

Critically, the demes and revamped tribes also served as the basis for representation within the new council—the Boule—a five-hundred-member body that set the agenda for the people's assembly. Each year the demes would nominate candidates to fill their preallotted seats on the council, and a lottery would be used to select which of those candidates would serve in the Boule. Athens's bona fides as a true democracy has been burnished by the egalitarian qualities of lotteries in comparison to election (Manin 1997). But replacing selection by kinship groups with random assignment had a more practical effect: it increased the costs of translating social standing and wealth into institutional influence by disrupting the kinship-based mechanisms linking the powerful with their clients (Sinclair 1988, 18; Hansen 1991, 84).[8]

Did these reforms foster a competitionless form of democracy, a form of democracy where people talk and deliberate but do not contest for influence? No, the scholarly consensus is that a vibrant form of regulated rivalry marked Athenian life (Rhodes 1986, 135). As a result, citizens had numerous opportunities to exercise political agency together. Key decisions were made directly in the assembly, and official positions were filled via lottery. But elites vied with each other to influence their fellow citizens as *rhetors*. They sought election as *strategoi* or generals. And those same elites exercised influence via *philoi*—groups organized along lines of friendship and personalistic influence (Connor 1971, 134; Rhodes 1986, 139; Strauss 1987, 17–31). The objects of that competition were power itself, of course, but also honor, influence over the polis's military engagements, and the distribution of fiscal responsibilities and wages.

If Athens really did feature legitimate opposition, we would expect the practice to generate the by-products that we closely associate with it. And that is what we observe. For example, Athenian modes of contestation plausibly increased the cost of engaging in corruption or misrule. Those who sought to gain or cement their positions as leaders of the Athenian polis predictably possessed incentives to uncover and expose the negligence and misconduct of their competitors. Thucydides, son of Melesias, famously wrangled with Perikles on questions of both military strategy and the cost of constructing the Parthenon. Thucydides charged Athens's most famous leader with having "squandered away the public money, and made havoc of the state revenues" (Plutarch 1916, 14). In response to this charge, Perikles was compelled to justify his expenditures to the people.[9] Forcing one's political opponent to explain and defend his approach to fiscal and military policy fits any defensible conception of legitimate opposition.[10]

The Athenian game of democracy, moreover, provided a forum for opponents of current policies to seek changes to the status quo and raise the profile of policy alternatives. We have substantial evidence that Athenian elites and the Athenians themselves could raise objections (Monoson 1994; Balot 2004; Saxonhouse 2006, esp. chap. 4).[11] But beyond the ability to dissent, Athenians could seek actual changes in policy. The Mytilene debate is the most celebrated example of this type of political action (Thucydides 2009, 3.36–49). Thucydides, the historian, describes the aftermath of a rebellion against Athenian influence by the leaders of the city of Mytilene on Lesbos. The Athenians determined that they would punish not only Mytilene's leaders but its people as well, killing the adult males and enslaving women and children. The next day, a large number of Athenians reconsidered their decision. A second debate was held between those, like Kleon, who supported the initial decision and those, like Diodotus, who opposed the policy. As reports of the speeches make clear, efforts to force the reconsideration of past decisions were familiar to the Athenians—Kleon criticizes the practice, while Diodotus, not surprisingly, defends it. Thucydides informs us that "with the two views expressed so evenly matched the Athenians continued to agonize over the decision and the final show of hands was very close, but Diodotus' motion was carried" (2009, 3.49.1). That the outcome of the famous Mytilene debate was not unanimous, or not described as such, befits a regime where outcomes were not foreclosed and where adversarial rivalry was lively, entrenched, and normal.

The Kleisthenic reforms altered the base elements of Athenian political life. A far-ranging combination of institutional innovations and adjustments, they constrained individuals' ability to wield monopolistic power but not their ability to express themselves. They also allowed critics of the political status quo to seek changes to current policy via a regularized form of political competition. In other words, Athens featured a recognizable and distinctive system of legitimate opposition, one that quite obviously instantiated respect for its citizens' agency. That conclusion gains further credibility once we turn to another fifth-century institution: ostracism.

Ostracism and the Limits of Legitimate Opposition

Athens's new democracy inherited a number of laws and practices aimed at safeguarding preceding regimes. One law penalized those who sought to establish a tyranny with outlawry—a punishment that allowed anyone to kill the convicted without fear of sanction (Forsdyke 2005, 83; Ostwald 1955). Another law allowed political trials for those who were suspected of treason, conspiracy against the regime, and the acceptance of bribes. And leading political figures, including Themistokles, Kimon, and Perikles (who are discussed later in this chapter), were subjected to these trials. Each of these institutions illustrates the Athenian tendency to employ popular action, like an assembly trial, to enforce limits on political activities (Teegarden

2013). Yet these protodemocratic institutions are not evidence of the practice of legitimate opposition. Why is that? Because these institutions were not created to defang a regularized form of competition. Engaging in treason, accepting a bribe, and seeking to establish a tyranny were beyond the pale even if one was not a contestant for influence.[12] Political communities use rules of this sort to sustain themselves, no matter how power is distributed or the form political rivalry takes.

Among the most famous innovations of Athens's transition to democracy was ostracism—the temporary expulsion of a citizen from the polis.[13] Ostracism was a critical mechanism for regulating and regularizing elite competition. Accordingly, it provides an especially revealing vantage to assess Athenian opposition. Its use should strengthen our confidence in the distinctive qualities of Athens's system, while diminishing our confidence in the view that legitimate opposition and its characteristic dilemmas only arose with the invention of political parties. Consistent with other Kleisthenic measures, ostracism was aimed at aristocrats and elites with excessive clout (D. Kagan 1961, 400).[14] As Aristotle observed in *The Politics*, democracies ostracized "those who seemed to predominate too much through their wealth, or the number of their friends, or through any other political influence" (Aristotle 1996b, 1284a15–25; on Athenian ostracism, see Aristotle 1996a, 22.6; Thucydides 2009, 8.73.3).

How did ostracism work? Every year, the assembly decided whether to hold an ostracism at all (Forsdyke 2005, 147). Citizens often voted with a specific candidate or candidates in mind (see the story of Kimon shortly). If a majority of the assembly voted to ostracize someone, the actual ostracism was held a short period later. Citizens had the ability, if they wished, to hide the content of their vote from others, making it more difficult for the powerful to monitor voters' choices (Missiou 2011, 53). And if six thousand votes or more were cast, the individual with the greatest number of votes had to leave the city for ten years.[15]

Aristotle reports that the first three citizens to be ostracized were tied closely to the tyrants who had recently ruled the city. The Athenians ostracized a fourth person, Xanthippos, the father of Perikles, because he "seemed to be too powerful" (Aristotle 1996a, 22.6). Aristotle's observation fits neatly with my account of Athenian ostracism. Yet we cannot place too much weight on his analysis of these cases, since we know so little about the people involved. To flesh out our understanding, I focus on three cases about which we possess more information: Themistokles, Kimon, and Thucydides (son of Melesias).

The ostracism of Themistokles, an architect of Greek victory at Salamis and of Athens's development into a sea power, indicates that the practice was not reserved for ideological opponents of self-rule. Themistokles was not a known critic of democracy. And though historians are always careful to highlight the antidemocratic biases of Aristotle and Plutarch, both authors identify Themistokles as a key player in the consolidation of the demos's power (Aristotle 1996a, 22.6; Plutarch 1914c, 19.4).[16] At the time of his ostracism in 470, Themistokles was locked in a contest with rivals, like Xanthippos, Aristeides, and Kimon, over the course of Athenian foreign policy. He believed that Sparta constituted the primary challenge to Athens. The others rated Persian influence in Ionia a greater priority (Frost 1968, 186). Despite Themistokles's democratic leanings, he was not an average citizen. He was an aristocrat who masterminded several military triumphs. And during his time at the center of Athenian political life, he also built a great fortune, one he famously deployed to extend his influence and reputation. Given these facts, the ostracism of Themistokles should reinforce our understanding of the Kleisthenic reforms. A leading political competitor, he possessed substantial sources of clout that were independent of the people.

The trajectories of two of Athens's most influential fifth-century leaders—Kimon and Perikles—also support the non-ideological, antimonopolistic understanding of the boundaries of contestation.[17] Kimon and Perikles occupy central places in the polis's history. And their similarities extend beyond their exalted historical status. Both led troops into war. Both were leading politicians in the new Kleisthenic regime. Both hailed from aristocratic stock. Kimon was ostracized. Perikles was not. According to Aristotle and Plutarch, what chiefly distinguished the two figures were their wealth and the ability to transform that wealth into influence. "Kimon possessed a kingly fortune," Aristotle reported. "[He] maintained many of the members of his deme, for any member of the deme Laciadae who wished could come to him every day and receive adequate maintenance, and all his estates were unfenced so that anyone who wished could help himself to fruit." Kimon's beneficence extended to the city as whole. He played a key role in the building of Athens's long wall, ensuring the polis's access to the sea. Perikles's resources, by contrast, were "not adequate to match such liberality" (Aristotle 1996a, 27.3).

A political anachronism, Kimon used his extensive connections and exaggerated wealth to wield power without pandering to the people. He developed a famously close relationship with the Spartans. And he did not flinch from putting his fortune to work. As Gorgias observed, "Kimon made money to use it and used it to be honored" (Gorgias, VS 21 B20, qtd. in Connor 1971, 20). In contrast, Perikles, as he rose to prominence, embraced the democratic cause. For example, he joined the effort to weaken the Areopagus—a bastion of aristocratic power that tried major offenses and played an important procedural role in Athenian government.

Kimon was well known for his discomfort with the victory of democratic forces in Athens (Plutarch 1914b, 15). But Athens's democracy had numerous antagonists, relatively few of whom suffered the penalty of ostracism (Ober 1998; Rhodes 2000). What distinguished Kimon from other Athenians, both democrats and nondemocrats, were his wealth and his relationship with a rival city. His substantial public influence was not drawn from the well of the people's power.

Perikles not only outlasted Kimon but also outlasted Kimon's successor, Thucydides, son of Melesias, who was ostracized as well. Thucydides, unlike Kimon to whom he was related by marriage, remains something of a mystery, and his legacy is debated (Raubitschek 1960; Frost 1964; Andrewes 1978; Krentz 1984). Nonetheless, three elements of his life are relatively well established. First, he was a prominent figure in Athens (Plato 1981, 94d). Second, he was a rival of Perikles, leading many of those who had supported Kimon. Finally, he was an organizational innovator. Thucydides was known for his ability to get Perikles's opponents to act in unison. The best-known example of his talent for political mobilization was the grouping of his supporters in the assembly (a practice that was later outlawed in the Boule; Plutarch 1916, 11; Strauss 1987, 28–31; Rhodes 1986). Kimon used his wealth and familial connections to exercise outsized power. Thucydides's proto-organization was used to advance the same ends and also cut against the grain of Kleisthenes's democratic reforms. Scholars have quarreled over many parts of Thucydides's story. Accordingly, placing too much on this single case would be a mistake. But considered against the background of the Kleisthenic constitution, Thucydides's ostracism is not surprising.

What of Perikles? Rid of his rivals, Perikles famously dominated the heights of Athenian political life, exercising unrivaled influence over the polis. Of course, Perikles's father, Xan-

thippos, was ostracized. And Perikles was a candidate for ostracism, surely perceived by some Athenians to be a threat to the
regime. Yet he was never successfully removed from the city. What
kept ostracism at bay? As Josiah Ober emphasizes, though Perikles
wielded significant power and was subject to energetic criticism,
he did not pursue independence from the people. His clout
rested on his ability to persuade the demos and on his capacity
to advance Athenian interests (Connor 1971, 120; Ober 1989, 90).

We might also ask, Did each Athenian always vote with the
aim of hobbling people with oppressive power? Were ostracisms
uncontaminated by the pursuit of political advantage or personal distaste? That seems implausible. Inscriptions on *ostraka*
(ballots) suggest that voters were moved by a variety of motives
(Forsdyke 2005, 155). A well-known story, for example, concerns
Aristeides, whose propensity for upright action earned him the
informal title "The Just." In the moments before a final ostracism
vote was to take place, an illiterate citizen asked Aristeides for a
favor, without realizing to whom he was speaking. The man
asked to have a name inscribed on his *ostrakon*. As the story goes,
the name that the citizen asked to have written was "Aristeides,
The Just." When Aristeides inquired what wrong he had committed, the man is said to have responded, "None whatever. . . .
I don't even know the fellow, but I am tired of hearing him everywhere called 'The Just'" (Plutarch 1914a, 7.1–6). Historians
do not credit the story. It attests nonetheless to the reality that
ostracism could be used to banish those who did not possess
destabilizing forms of undemocratic power.[18] And given the
intense, adversarial rivalry shaping Athenian political life, it
would be naive to assume that ostracism would not be a site of
contestation.

Still, I do not think that these important reservations
should alter our conclusion. Laws and institutions are not always
used consistently. In the United States, if prosecutors seek an

indictment on the basis of weak evidence, as they have the power to do, we would not be justified in concluding that prosecutors are afforded discretion in the name of prosecuting the innocent. And the Athenians deployed a range of institutional measures to limit the possibility of misuse. Ostracism required multiple votes over an extended period of time. Citizens possessed time and space to reconsider their decision. Each voter cast a secret *ostrakon*. And a large quorum was required to successfully ostracize someone, increasing the difficulty of gaming the system. These measures were not foolproof: misuse remains an indelible possibility whenever individuals are allowed to exercise their judgment. Assessing the aim or force of ostracism, I have placed it in the context of contemporary reforms. Despite the possibility of misuse, it seems sensible to treat ostracism as one part of a comprehensive institutional effort to rein in those who wielded undemocratic power and to ensure the integrity of Athens's regularized system of political competition.

In modern polities, when states limit competition, we assume, almost axiomatically, that their actions indicate official disapproval of the views or the actions of the affected (Brettschneider 2010). States' capacity to chill debate is a familiar source of anxiety, an anxiety spurred by ideological approaches to opposition's boundaries. A remarkable feature of ostracism and of the Athenian approach to opposition, more generally, is that these institutions did not constitute an ideological moat, keeping Athens free from malevolent ideas. What supports this conclusion? Known opponents of the demos's rule were allowed to play a large role in Athenian political life, and they did so. And supporters of the ostracized were not punished. Meanwhile, known supporters of the demos were ostracized. Finally, though it is counterintuitive, ostracism was not a mark of disloyalty or illegality. The status of the ostracized reflects this fact. They remained citizens, and they retained their property. As full members of

Athenian society, the ostracized, including Megakles, Xanthippos, Aristeides, and Kimon, could, and were, called back to the city if a new, greater threat to the demos emerged (Forsdyke 2005, 152, Plutarch 1914b, 17). "The framers of ostracism were neither fools nor incompetents," Robert Connor has observed. Athens's institutions reflected "a recognition that was most to be feared was not ideas or policies but men" (1971, 74). Taken together, it is apparent that the institutions and practices of fifth-century Athens constitute a critical alternative to an overly ideological approach to opposition's boundaries, an alternative that turned on men's status and on their ability to wield outsized influence.

Why Ancient Opposition Matters: Ideology, Status, and the Limits of Legitimate Opposition

How ought we think about the boundaries of legitimate opposition? As I noted earlier, contemporary analysts of this question focus on the claims of those who avowedly reject a constitutional order, democracy, or legitimate opposition itself. Perhaps politicians and citizens who question the basic features of a political system render themselves liable for some kind of sanction. Political theorists have arrayed themselves for and against that proposition. And these debates have only gained in intensity with the cresting of populist forces that routinely question the legitimacy of their rivals and of contestatory political systems.

This chapter has taken a genealogical approach to rethinking the relation of parties to legitimate opposition. And that effort offers us the chance to reconsider the debate about the boundaries of opposition, a debate in which each side's position is well known and entrenched. Rather than resolving that debate, the Athenian example suggests that it has been unnecessarily constricted, arguably overfocused on what political actors do and say and insufficiently attentive to who they are and what forms of power they wield. One might reject the practice of ostracism itself, because it is inconsistent with the strictures of due process and the rights of citizens, and still draw from the Athenian experience. Perhaps, consistent with the Athenian example, parties should be sanctioned in some way if they draw too much support from the wealthy and powerful. Or perhaps those with outlandish wealth should be blocked from holding office or certain offices (McCormick 2011). Much more work would be needed to identify and master all the nuances raised by policies of this sort. What interests are unjustifiably set back by the political participation of the wealthy? Perhaps their influence perverts the policy-making process and undermines the well-being of others. Perhaps their influence is inconsistent with the relationships that ought to characterize a democratic society. A full analysis would inevitably have to consider the toll of policies of this sort and whether they are compatible with the rights and status of the wealthy.

At a minimum, the Athenian case suggests that a policy of this sort may be consistent with democratic values. Moreover, the Athenian model was not an ideal hatched in an academic's office; it was a genuine, working response to the challenge posed by people wielding unequal power. And once we acknowledge Athenian opposition, we ought to carefully reassess more familiar, ideologically oriented approaches to competition, just as the Athenians' use of sortition has caused modern political theorists to reconsider the practice of election (Manin 1997).

Why Ancient Opposition Matters: The Superficiality of Clockwork Constitutionalism

Can contemporary political reformers, in the United States, for example, take encouragement from Athens's system for managing opposition? Since the mid-1980s, US inequality has increased dramatically, and political outcomes arguably reflect the preferences of a narrow economic elite (Gilens 2012; Saez and Zucman 2014). Influential political reformers and academics, like Lawrence Lessig, contend that reforming campaign finance is the best strategy for reshaping the political system and for making progress on a host of additional issues (Ackerman and Ayres 2002; Lessig 2011). Lessig's approach is a paradigmatic example of clockwork constitutionalism. Again, by that I mean that his proposal assumes that political institutions function predictably, like elements in a very complicated clock. On this view, political actors will act in accordance with the desires of institutional designers. Empowered by this kind of belief, reformers like Lessig have repeatedly sought to increase the cost of converting economic power into political influence. In 2002, the United States Congress passed the Bipartisan Campaign Reform Act (BCRA), making it more difficult to spend money on political campaigns outside limits already established by federal campaign-finance law. The law restricted the ability of corporate entities, like unions and businesses, to fund political advertisements. It also sought to block outside organizations from acting in the stead of more highly regulated campaign organizations.

The United States Supreme Court has overturned key elements of BCRA because it violates the Court's free-speech doctrine. Since the 1970s, the Court has distinguished contributions made directly to campaigns and parties, which are subject to significant limitation, from independent expenditures, which are treated as expressive and therefore subject only to regulations that meet the highest justificatory standards. The Court has held that the federal government has a compelling interest in reducing direct forms of corruption, where individuals give money to candidates in exchange for favors. This focus on direct corruption, however, has not stanched the ability of individuals to convert wealth into political influence. Federal and state governments, the Court has held, do not have an especially weighty reason to make that conversion more difficult. In effect, the Court remains wedded to an ideological model of legitimate opposition, one in which the chief danger to the system is not individuals wielding undemocratic power but political officials silencing views they reject. Any but the most finely tailored efforts to limit the influence of the powerful are, from the Court's perspective, potentially chilling and democratically suspect.[19] The Athenian approach to political opposition illustrates the democratic pedigree of alternatives to narrowly ideological approaches to the issue. And political reformers and critics of the Court's rulings may take sustenance from that fact.

On the other hand, the Kleisthenic solution to the problem of concentrated power was not an example of clockwork constitutionalism; it was an elaborate and overlapping system of regulation, one that included mechanisms to sanction those who did not conform. It is comforting to believe that a single institutional change could neutralize undemocratic sources of influence. That belief is consistent with clockwork constitutionalism. But these beliefs are probably mistaken. Political processes impact key areas of our social and economic lives. Meeting an obstacle along one path to political influence, elites will scour for alternative routes. The Athenians, it seems, were aware of this truism, establishing an array of institutions to alleviate the threat posed by undemocratic concentrations of power—for example, laws concerning citizenship, the restructuring of the demes and trittyes, the use of lotteries to select officeholders, and, of course, ostracism itself. These far-ranging reforms altered the character of Athenian political competition. Just as critically, they placed responsibility for maintaining that system in new hands—that is, the people's. In doing so, they increased the likelihood that the changes made to the system would be enforced.

The scope of the Athenians' project may actually lend weight to the arguments advanced by certain skeptics of campaign-finance reform. The prominent constitutional and election-law scholars Samuel Issacharoff and Pamela Karlan, for example, have repeatedly drawn attention to the limits of silver-bullet approaches. "If money has the outcome-determining effects on the electoral process that reformers have identified," Issacharoff and Karlan argue, "then moneyed political interests will continue trying to use money to influence outcomes whatever the regulatory regime" (1999, 1709). Efforts to restrict the flow of funds to campaigns and parties, they predict, will have unintended consequences, diverting money to organizations that are even less accountable than parties and candidates. Moreover, they argue that reforms must reflect the environment in which campaign finance is embedded. By "environment," they mean the social and economic characteristics of the society as well as its institutional ecosystem—for example, the role of the Supreme Court, the dominance of first-past-the-post representation, territorial districting, the two-party system, and political control over reapportionment. Shifting a single dial on this unwieldy institutional contraption is unlikely to achieve the desired outcome. And actually altering the US approach to legitimate opposition, on this view, would require a more thoroughgoing effort—for example, like Athens's popular revolution. That reality, I think, actually underlines the Athenians' achievement. If we accept that the Athenians domesticated elite rivalry, while reaping the benefits of legitimate opposition, then we ought to acknowledge the massive scope of their ambition.

Conclusion

In the seventh book of Herodotus's great work *The Histories*, he describes an encounter between the Persian king, Xerxes, and his counselor Mardonius. While other members of Xerxes's court were afraid to contradict the king, Mardonius outlined the benefits of disagreements: "My lord, when no opposing opinions are presented, it is impossible to choose the better, but one must accept what is proposed. When such opposites are stated, it is as with gold, the purity of which one cannot judge in itself, but only if you rub it alongside other gold on the touchstone and see the difference" (Herodotus 1987, 7.10.1, qtd. in Anastaplo 2003, 1009). Through Mardonius, Herodotus outlines one of the benefits of political rivalry: that it brings novel alternatives to the fore, improving the decision-making process. But Mardonius's analogy also captures the benefit of allowing ourselves to reinvestigate the origins of legitimate opposition. By comparing it with its ancient predecessor, we gain a better sense of the work performed by the modern practice.

The Athenians did not participate in organized political parties, but they did draw a line between acceptable and unacceptable forms of political contestation. Allowing aristocrats to wield undemocratic forms of power might have threatened constitutive elements of the regime. Not to allow adversarial competition would have been a form of self-mutilation, compromising the capacity of the demos to rule itself. The Athenians identified a potential equilibrium between those two poles and worked to maintain it. That balance is the distinguishing mark of legitimate opposition.

Athens functions as a stockroom of institutional ideas for democratic innovators. Perhaps its system of opposition too could serve as a model for reform. But reformers who pick over the city-state's institutional bones give less than sufficient weight to the source of its egalitarian features. The Kleisthenic reforms were the product of a violent political transition, a revolution (a fact that might reasonably influence one's assessment of the costs of egalitarian reform). Popular power was the precondition of its egalitarian system of opposition, not the result. Chapter 5 elaborates on this line of thought, considering how violence shaped the Roman Republic's undemocratic system of opposition and outlining how the shadow of violence should influence our assessment of opposition's rivals.

5

Opposition without Democracy
Roman Competition, Violence, and the Limits of Clockwork Constitutionalism

The nobility still maintained an ascendency by conspiring together; for the strength of the people, being disunited and dispersed among a multitude, was less able to exert itself.

—Sallust

Plutarch reports that in 121 BC, after masterminding the death of Gaius Gracchus and summarily executing three thousand of Gaius's supporters, the consul Lucius Opimius rebuilt an important temple to the goddess Concordia. The temple ostensibly represented Romans' love of social harmony. Evidently, the irony was too bitter for many Romans. Concord was a much-lauded Roman value. Opimius's monument was defaced nevertheless. Hidden by the night, someone carved into the temple, "A work of mad discord produces a temple of Concord" (Plutarch 1921, 238–39).

Plutarch's tale is an appropriate starting point for an assessment of Rome's system of opposition. Even if the city's best-known political philosopher, Cicero, embraced concord, Roman Republican political practice was vigorously competitive (Cicero 1928, *Republic* 2.69). And that competition famously overran the banks of the Republic's established institutions, surging into waves of violence that sped the Republic's end.

In the first two sections of this chapter, I demonstrate that for much of the last two centuries of the Roman Republic (roughly 250–50 BC), individuals could seek changes to the current officeholders and current policy through a rule-based, nonviolent system of political contestation. Participants had the option to engage in joint efforts to change policy and law. The system was consistent with the adversarial conception of legitimate opposition, instantiating a kind of respect for the agency of those who could participate. The evidence discussed in this chapter should bury any lingering concerns that Athens was an outlier, that legitimate opposition does not predate the advent of representative democracy, or that the traditional party-focused view of opposition, typical of the democratic conception, accurately captures the history of the practice. As one of the deans of Roman historiography, Andrew Lintott, has observed, "perhaps the most enduring legacy of the Roman Republic to western political thought is the legitimacy and desirability of opposition and competition as constituents of liberty and stimulants of effective government" (1999a, 254).

Contra the democratic conception, the Roman experience demonstrates in clear-cut terms that opposition is not chained, practically or conceptually, to democracy—a conclusion with evident implications for our assessment of regimes currently defined by opposition.[1] Most Romans did not think they lived in a democracy, and by today's standards, they did not. Many citizens could engage in joint efforts to effect law and policy. For many more, the opportunities to engage in political life were comparatively and unjustifiably restricted. For instance, many inhabitants, including citizens, did not live near enough to Rome to exercise any influence over decisions that impacted them (Mouritsen 2001, 16). Still, opposition existed, and Roman institutions clearly reflected the dilemmas typically involved with harnessing it. Rome boasted a variety of measures, not ultimately successful, aimed at mitigating competition's costs.

This chapter and chapter 4 make plain the sheer range of political conditions in which opposition can be used to organize political life. It is a virtue of such systems that they can facilitate the peaceful exercise of collective agency in difficult and unjust conditions. This is no naive apologia. My aim is to thread a normative needle, seriously weighing the practice's value without treating it as something it is not—that is, reliably democratic.

Should opposition's flexibility really be considered a virtue? Not if there is an alternative to opposition that would avoid compromises with those who are intent on safeguarding unjust and inegalitarian states of affairs. This is what many critics of political competition posit. Since we assume that unequal competition is democratic or uniquely feasible, we overlook more attractive alternative arrangements, like sortition (Manin 1997; López-Guerra 2011; McCormick 2011; Guerrero 2014; Landemore 2020).

When political philosophers and theorists critique opposition in this way, they often embrace clockwork constitutionalism. Again, by "clockwork constitutionalism," I mean that these assessments proceed as if political institutions can be easily changed and that they will function as intended, like the precise elements of a Swiss clock. The approach has two common elements. First, it assumes that those who are subject to the proposed institutions will mechanically accept and abide by institutional rules, even if the imposition of those rules would set them back substantially. In other words, the institutions that structure political decision-making are assumed to be *discon-*

nected from political actors' capacity to wield force or other de facto forms of influence. Second, because institutions are assumed to function as they are proposed, theorists and philosophers tend to conclude that political institutions are not as egalitarian or just as they might be for ideological reasons, principally because the actors involved did not appreciate that more equitable or more just institutions were possible or feasible. It is important to note that adopting clockwork constitutionalism does not require one to trade in ideal theory. Frequently enough, those who assume this perspective are self-consciously offering *proposals* to mitigate features of nonideal political life, for example, political inequality.

Using the history of ancient Rome, I illustrate why this approach may be mistaken in most cases of interest, that is, cases in which institutions reflect inequities and injustices. By implication, many critiques of opposition will miss their target. In other words, consistent with the adversarial conception, I continue to illustrate the value of opposition relative to its most prominent theoretical rivals. This chapter's third section shows that the inegalitarian character of Roman opposition was not, fundamentally, the product of a lack of information about how to improve the political system. The character of Roman opposition was set by elites' and plebs' capacity to credibly threaten physical resistance against each other. Contra clockwork constitutionalism, the system was not disconnected from political actors' capacity to act violently; it was the product of that capacity. Moreover, there is little reason to think that Rome is unique in this respect. By implication, systems of opposition cannot be assessed adequately, I believe, without weighing the possibility of violence.

The fourth section mines a different vein of the violence-opposition connection, exploring the failure of Roman opposition. If clockwork constitutionalism was correct, if institutional change was driven in the first instance by ideas, we would expect the decline of Roman opposition to be married to a decline in support for republican ideology. But a rising tide of antirepublican ideology did not presage the end of opposition. Instead, the consensus is that the system failed when it became sufficiently detached from the distribution of de facto power. Of course, individuals did not stop competing for power. Instead of building institutional support for their aims, they resorted to arms. Eventually this instability brought an end to rule-based contestation. Rather than ushering in a more egalitarian and less adversarial set of institutions, the Republic's failure brought a monarchy into power. The upshot here is clear: institutions that are disconnected from political actors' de facto influence may not be stable. And if theoreticians propose clock-like institutions totally removed from the underlying realities of political life, then an accurate assessment of those institutions would incorporate the probability of instability and conflict that would be likely to greet their establishment.

Examining recent proposed alternatives to opposition, the final section continues to measure clockwork constitutionalism's theoretical limitations. The perspective is seductive, suggesting that an inventive theoretical argument might be something more: a plausible solution to an obdurate malady. Political scientists have long recognized that electoral competition is a substitute for violent competition. But as I show, political philosophers who consider opposition and its alternatives typically do not give due weight to this reality. As a result, clockwork constitutionalism fuels misunderstanding of practices like legitimate opposition. On the one hand, by assuming that institutional inequity comes down to a lack of intellectual creativity or vision, these approaches exaggerate the attractiveness of idealistic proposals and underestimate the value of institutions that allow individuals to peacefully exercise mass agency under less-than-ideal conditions. On the other hand, these approaches bolster the intuition that to be valuable, institutions must be consistent with ideal schemes of government. Typically, this implies that valuable institutions must be democratic institutions. Yet this simply contributes to misunderstanding and confusion. If we think that opposition must be essentially democratic, the actual practice will be vexingly and resolutely distant from the ideal. Once we relinquish that supposition, as this chapter argues we ought to, the real value of opposition, such as it is, comes into view.

Roman Opposition

A single example, Athens, may not suffice to undermine long-held notions about the origins and character of legitimate opposition. The Roman Republic's complex structure of customs, rights, and laws also featured a version of this practice.[2] And the case for this proposition is sufficiently straightforward, I believe, that after laying it out, any lingering credulity about the orthodox account of legitimate opposition will be easily shed. This conclusion stands even if we do not accept the democracy-hued vision of Roman politics most famously advanced by Fergus Millar (1984, 1986, 1998). The conclusion does require, however, that we understand republican institutions as more than a mere facade for elite contestation and collusion (Münzer 1999; Gelzer and Gelzer 1969; Syme 2002). In this chapter, I follow the moderate course set out by those who interpret Roman politics through a more permissive frame. That frame allows for the possibility that Roman institutions guided political activity and gave a reasonably broad swath of the city an important role in Republican politics. It also recognizes the existence of radical disparities in de facto and de jure political influence (Flower 2010; Morstein-Marx 2004; Mackay 2004; Lintott 1999a; North 1990). On this view, patrician privilege distinguished the early Republic, placing sharp limits on political practice. With the loosening of those restrictions, Roman politics came to illustrate "that within limits vigorous conflict could be creative" (Lintott 1999a, 66).

The array of powerful positions or magistracies that were filled using competitive elections attests to that conclusion. These positions included the consuls, praetors, censors, aediles, quaestors, and tribunes. Elected magistrates waged wars, governed Roman provinces, and wielded significant, if more limited, influence within Rome itself. Individuals sought these positions because officeholders guided policy and gained public honor. In addition, achieving one office increased the likelihood of holding positions of greater influence (Flower 2010, 61).

Some positions, such as the tribunes, were elected by the Concilium Plebis, a plebian assembly. Most other magistrates were annually elected by the Comitia Centuriata or the Comitia Tributa, assemblies roughly organized around property classes (centuries) and a citizen's traditional geographic district (tribes), respectively. Neither body featured voting systems that treated voters equitably. The tribes and centuries were unbalanced—in the same way states are unbalanced in the US Senate today. Each unit had equal absolute voting influence in processes requiring a majority of those units. But they had radically divergent populations associated with them—that is, each of the tribes and centuries associated with the lower classes had many more members (Taylor 1966, 88; Lintott 1999a, 61).

The inequity of the annual electoral system in combination with persuasive evidence that elites could exercise extrainstitutional influence, via bribery, for instance, regularly engenders doubts about Rome's system of opposition. We might view it as closer to the biased and unfair electoral systems that modern-day autocrats employ to subvert and distort the agency of their citizens (see chapter 3). As Cicero remarked, the system could be seen as a mechanism to "avoid insolence" by ensuring that popular classes were not excluded from the vote, while also "avoid[ing] danger" by sharply restricting their ability to exercise collective influence (1928, *Republic* 2.39).[3]

So, were outcomes really determined by political competition? The weight of evidence suggests that they were. Defending the virtues of the *optimates*, supporters of the Senate and skeptics of popular causes, Cicero conceded that their strategy entailed risk. Thwarting the felt interests of the popular class left some men "not acceptable to the masses," and as a result, "their purpose was often thwarted by the voters" (Cicero 1958, *Sestio* 49.105). And despite the frequency of elections, the sources contain many descriptions of elections in which there were more candidates than positions. For example, Livy suggests that in 189, there were six candidates for consul—of which two would be selected (2018a, 37.58). And this was not unusual (Rosenstein 1993). Moreover, candidates engaged in time-consuming campaigning. The character of a Roman political campaign is made vivid by the *Handbook of Electioneering*, a brief work ostensibly authored by Cicero's brother, providing advice on how to win election as consul (Q. Cicero 2012).[4] Glad-handing fellow citizens, organizing one's friends, offering promises without compunction, and launching abuse at one's electoral rivals are necessary tactics for the successful Roman office seeker, according to this work. Cicero famously won his contest, though he was a "new man," a nonaristocrat, and his rivals for the consulship were highborn. Electoral victory sometimes required extensive efforts to bribe and bring on board the broader populace. But this practice supports rather than contradicts the notion that Roman politics was defined by competition. The adversarial character of elections drove rivals to pay off supporters (Yakobson 1999, 22).

Beyond elections, Roman institutions provided multiple paths for groups to collectively impact policy. Elites could use the Senate to deliberate and vote on motions. Doing so, they could shift the course of public policy. Senate motions were not law. Yet a powerful magistrate who might have ignored the protests of a single member of the elite would have weighed carefully ignoring the collective counsel of the military and political establishment—that is, the Senate (Lintott 1999a, 86–87). Similarly, a magistrate who wanted to build support for an initiative would be better served gaining the assent of the Senate than of any single individual.

Only a select group of people could exercise their agency via the Senate. Rome, however, offered additional mechanisms for resolving disputes and hammering out policy. Probably the best-known mechanism was the position of the tribune, an officeholder elected by the plebs. Among other powers, tribunes could intercede on behalf of citizens to determine the legality of a magistrate's actions, veto the proceedings of an assembly before a vote, prevent the Senate from convening, orchestrate support for legislation, and put legislation before the Plebian Assembly. A tiny percentage of the populace ever served as a tribune. It was a stepping-stone to additional political influence for ambitious plebeian elites. According to Polybius, tribunes were "always obliged to act as the people decree and to pay every attention to their wishes" (2011, 6.16; see also Livy 2018b, 38.36; Lintott 1999a, 126; Morstein-Marx 2004, 125). Most contemporary historians regard Polybius's claim as too strong. Still, they credit the view that tribunes were generally expected to act as the popular class's agents, opposing the subversion of their political power and forwarding their interests. The tribunate was unmistakably associated with *popularis* activity. Yet it was often held by plebeians with ambitions to reach the highest echelons of Roman political life. This indicates that advocating on behalf of lower orders did not mark one as an outsider—this kind of contestation was accepted. Cicero is not often mistaken for a *popularis* sympathizer. Still, even he makes room for the tribunate in his ideal regime (Cicero 1928, *Laws* 3.9). In sum, the tribunate was broadly understood as a permanent and attractive feature of Roman political life. It was an institution that provided the lower orders with a powerful advocate, a mechanism for swaying political outcomes, allowing them to confront the status quo. For this reason, in Lintott's estimation, the tribunes amounted to a "sort of legitimate opposition" (Lintott 1999a, 208).

The election of a tribune was not the only avenue for mass collective agency. The *contiones*, popular meetings that always preceded legislative assemblies, supplied additional opportunities. During these meetings, politicians offered their cases for policy change and rained criticism on their rivals (Morstein-Marx 2004, chap. 5). The meetings were used to coordinate and charge popular support before a vote occurred. We know of very few instances in which proposed legislation was actually rejected. This can be explained, the historian Robert Morstein-Marx contends, once we grasp the dynamics of the *contiones*. The reaction in a *contio* presaged the level of support for a given action (Morstein-Marx 2004, 124). Unfavorable popular responses to proposals or arguments could wound the prospects of one's efforts, potentially causing magistrates to withdraw a proposal (Thommen 1995, 365; Morstein-Marx 2004, 147). In other words, the popular debates had significant practical import.

The passage of legislation, unlike in Athens, was procedurally distinct from the speech-making forum of the *contiones*; it occurred in the assemblies. And when conditions were propitious, those bodies passed legislation that cut against elite interest. After 287, the Concilium Plebis, an assembly made up of plebian tribes, had the authority to ratify legislation that bound

all of Rome's citizens. And popular agitation could instigate
legislative proposals advancing the interests of the people
(Lintott 1999a, 205).

Popular political and economic reform was not an everyday occurrence in Rome. The institutions I have briefly canvassed, however, not only allowed groups to defend their
interests but allowed political actors to orchestrate lasting
change (Lintott 1999a, 64–65; Flower 2010, 62). For instance,
during the late Republic, redistribution of land and grain became regular subjects of legislative contestation. And that
contestation generated tangible change. Rome's competitive
political system facilitated the exercise of collective political
agency. The Republic featured legitimate opposition.

Limiting the Costs of Roman Opposition

Roman opposition was not democratic opposition. It was not
a strain of collegial rivalry either—engaged in by individuals
who ultimately saw themselves as collaborators motivated to
advance their rivals' fundamental interests. As a result, Rome's
adversarial system generated all the typical costs of political
competition. And, not surprisingly, those costs sparked efforts
to limit the damage. For instance, the intensity of competition
was tamped down by the surfeit of opportunities provided to
ambitious Roman individuals and families (Flower 2010, 26).
Nonaristocrats faced substantial obstacles reaching the highest
echelons of political life. But they were not blocked entirely (Q.
Cicero 2012). Beginning in the fourth century, elected positions
were open to all who met the property requirements and had
undertaken ten years of military service. Office terms were kept
short. New magistrates were sought each year.

From my perspective, from the perspective of a nonexpert
interested in legitimate opposition, *the* distinctive aspect of

the Roman system for managing competition was the *cursus honorum*—the fixed ladder of political offices and positions that aspiring political leaders climbed as they sought higher office and increased influence (Livy 2018b, 40.44). One generally had to give ten years of military service before seeking elective office and could not become an aedile without first serving as a quastor. This clever reform was entrenched in law in 180 BC with the passage of the Lex Villia Annalis. It limited competition for any given position without choking off the possibility of advancement for the truly ambitious. Moreover, the perceived benefit of reducing the intensity of competition must have been significant. As Cicero observed, the program was not costless. It bridled the ambitious, keeping qualified candidates from positions they might have filled honorably (Cicero 2010, 5.47).

The institutional history of the *res publica* is replete with examples of efforts to harness competition, preserving its key functions, while restraining its excesses. These efforts included the introduction of the secret ballot in elections (Lex Gabinia, 139 BC) and other measures to protect voters from pressure and intimidation, such as the Lex Maria, 119 BC (Cicero 1928, *Laws* 3.33–39; Plutarch 1920, *Marius* 4; Yakobson 1995; Lintott 1999a).[5] Related measures were established to curtail electoral bribery, *ambitiu*. Lintott argues that the initial effort to limit bribery in 181 was part of the same program of competitive reforms that included the Lex Villia Annalis. Numerous other measures were put in place to constrain bribery—though eradicating all forms of "generosity" was unlikely to have been the aim of those efforts (Lintott 1990; Yakobson 1992, 35). The punishments for being convicted of bribery could be severe. In 65, two consuls-elect were convicted and exiled for engaging in the practice (Yakobson 1992, 36).

Had Rome not featured a system of legitimate opposition, many of the institutional changes just described would be utterly

baffling. If elections were not competitive, if outcomes were forgone or meaningless, there would be no plausible reason to con-
struct and adhere to the *cursus honorum*. Nor, presumably, would
it have been in the interest of the plebs to seek a private ballot. As
discussed earlier, electoral payouts, one assumes, would not have
flourished if nothing was at stake in Roman politics. And it would
have been unnecessary to curb the practice if Romans did not
sense that certain modes of competition were costly. These institutional limits on competition reinforce the case against the
democratic conception.

How Violence Defines Opposition

When criticizing electoral competition's status as the default
mechanism for distributing political power, political philosophers are apt to contend that this status is the product of intellectual misapprehension. "The political use of lot," Bernard
Manin argues in his well-known work on representative government, "is virtually never thought about today" (1997, 9). As a
result, "institutional choices made by the founders of representative government have virtually never been questioned" (3).
For Manin, the association of democracy with electoral competition amounts to a form of ideological pacification, occlud-
ing the possibility of achieving more representative and less
elitist political institutions. Despite the passage of almost a
quarter century since Manin published his treatment of sortition
and representation, Alexander Guerrero makes the same argument in his defense of a lot-based alternative to democratic
competition. "It is widely accepted," Guerrero observes, "that
electoral representative democracy is better—along a number
of different normative dimensions—than any other alternative
lawmaking political arrangement" (2014, 135). Like Manin, Guerrero criticizes electoral competition as instrumentally ineffective

and subject to elite capture. And the implication of his argument
is that, if we were aware of electoral competition's shortcomings
and the existence of a "normatively attractive alternative," we
might be able to achieve a more attractive institutional state of
affairs (136). This is an ideological explanation of electoral
competition's persistence, and this kind of explanation is a common feature of clockwork constitutional approaches.

The Roman case suggests that these critiques of electoral
competition, and clockwork constitutionalism more generally,
may not account sufficiently for the role that force and violence,
as opposed to lack of information, play in shaping political
institutions. Historians of Rome, like Robert Morstein-Marx
and Valentina Arena, have argued that by the late Republic, if
not before, contenders for political power sparred using a common political language. Debates centered on notions of *libertas*
and on whether Roman institutions properly instantiated citizens' status. Since political debate occurred within a limited
theoretical register, one might credit an ideological explanation
of Rome's institutional setup: elitist ideology led to elitist institutions. Yet both Morstein-Marx and Arena describe how
popularis opponents of the political status quo used the language
of *libertas* to make the case for their causes. That language was
deployed, for instance, to justify passage of the Leges Gabinia
and Manilia. Both laws impinged on Senatorial authority, shifting the balance of influence toward politicians allied with the
people (Brunt 1988, 321–30; Morstein-Marx 2004, 218; Lintott
1999a, 201; Arena 2012, 6). Supporters of these measures characterized their opponents as enemies of republican institutions
and practices. Defenders of the status quo, like Cicero, employed
similar language but, naturally, sought to cast their opponents
as the true antirepublican menace. These examples suggest that
the barrier to political and social equality was not primarily
ideological and was not grounded in an inability to envision

something more attractive. Constrained by a limited ideological repertoire, Roman actors still came to divergent assessments about the appropriate course of action and the appropriate balance of power among Rome's political institutions. If we are to look for the source of the elite's long dominance over Rome, or over polities with similar characteristics, an explanation that focuses on the horizon of the political imagination, an ideological account, may be partial, at best.

Here is an alternative account of the persistence of electoral competition, one inconsistent with clockwork constitutionalism. Powerful political actors are often willing to wield physical force if institutions do not adequately advance their interests. A given institutional system is likely to persist when those actors find abiding it less costly than seeking power via alternative means, like force. By implication, stable political institutions will reflect, in some rough way, actors' de facto power. And the powerful will resist institutional changes that set back their interests, including efforts to make institutions more equal. Call this the nonideological account of competition's persistence. What if this view were correct in the Roman case? If the mass of Roman citizens understood that Rome's institutions were inegalitarian, less oriented toward their interests than they might be, they still might be unable to make those institutions more egalitarian. Why? Because defenders of the status quo may have been sufficiently adept at using violence to maintain their dominance.

The nonideological account gains plausibility if we consider the case of Tiberius Sempromius Gracchus (Tiberius).[6] The Gracchi were one of the Republic's most prominent families. As a tribune, however, Tiberius used popular support to advance legislation challenging essential elements of Senatorial influence. For instance, on taking up his tribuneship in 133, Tiberius proposed a law establishing a board to oversee the disbursal of public land (*ager publicus*) to landless citizens. This was followed by proposals to sidestep the Senate's opposition to redistribution. Facing the possibility of prosecution once he was no longer a magistrate, Tiberius sought reelection. His reelection would have protected him from prosecution but contravened the norm against reelection. And he attempted to secure the position by keeping his opponents from voting. At a minimum, Tiberius's actions demonstrate that the inegalitarian state of Rome's institutions cannot be attributed to an incapacity to imagine a preferable state of affairs.

Ultimately, a group of senators, led by the pontifex maximus P. Cornelius Scipio Nasica Serapio, bludgeoned Tiberius and killed more than three hundred of his supporters (Plutarch 1921, *Tiberius* 19). Cicero offered the standard justification for meeting a challenge of this sort before it developed into something graver. "Revolution creeps on imperceptibly at first," he observed. But "once it has acquired momentum, [it] rushes headlong to ruin" (Cicero 1923, *On Friendship* 152). A challenge to the status quo was blocked, not because some participants never pondered a preferable economic and political order but because those in favor of the status quo wielded force to maintain it.

The famed case of Tiberius Gracchus illustrates how violence can limit institutional reform. Yet the claim that violence gave shape to Roman competition requires more substantial evidence. Here is an abbreviated list of those who were killed in the name of Senatorial dominance. In 121, Gaius Gracchus, Tiberius's younger brother, who also pursued a reformist strategy, committed suicide to avoid the same violent end as his sibling (Plutarch 1921, *Tiberius and Gaius Gracchus* 17). While we possess less information about the details of the rise and fall of Saturninus, he was yet another high-placed challenger to the Senate's dominance. He was killed under a Senate mandate (Mitchell 1971, 52). Livius Drusus, another reformer and one who did not shy from using violence, was assassinated in 91 BC (Cicero 1931, *Milone* 7). And after decades of political turbulence, P. Clodius Pulcher, who hailed from a patrician background but pressed to be adopted by a plebeian, challenged Cicero. In 52, he was dispatched by Titus Annius Milo.[7] These examples do not suggest that all of those who opposed Senatorial dominance were murdered. But they further demonstrate that what blocked egalitarian reform was not an incapacity to imagine a better political system.

Optimate violence was not the only factor influencing Roman opposition. The persistence of popular institutions like the tribunate would be impossible to comprehend if that were the case. In *De Legibus*, Cicero described the institutions of his ideal regime. In it, he offered a tempered defense of the tribunate. Marcus, one of the participants in the dialogue, observes that the tribunes of the plebs "have too much power." Yet he resists the conclusion that there should be no such bodies. The masses, on his view, were not owed a voice in government. Rather, the tribunes' influence was warranted because the people themselves were capable of cruelty and force. Here, a capacity for violence remains the dominant factor shaping Roman institutions. But that capacity is not assumed to inhere only in the elite. On Cicero's account, the ancestors of Rome's elite had not established the tribunate enthusiastically. Instead, once "the Senate had granted this power to the plebeians, conflict ceased, rebellion was at an end, and a measure of compromise was discovered which made the humbler believe that they were accorded equality with the nobility; and such a compromise was the only salvation of the State" (Cicero 1928, *Laws* 2.23–25).

The exact conditions that led to the tribunate's establishment are difficult to pin down. The historical record is imperfect, at best. The larger point remains, however. Plebeian rights were assumed, with some reason, to flow from the plebs' ability to wield physical force (Raaflaub 2005). Beyond the mere existence of the tribunes, the peculiar powers of the office, including their legal right to interpose themselves between a magistrate and plebeian, derived from the widely shared understanding that the plebs would collectively and forcefully defend their representatives. The legal instantiation of the tribune's inviolability, in other words, followed the emergence of a credible threat of plebeian violence (Lintott 1999b, 24). In light of the *optimates'* capacity and willingness to use force to guard their institutional privileges, it is not surprising—indeed, it probably amounts to a practical necessity—that the extension and the maintenance of plebeian institutional rights and influence also depended on the threat of physical force.

It is worth pausing here to consider how little support Roman history lends to a clockwork constitutional perspective. On that approach, the shape of an institution, like a system of opposition, is determined, fundamentally, by a conception of what kinds of institutions are legitimate or preferable. Rome's history, captured by Cicero's description of the rise of the tribunate, suggests that the shape of institutions like legitimate opposition are determined, in significant part, by the shadow and use of violence.

We might worry, of course, about whether an ancient Roman example bears any relation to modern institutional systems and how they develop. There is a traditional strategy for meeting this challenge. One simply points out that many of the institutions characteristic of modern political systems were inspired by Roman institutions and interpretations of Roman history (Pocock 2003). An alternative and more promising strategy is to note that contemporary popular systems are shaped by the same forces. Representative regimes, contemporary political economists argue, reflect rival groups' capacity to impose costs on one another if they are excluded from the decision-making process (Boix 2003; Przeworski 2005; Acemoglu and Robinson 2006). Modern regimes, then, like their precursors, are constructed within the penumbra of violent conflict.

When Violence Replaces Opposition

Opposition can contribute to the cessation of violent competition. How? By reflecting different groups' capacity to wield de facto influence while still allowing them to pursue their ends. The resulting inequalities, though objectionable, do not block fully the exercise of political agency. This flexibility is a key element of opposition's value. But the absence of violence is typically taken for granted by contemporary political theorists when assessing political institutions. As I discuss at length in the next section, resolving the Hobbesian problem of political stability is assumed not to be a task for political institutions, or it is assumed to be a task that simply does not exist in well-functioning regimes. Preparing the ground for that discussion, this section emphasizes the import of that Hobbesian problem and its relation to systems of opposition. The late Roman Republic provides a dramatic image of what opposition should prevent. Indeed, until the constitutional implosion of the Weimar Republic, Rome was *the* example of a political system that failed to channel political contestation through its institutions. "In any interpretative scheme that has been or could be proposed," the historian Harriet Flower observes, "political violence is a characteristic—and perhaps the best-known—feature of the urban landscape in Rome after the time of the Gracchi" (2010, 80).

In the late Republic, the primary currency of political influence was no longer issued by Rome's formal institutions and rules. Violence came to the fore and was disbursed in every institutional domain. During prelegislative debates (*contios*), audience members intimidated speakers, even stoning them (Sallust 2013, *Jugurtha* 34.1; Morstein-Marx 2004, 165). Elections were polluted. Appian reports, for example, that Saturninus only gained office as a tribune after his supporters killed the recently elected A. Nunnius.[8] Force was used to influence the passage of legislation and obstruct other legislative efforts. Q. Servilius Caepio and a gang of fellow conservatives famously blocked the procedurally dubious passage of an agrarian reform bill. They demolished the bridges that Roman voters crossed to cast their votes and toppled the ballot boxes (Cicero 1954, 1.21). Even trials, which were frequently political in character, became arenas in which violence was applied (Asconius 2006, 59–60; Cicero 1976, *Sulla* 15; Lintott 1999b).

The rise and ubiquity of organized political gangs is the clearest indication of the shift from regulated rivalry to organized force. On becoming a tribune in 58, Clodius championed legislation advancing the interest of associations whose membership also served in the gangs that supported him. And Clodius was killed during a clash between his own retinue and that of Milo, Cicero's associate (Asconius 2006, 65; Lintott 1999b, xii–xv, 77–93). Perhaps unsurprisingly, armed rivalry did not reach its climax with gangs; competitors ultimately graduated to armies. That escalation led to the final subversion of Rome's system of legitimate opposition. In 49 BC, Caesar ran out of institutional resources for maintaining his claims to leadership, resorting to a military invasion of Italy. Caesar's famous act stands as the natural end point of the transition from regulated, rule-based, adversarial rivalry to military competition.

Here is a potential explanation for the failure of Rome's system of regulated rivalry: Romans stopped believing in republican principles—whether of the *optimate* or *popularis* versions. If that were plausible, proponents of clockwork constitutionalism would have an additional reason to be confident in their argu-

ments. They would have an additional reason to be confident
that what fundamentally determines the fate of an institutional
setup is whether individuals embrace principles consistent with
that setup. In this canonical case, however, that explanation fails
to match facts. The collapse of republican institutions was not
accompanied by a corresponding collapse in republican ideology. Though violence became a familiar part of political life in
the late Republic, a variety of measures were deployed to stem
the tide. These policies demonstrate that violence had not been
accepted, folded into republican conceptions of legitimate rule.
Efforts to stanch the violence included laws against the organization of political gangs, laws allowing the annulment of measures
passed through the use of violence, and laws authorizing trials
for those who engaged in political violence (Lintott 1999b, 107–24,
132–48). Moreover, even the end of the Roman Republic, the
transition to a form of monarchical rule, was not wedded to a
rejection of republican values. Julius Caesar famously did not
think of himself as pulling down basic republican institutions
but as defending the fundamental privileges of the tribunes. Nor
did the emperor Augustus boast that his ascension eclipsed republican institutions (Brunt 1988, 2, 7).

The fall of the Roman Republic probably cannot be attributed to the rise of an antirepublican ideology. For many
prominent historians, however, the Republic was destabilized
by changing political fundamentals. Late Rome was marked by
a dual expansion in people and territory. And its institutions
were not adequately refined in light of these changes (Montesquieu 1965, 91–95; Brunt 1988, 68; Flower 2010, 98; Mackay 2004,
176). In particular, those institutions did not reflect competitors'
access to the resources required to govern a much larger polity,
that is, large armies (Flower 2010, 111). This development made
it less costly for the powerful to engage in violent conflict than
to accept the outcomes of the Republic's rules, regulations, and

procedures. Violence, on this view, moved to the fore once the political reality described by Rome's institutions pulled free from the underlying distribution of power in Rome.

Violence and Alternatives to Legitimate Opposition

Racing through the institutional history of the Roman Republic, this chapter has provided further evidence that the traditional, democratic view of opposition has been constructed on corrupt foundations: opposition was not invented in the nineteenth century, and it is not securely linked to democracy. I have also sought perspective on the relation between violence and opposition. That history reveals an intimate, dynamic relation: Rome's competitive institutions were bent into shape and then crushed by participants' capacity to wield de facto influence and resort to violence.

So what? What implications does this relationship actually hold for our understanding of opposition's value? Applying what we have learned from Rome's history, this section explores how a comparative assessment of opposition, one that considers that practice against its rivals, will be distorted if we sidestep the possibility of violence. Proposals assuming a clockwork-view of political institutions typically follow this path. Showing how this strategy colors analyses of political institutions, I consider recent efforts to defend an alternative to competition: lotteries or sortition.

Lotteries have been used as an alternative to elections for more than two thousand years. They have a multimillennia pedigree. And contemporary political philosophers have now rediscovered the practice (López-Guerra 2011). Alexander Guerrero, for example, has developed a nuanced and insightful argument for a "lottocratic alternative" (2014). Instead of filling

political positions competitively, officeholders are selected via
a random procedure. My comments are not intended to question
(or support) the view that a lottocratic system would be a feature
of an ideal regime. Instead, I focus on the following fact: Guerrero's critique of competition turns on the opportunities it
provides for the powerful to exert unjustifiable influence over
elected officials. Yet, consistent with most critiques of opposition,
Guerrero sidesteps the potential capacity of those individuals
to pervert lottery-based institutions or take up arms to prevent
their imposition, a possibility that the Roman experience makes
conspicuous. In other words, Guerrero embraces clockwork
constitutionalism. As a result, he offers a skewed estimate of
opposition's value relative to his favored alternative.[9]

Summarizing crudely, Guerrero contends that the quality
of decision-making in an electoral democracy is limited by two
factors. First, citizens have difficulty assessing political decisions
made by elected representatives. Second, the powerful can exploit that difficulty to influence elected officials, advancing their
interests at the expense of the larger population of constituents.
A background assumption here is that many or most individuals are self-interested. This is presumably why the powerful
manipulate political institutions to suit their own interests. And
it is why elected officials are willing to accommodate themselves
to that manipulation. If Guerrero assumed that individuals were
not motivated by their own interests, narrowly understood, his
critique of representative institutions would not go through.
Imagine an alternative world. In that world, individuals do not
pursue their self-interest but reliably seek to advance the commonweal. In such a world, citizens would continue to face difficulties assessing the decisions of their representatives. But in
that rosier alternative world, there would be little reason to assume that elected representatives would not rule well; they
would go out of their way to weigh alternative perspectives, seek

consensus, reveal exactly why they had made their decisions, and even step down from office if other actors would be more effective at advancing the polity's welfare. In such a world, one assumes, there would be relatively little reason to create a lottocracy. As this example illustrates, the likelihood that self-interested, real-world representatives will make suboptimal decisions sets the table for Guerrero's proposal. It is an indispensable presupposition of the argument.

In Guerrero's lottocratic alternative, legislation is created by multiple, single-issue legislatures, composed of roughly three hundred members, who are selected by a rolling system of lotteries: each year, one hundred new members are chosen, and one hundred leave. Experts provide information to the legislative assemblies at the beginning of each session. Assuming that these institutions work as intended, Guerrero adduces many comparative benefits to this system of decision-making, focusing especially on the high quality of decisions it would produce. For the purposes of this discussion, I leave these claims unanalyzed.

What would it mean for our assessment of this clockwork proposal if we took the implications of the Roman case seriously? Guerrero counsels us to compare "apples to apples" when weighing the value of alternative political systems. Heeding that counsel, we would have to imagine how the proposed lottocratic system would function when the powerful could wield their de facto influence and even resort to violence. Doing so gives us three reasons to doubt whether Guerrero's alternative to electoral competition could function as he predicts or that it would be substantially preferable to the status quo.

First, as the Roman case indicates, presumably the well-off would corrupt Guerrero's lottocratic system just as they have corrupted the electoral systems he bemoans. We have no reason to believe that the door to corruption is only opened by elections. Guerrero, to his significant credit, anticipates this concern. He suggests that measures could be taken to protect lottery-based assemblies from malign influence, for example, by paying legislators a million dollars a year (Guerrero 2014, 164). But the persuasiveness of this response is limited. Guerrero rejects the feasibility of barricading electoral institutions from similar influence. And there is no principled reason to think that these institutional barricades would be effective in one case and not the other. Indeed, we have relevant experience with institutions that incorporate sortition. Sortition was famously used in both republican Venice and Florence. Both polities erected intricate and clever barriers to block corruption. And in both polities, wealthy families manipulated those procedures, corrupting them to suit their ends. They changed the timing of selections, influenced who could be a candidate for random selection, played games with selection procedures, and even banished their rivals (Finlay 1980; Rubinstein 1997). Of course, these examples occurred hundreds of years ago. Here is a more proximate case: the US experience with a military draft organized around the random selection of young men via their birthdates. The wealthy and powerful famously still found ways to avoid military service, frustrating the point of the random procedure. That history dramatically illustrates the vacuity of claims that lottery-based systems of decision-making are immune from corruption (Card and Lemieux 2001; Seelye 2004). The implication here is not that sortition is a less-effective corruption stopper than opposition is. The implication is that we have no reason to believe that sortition would be better at blocking elite influence *in the kinds of situations* in which we use opposition. And we cannot assume that it is so. By implication, if the comparative attraction of alternatives to opposition depends on their immunity from the influence of the powerful, then those alternatives cannot be considered comparatively attractive.

Here is the second reason to doubt the attractiveness of Guerrero's proposal. Once we acknowledge that some indi-

viduals can exercise outsized political influence, there is little
reason to assume that a lottocracy could be instituted in the
way Guerrero imagines. As in Rome, the powerful would ensure
that these systems would reflect their influence. Here the issue
is not corruption, which implies that the influential can pervert
existing institutions. The issue is that in a world in which certain
groups exert extra influence over elected officials, the powerful
would embed their influence and interests in the very design
of lottocratic institutions. That political institutions reflect the
relative power of those who create them is not a theoretical
deduction. It was true of the Roman case. And it remains an
empirical regularity (Boix 1999).

What if we imagined that an ideal form of the lottocratic
system could, in Guerrero's words, be "superimposed" on a
society like ours? Could we straightforwardly compare it to an
existing system? I do not think so. As Guerrero makes clear, the
groups most likely to suffer under his proposal would be those
that currently exercise inordinate influence. By implication,
assessing the "lottocratic alternative" requires us to consider
how they would respond to the imposition of such a system.

The Roman experience suggests that they would not respond well. And most contemporary theories of regime stability assume that political systems must reflect, in some crude
way, the underlying distributions of power and interests, or
they will generate conflict. Of course, it is difficult to outline
exactly what the costs of their resistance would amount to and,
perhaps more importantly, who would bear those costs. For
instance, the outcome of any assessment would probably depend
on whether those who play no blameworthy part in maintaining the current flawed system—the innocent—bear the costs
of elite resistance (assuming, for the sake of argument, that the
new, imposed system is not flawed). Under the right conditions,
superimposing institutions might still be justified. But if the

innocent would be the most likely to suffer and if the new system would be unlikely to remain in place, then, presumably,
superimposition would not be warranted. Regardless of how
this challenging calculation turns out, any proposal to replace
opposition that does not account for the potential for violence
will be systematically and unjustifiably biased against legitimate
opposition.

Guerrero's imaginative proposal to inoculate collective
decision-making from the worst symptoms of inegalitarian
political competition is not unique in embracing clockwork
constitutionalism, a perspective inconsistent with the Roman
experience. John McCormick advances an arguably less-ideal
palliative to the very same disease in his striking, agenda-setting
book *Machiavellian Democracy* (2011). Like Guerrero, McCormick
laments how elites corrupt competitive elections, undermining
mechanisms of political accountability. And like Guerrero,
McCormick outlines a lottery-based fix to legitimate opposition:
a legislative body that would specifically exclude elites from
eligibility and possess the power to veto government actions, to
call national referenda, and to impeach federal officials. Inspired
by Machiavelli's laudatory analysis of the Roman system,
McCormick calls his proposal the "People's Tribunate." Machiavelli, McCormick emphasizes, knew well the political import of
violent conflict and believed that an armed citizenry was a key
source of popular empowerment (2011, 31). Nonetheless, even
McCormick's proposal does not weigh the (high) probability
of intense discord entailed by the imposition of class-specific
institutions in a regime afflicted by outrageous political inequality. Any straight comparison of his proposal with the current
system of legitimate opposition would surely have to take that
possibility into account. But, adopting a clockwork perspective,
McCormick does not do so. And that means that McCormick's
assessment of the People's Tribunate is either inconsistent with

the premises of his argument (assuming advantageous conditions for its establishment) or distorted to appear more attractive than it is.

That McCormick does not fully attend to the way violence and discord shape electoral institutions can perhaps best be seen in his consideration of why James Madison and his contemporaries did not settle on class-specific institutions when designing the US Constitution (McCormick 2011, 170, 179). McCormick considers different possibilities. Perhaps Madison and his contemporaries were swayed by the theories of popular sovereignty and political pluralism? Perhaps they were moved by simple class prejudice? But in keeping with clockwork constitutionalism, McCormick, like another defender of lotteries, Bernard Manin, does not give due consideration to concerns related to institutional efficacy and conflict. Such concerns surely occupied the minds of those who had experienced the Articles of Confederation (Amar 2005). McCormick specifically discusses Federalist 10 (2011, 170, 179–80). The title of that famed argument offers information about whether the "Founders" connected the form of the political system and its capacity to engender or subvert violence. The title is "The Utility of the Union as a Safeguard against Domestic Faction and Insurrection." Indeed the first line of that work specifically considers the connection between electoral competition and force: "Among the numerous advantages promised by a well-constructed Union," Madison famously observed, "none deserves to be more accurately developed than *its tendency to break and control the violence* of faction" (1961a, 56; emphasis added). Whatever the faults in Madison's institutional vision, he cannot be accused of ignoring the institutional dynamics highlighted by the Roman experience.

Of course, we may have very good reasons for abstracting from unjust realities when trying to specify our political ideals

(G. Cohen 2008). The Roman case may counsel us to consider how power shapes political institutions and how the threat of violence can undermine opposition. But incorporating unjust power relations and the possibility of violence into our political ideals will necessarily lead us to misperceive what justice entails.

Still, those who adopt a clockwork perspective when assessing opposition are not aiming to divine the *principles* and *ideals* that should guide our assessment of existing institutions. They seek to show that an alternative set of *institutions* would be comparatively more attractive than opposition given current conditions. As a result, these accounts are not immune from complaints if they fail to consider the conditions necessary to instantiate their proposals or how their proposals would be impacted if those conditions were not achieved.

One might contend that it is unrealistic and unnecessarily restrictive to ask political theorists and philosophers to consider the implications of the Roman case, to take all manner of side effects into account when developing institutional proposals. Arguments in favor of creative, even ingenious alternatives to opposition, like those developed by Guerrero and McCormick, offer *pro tanto* reasons to embrace their proposals. And they ought to be assessed as such.

There are two reasons to reject this argument in *these* cases. First, it seems to me that proposed solutions to a specific problem—a problem like elite influence—should not require that that problem be addressed *before* those solutions could be implemented. Imagine, for instance, that you had discovered a technical solution that would arrest climate change. Imagine further that a condition for the successful implementation of your proposal was that climate change had stopped. We might, of course, have good reason to find your proposal pretty attractive. It necessarily entails a cessation of climate change. Yet once we have assumed that the problem has been addressed, there is little reason to value the proposed solution—that is, given current conditions, there is no reason for us to embrace the proposal. The same logic applies to these proposed alternatives to legitimate opposition. They identify political inequality as a central defect of electoral competition. And they propose solutions that could only be instituted if political inequality were not as grave an issue as they contend.

Second, and more importantly, contributing to the cessation of violence is not a peripheral or secondary effect of legitimate opposition. It is, I believe, a core or essential function. Examining the Roman case, I illustrated how oppositional systems are forged and developed within a penumbra of violence. There is little reason to think that this canonical case is unrepresentative. Proposing a system that dodges this task is like proposing institutions to foster religious toleration that would predictably lead to religious violence. Limiting violence cannot be the only recognized aim of tolerant institutions; clearly the autonomy to worship within reasonable limits looms large. But any institutional proposal concerning religious toleration that ignored the possibility of violence would be incomplete. And the same holds true for institutions aimed at processing political conflicts (Przeworski 2011).

Am I defending a kind of political determinism? If we accept that stable political institutions reflect the de facto power of key players, does that imply that no change or reform is possible, that collective agency of the sort I have defended is implausible? I do not think so. The Roman political system reflected an inegalitarian balance of power. Popular forces were still able to organize, to shift the balance of de facto influence, press for significant changes to the political structure, and seek redistribution. The upshot is that serious proposals to replace or reform systems of legitimate opposition should weigh the possibility of disorder. And actually weighing that possibility will allow us to properly evaluate the real political achievement of legitimate opposition.

Conclusion

"[The tribunate] is a pernicious thing, born in sedition and promoting sedition" (Cicero 1928, *Laws* 3.19). This was the negative verdict of Quintus, a character Cicero used to defend an elitist perspective in the dialogue *On the Laws*. Quintus's aphorism echoes the accepted view that the tribunate was the product of popular resistance to elite dominance. Nonetheless, it is also an admission: despite the radically undemocratic and inegalitarian character of Rome's institutions, the tribunate provided popular actors with a credible institutional avenue to advance their ends—it was an element of an adversarial system of opposition. Quintus's argument thus aptly captures two key features of legitimate opposition. It cannot be divorced from groups' capacity to exercise extrainstitutional influence. And it is a virtue of the practice that, notwithstanding the existence of inequality, it provides citizens with the institutional means to exercise valuable forms of collective agency.

This chapter and chapter 4 pose a fundamental challenge to the democratic conception. Opposition precedes the development of political parties. We have misunderstood the intellectual revolution that ended with a partisan, organized form of legitimate opposition becoming synonymous with democracy. Can my claims possibly be correct? Chapter 6 makes the case, illustrating why the key to understanding modern opposition is not intellectual acceptance but the power of the modern state.

6

It's the State, Not Parties
Why Legitimate Opposition Is a Preeminent Constitutional Principle

David Hume plays an important role in the traditional story of opposition's invention. He is used to illustrate the widespread aversion to the practice that was ostensibly prevalent during the eighteenth century (Hofstadter 1969, 24–27). Hume's writings wielded significant influence on the political thought of the American founders.[1] And he was famously ambivalent about parties, decrying some while allowing the value of others. According to the orthodox view of legitimate opposition, this marks Hume as someone who did not accept the legitimacy of opposition.[2] According to that view, it would be inconceivable for Hume to have accepted legitimate opposition, since he did not consistently embrace partisan competition.

Hume's essay "Idea of a Perfect Commonwealth" demonstrates the considerable limitations of the orthodox view (Hume 1994a).[3] In the essay, Hume outlines his ideal regime. The essay barely mentions parties. When it does, it is not clear that Hume is referring to political organizations. Yet power in Hume's system was gained via electoral contestation. This was a competitive political system, one that allowed individuals, both candidates and supporters of those candidates, to advance ends they cared about and seek to block or mitigate projects they objected to. Moreover, the Scot recommends the creation of a "court of competitors." The body consisted of runners-up for senatorial election. It would inspect public accounts, accuse men in the senate or in a special court, and propose laws to the senate or to the people. This is hardly a proposal of someone who rejected regular, regulated competition for power. Challengers in this system were not ostracized or punished. They were encouraged to popularize alternative proposals, exercise a measure of power, and bide their time before seeking greater influence. Hume's system was not a party system, but it was clearly a system in which those who wielded formal political influence could be judged and displaced by those who were out of power, via a regular, rule-based system of competition. Power holders would tolerate their rivals and let them exert political influence. It was a system of legitimate opposition.

On the orthodox view of legitimate opposition, my reading of Hume has to be judged nonsensical. On that view, eighteenth-centuries theorists of representative government, like Hume, did not fully grasp the value of opposition. They understood opposition as essentially party based, essentially factional, and essentially anticonstitutional.

That dogma is wholly contradicted by a plain reading of Hume's institutional proposal, a proposal that is self-evidently a competitive system of opposition. In his ideal system, power holders would have to yield their places to those who defeated them in an election. Hume just did not conflate a system of opposition with a system of party-based competition. And he did not conflate electoral competition with factional anticonstitutionalism. As this brief discussion illustrates, collapsing the acceptance of opposition into the acceptance of political parties obscures a proper understanding of Hume's arguments and of the "invention" of legitimate opposition, more generally.

This chapter tallies the intellectual payoff for this historical volte-face. Influential assessments of opposition's development have mapped the *diverging* attitudes toward parties of figures like Viscount Bolingbroke, David Hume, and Edmund Burke (Mansfield 1965; Rosenblum 2008). In sharp contrast, I track the *consistent* intellectual threads binding their arguments to each other. I argue that each of these authors *accepted* the legitimacy of opposition. Yet they surveyed a radically different political landscape than ancient actors who engaged in the practice. Modern regimes are separated from their ancient analogues by many factors: the nature of their economies, size, and so on. But they are critically distinguished by the existence of a modern state and the complicated apparatus that enterprise entails.

What difference do states make? Put simply, states' offices and resources are deployed by governments to organize collective action. Crucially, these efforts need not be contained within a single body or division of the government; the state's resources can be wielded, for instance, to coordinate activity within legislative bodies and to generate electoral support. It is a truism of modern political science that parties facilitate legislative and electoral collective action (Aldrich 1995). There is little reason, however, to assume that parties are the *only* institutions capable of this activity. As each of the authors I discuss here recognized, the executive's ability to coordinate collective action in both the legislature and the electoral domain did not render opposition illegitimate; it rendered unorganized opposition ineffective and self-defeating. Real competition for power, real opposition, required those who did have immediate access to the state's resources to organize. By implication, if opposition was legitimate in a modern state, if power could be pursued competitively, then organized opposition had to be legitimate too.

In this chapter, I tackle the question of why some of the most important theorists of "organized" opposition embraced that conception of the practice. To be clear, my aim is not that of a historian, rewriting intellectual history. Instead, my goal is to draw out and develop the theoretical import of the conclusions arrived at in preceding chapters.

Shifting focus from parties to opposition reveals the import of legitimate opposition as a constitutional principle.[4] By "constitutional principle," I mean a rule or practice that generally warrants legal protection and political deference in imperfect, real-world polities. Using this term, I mean to emphasize opposition's institutional significance without implying that it is a necessary feature of a just or ideal regime. And by using this term, I also mean to counterpose opposition to other constitutional mechanisms that might be employed instead of *or* in addition to a system of opposition—for example, the separation of powers, a lottery-based mechanism for selecting office holders, or J. S. Mill's division of the executive and legislative functions.

Having reread authors like Bolingbroke, Hume, and Burke in light of the preceding chapters, I now believe that it is difficult to correctly assess modern systems of opposition unless one takes as a starting point the capacity of the executive to coordinate political activity across institutional barriers, to engage in legislative *and* electoral politics, to co-opt and divide the opposition.[5] Once we divest from the assumptions of clockwork constitutionalism, an approach to constitutionalism that assumes that institutional barriers will be respected and that specified roles will be fulfilled, it becomes apparent that a system of organized opposition plays a *special* role in allowing those who disagree with the government to affect policy and limit the ambitions of those who hold power.[6] It can play this role as long as opponents of the government can mobilize and organize. Organization allows even those who do not have the resources of the state to effectively compete; it is why opposition can remain a constitutional principle even when officials put the resources of the state to work.[7] And it is because of the power of organization that opposition is not merely one constitutional principle among others but a rival in import to better-known principles like the division of powers.

This chapter is composed of several sections. Reexamining the writing of three well-known authors—Bolingbroke, Hume, and Burke—the first through third sections illustrate the role that executive action played in justifying a system of sustained and organized opposition. The fourth section considers and defends the applicability of this analysis beyond eighteenth-century Britain. The fifth section critically considers J. S. Mill's influential, deliberative system of legitimate opposition. Mill's proposals have inspired an entire genre of theorizing about legitimate opposition that I have referred to as collegial rivalry. As I have used the term, it refers to a largely intellectual, well-mannered, restrained form of competition, a form of competition that reliably advances the ends of the commonweal. The attraction of Mill's conception of legitimate opposition depends on dodging the problem of executive advantage. As a result, Mill's institutional proposals, and those that suffer the same limitation, may have severely limited relevance for regimes featuring a modern state.

A word on terminology: I have asserted that the heart of legitimate opposition is the capacity for groups or individuals to seek power via a competitive process. This has allowed me to consider whether the practice predates its ostensible acceptance in the late eighteenth century. As our attention shifts to the eighteenth century, we now will have to distinguish a system of legitimate opposition, which is my focus, from the terms "formed opposition" and "partisan opposition." As I understand it, a formed opposition is a group of elected delegates, representatives, or lawmakers organized to consistently oppose the people in power and to seek office and influence for themselves within a system of legitimate opposition. By "formed opposition," I mean something more general than a party. I take a party to be a group joined across *an extended period of time* with the common aim of winning elections and wielding legislative influence together. Partisan opposition is therefore a party that seeks power via a system of legitimate opposition. A system of opposition might feature formed opposition groups, but it might not feature parties. For instance, a formed opposition might simply be a group that joins together during a single legislative term, with the aim of systematically frustrating a particular government, without any intention of working together during the next election or of seeking common ends during the next legislative term. A competitive system of legitimate opposition, a formed opposition, and a party are related practices, and they are easily conflated; but running them together results in confusion.

Lord Bolingbroke and the Simple Logic of Formed Opposition

Henry St. John, Viscount Bolingbroke, is well known for offering an "eschatological" defense of formed opposition: a defense of formed opposition that would render it unnecessary (Foord 1964, 150; Rosenblum 2008, 36).[8] This section focuses on Bolingbroke's defense of formed opposition and his essay "On the Spirit of Patriotism" (1736). In a later work, 'The Idea of a Patriot King" (1738), Bolingbroke famously contended that a king who pursued a constitutionally legitimate policy would win broad support and end the need for *formed* oppositions (but as I will claim shortly, Bolingbroke did not call for the end of legitimate opposition in toto).[9] This amounted to an inelegant intellectual pirouette, one that leads historians to treat Bolingbroke's writings on opposition as exemplars of opportunism, not principle (a conclusion well supported by Bolingbroke's unsteady political allegiances). But even if Bolingbroke's arguments were entirely strategic, he intended those arguments to be persuasive. They therefore provide insight into the intellectual currents of the period (Skinner 1974). The impurity of Bolingbroke's intentions aside, his writings may also contain independently defensible claims.

Grappling with Bolingbroke's contribution requires understanding the incipient system of legitimate opposition characterizing eighteenth-century British politics. Competition for political influence had a number of elements. And these cannot be boiled down to the personalistic rivalries that characterize all political life. The first was regular elections. Elections were not fully fair. Few individuals could participate, and there could be little competition for office. Henry Fox lost a 1728 election to Thomas Pitt, two votes to one. The borough was entirely controlled by the Pitts, and they had simply assumed that their candidate would, as usual, be unopposed (Owen 1972, 369). Nonetheless, elections could turn political fortunes. The 1710 election brought the Tories, including Bolingbroke, into political influence, a turn of events that would be quite difficult to explain without an electoral intercession. "By the late seventeenth century," the historian Mark Kishlansky observes, "parliamentary selections were dominated by competition" (1986, 192). Royal favor constituted the second feature of the system. The monarch possessed the right to name his ministers. And during this period, high political ambition required competing for royal favor. A final element was support in Parliament, especially the Commons. Initially, support in the Commons made one more likely to be the target for inclusion in the administration; over time, it became necessary for holding a position in government (Foord 1964, 55–214).

The development of Britain's *system* of legitimate opposition is fundamentally a story about a shift in the relative import of these three factors. The waning influence of the Crown relative to the other, more regular and rule-based factors generated the system we recognize today. Yet the germinal, eighteenth-century version of the system would not have worked had some elements of legitimate opposition not been broadly accepted. Active support for the Jacobite cause was beyond the pale. So were direct attacks on the monarch. During the first part of the eighteenth century, those who served in a prior administration suffered threats of legal prosecution. But it was still accepted, in practice, that political elites could compete for office and the Crown's favor. And they could oppose the king's ministers, especially if those ministers threatened the constitution.[10] Rough-and-tumble Parliamentary politics and contested elections would be difficult to explain if this were not the case. Moreover, as everyone understood, the constitutional settlement in place during the lifetimes of Bolingbroke, Hume, and Burke, one that gave elected members of Parliament a significant political role, would not have been sustained had opposition been illegitimate.

Did Bolingbroke really accept a system of opposition? Consider his argument for a patriot king, a king who would be a focal point for public-minded collective action. Such a king would render *partisan* activity and factionalism unjustified. Yet, even in a regime justly ruled by a king, Bolingbroke saw a place for regular, rule-based opposition. "There may be abuses in [the king's] government," Bolingbroke observed, "mistakes in his administration, and guilt in his ministers, which he has not observed: and he will be far from imputing the complaints, that give him occasion to observe them, to a spirit of party; much less will he treat those who carry on such prosecutions in a legal manner, as incendiaries, and as enemies to his government. On the contrary, he will distinguish the voice of his people from the clamor of a faction, and will hearken to it" (1841a, 404). Here, Bolingbroke offers a familiar, even banal, principal-agent justification of systematic, rule-based competition, a justification outlining why it was sensible to tolerate outsiders seeking power. Regular competition among power seekers is defended as a service to the principal (the king, the queen, or the people), providing valuable information about the activities of its agents and ensuring the justice of its own rule. In other words, even with a patriot king, there "may be reason . . . sometimes for opposition" (404). Originating during a panegyric to monarchical power, Bolingbroke's defense of limited opposition illustrates, rather persuasively, that legitimate opposition was not beyond the intellectual horizon during the early eighteenth century. It suggests that the distinction between legitimate opposition and partisan opposition had potency at the time and is not merely a product of my own theoretical imagination.

Unfortunately, according to Bolingbroke, Britain was not led by a patriot king, a king standing above party, avoiding direct engagement in legislative politics. This fact justified a different kind of opposition, a system of opposition in which those who were out of power would *organize*. Bolingbroke stretched a broadly shared, if narrow, commitment to legitimate opposition to cover a specific version of the practice presumptively inconsistent with the king's right to choose his own ministers and have them govern, in the main, as he wished (Skinner 1974).

For convenience, we can divide Bolingbroke's argument for formed opposition in two. The first part identifies the problem requiring special action; the second specifies why formed opposition was an appropriate solution to that problem. I treat them serially. Why, Bolingbroke's readers might have asked, must groups organize given the protective mechanisms already incorporated into the English constitution? A question of this sort would have been motivated by the widespread acceptance of a clockwork view of the British constitution, in which balance was attained among the branches: monarchy, commons, lords (Robbins 1959). Each part of the system limited the liberty-threatening excesses of the others. The king chose his ministers, Parliament controlled the budget, and so forth. In principle, each of these branches represented distinct sections of the population. The different sections would, on this view, have no trouble coordinating their activities. They were assumed to share common interests and a political body to organize their activity. Because interests were shared among section members and not without, one could be confident that the different bodies would consistently check each other. In sum, each section would jealously and vigorously protect its interests against the others, perhaps even coming into conflict. But these conflicts would generate the institutional equilibrium or balance that many people found attractive at the time and that continues to inspire fidelity as a constitutional principle.

This was not at all the way the system functioned (or functions). Despite the formal institutional stability of the British constitution since 1688, the executive exercised significant influence within Parliament, materially changing the constitutional setup and its basic mechanics. "Parliaments are not only, what they always were, essential parts of our constitution, but," Bolingbroke observed, "essential parts of our administration too" (1841b, 362). Indeed, as I discuss in chapter 7, even Montesquieu, a reader of Bolingbroke and probably the person most responsible for winning the division of powers its preeminence among constitutional principles, did not think that the English constitution of this era approximated the ideal (Shackleton 1949; Gunn 2009, 15). Why not? The logic is simple.

The Crown had legislative, budgetary, and political interests at stake in Parliament. And it had the resources to support the ministry of its choice. Perhaps unsurprisingly, the Crown's ministers did not act like elements in a clock, moving mechanically forward, respecting the distinction between executive and legislative prerogatives. Instead, they enticed independent members of Parliament with the promise of valuable office. And they placed people holding executive offices in Parliament (Foord 1964, 68). The success of the government in putting those resources to work led Bolingbroke to refer to the dominant political figure of the period and the longtime head of government, Robert Walpole, as one of the "farmers of government" (1841b, 363).

The most interesting elements of Bolingbroke's argument are the most prosaic: those describing the difficulty of coordinating efforts among a diverse group of political actors. These difficulties meant that organization was the only plausible solution to the opposition's woes. The intrusion of the executive into electoral and legislative politics, the failure of the division of powers, Bolingbroke claimed, ironically provided the opposition with opportunities to influence the government's policy and even defeat its plans. They had done so in one instance in 1733, blocking Walpole's effort to impose an excise tax on wine and tobacco. "It is become so easy by the present form of our government," Bolingbroke argued, "that corruption alone could not destroy us" (1841b, 363). But potential opponents failed to consistently grab those opportunities. They were uncoordinated and had no leaders to get them in sync and no method for sanctioning shirkers.

Jean-Jacques Rousseau famously outlined the difficulty of cooperation and coordination using his "stag hunt" analogy in the *Discourse on the Origin and Foundations of Inequality Among Mankind* (1753). Bolingbroke developed a similar analogy almost two decades earlier, describing the difficulty of orchestrating an effective challenge to power wielders.[11] Those who were averse to the current ministry, Bolingbroke argued, seemingly shared common aims: "the reformation of the government" and the "destruction" of Walpole. "But when his destruction seemed to approach, the object of his succession interposed to the sight of many, and the reformation of the government was no longer their point of view. They divided the skin, at least in their thoughts, before they had taken the beast, and the common fear of hunting him down for others made them all faint in the chase. It was this, and this alone, that has saved him, or has put off his evil day" (1841b, 363). Given the common ambitions of Walpole's critics and the possibility that their efforts would result in the ascension of another, no one acted, facilitating Walpole's survival as minister.

Today, parties solve coordination problems of this sort (Aldrich 1995). But the Crown's ministry was not organized into a party. And one might assume that the challenges Bolingbroke complained of would also hobble the ministry's supporters. Parties are not, however, the *only* way to coordinate electoral and legislative activity. The ministry wielded the resources and offices of the Crown to organize and induce collective action. This gave it a persistent advantage even when members of the opposition wanted to act. "Look about you," Bolingbroke suggested, "and you will see men eager to speak, and keen to act, when particular occasions press them, or particular motives excite them, but quite unprepared for either: and hence all that superficiality in speaking, for want of information, hence all that confusions or inactivity, for want of concert, and all that disappointment for want of preliminary measures" (1841b, 369).

We now have our hands on each element of Bolingbroke's argument. The resources of the Crown and the ministry's willingness to wield them rendered a particular, clockwork constitutional principle invalid: the division of powers. What would take its place? Not disorganized opposition. That would lack effect. Yet if regular, rule-based opposition was legitimate, then legitimate opposition must cover strategies allowing the government's critics to succeed. In other words, the range of strategies legitimately employed in seeking to impact policy would reflect the executive's advantages. "Every administration is a system of conduct: opposition therefore, should be a system likewise; an opposite, but not a dependent system," argued Bolingbroke. Given the resource advantages enjoyed by the executive, the only option was organization: "a party who opposed, systematically, a wise to a silly, an honest to an iniquitous scheme of government, would acquire greater reputation and strength, and arrive more surely at their end, than a party who opposed occasionally, as it were, without any system, without any general concert, with little uniformity, little preparation, little perseverance, and as little knowledge or political capacity" (1841b, 370).

Traditionally, Viscount Bolingbroke is deployed as an exemplar of the vexed place of political parties in the history of political ideas. He acknowledged their promise and counseled their abolition. Focusing on legitimate opposition, not parties, I have identified a more promising vein in Bolingbroke's thought. He identified a basic, unresolved problem in an eminent constitutional principle—the division of powers—and outlined a credible and surprisingly comprehensive justification for its supplement, that is, legitimate opposition. A system of competitive opposition was legitimate, on this view. But the liberty to engage in *formed* opposition was not to be embraced in all circumstances. Organization was entailed *only* when the executive unfurled the substantial powers of the modern state to advance its political ends.

Hume and the Failure of Clockwork Constitutionalism

Ambitious, hypocritical, and disloyal, Bolingbroke is the poster theorist for the shortcomings of political partisanship. It would be wise to handle his claims with great care. David Hume has a different, justifiably superior reputation as a political observer and philosopher. The Scot did not share Bolingbroke's political preferences. And he offered a compelling critique of the unreasonable stridency with which Bolingbroke justified his political ends. Bolingbroke insisted that Britain's historic constitution was grounded in unimpeachable principles, burnished by centuries of experience. But if Bolingbroke's high estimation of the British constitution was accurate, Hume judged, then it was unreasonable to conclude that one corrupt minister, Robert Walpole, could have the irredeemably corrosive effect that Bolingbroke alleged (Hume 1994d, 28).

Still, Hume's own observations about the character of politics in Britain echo and corroborate key elements of Bolingbroke's arguments: the practical failure of the division of powers, the executive's ability to wield its resource advantage, and the legitimacy of a system in which formed oppositions sought to supplant their rivals.

For Hume, a "constitution is only so far good, as it provides a remedy against mal-administration" (1994d, 29). Normally, this risk-averse vantage on constitutionalism lends itself to warm embraces of the division of powers. And in Hume's essay "Of the Independency of Parliament," he outlined the standard logic of constitutional division. Such a plan *could* be valuable. But success required organizing political bodies so that they consistently advanced the public interest even as each order of the population pursued its own good. Organized poorly, such that the separate orders were unchecked, the result would be "faction, disorder, and tyranny." On the standard view, one Hume attributed to "such geniuses as CICERO, or TACITUS," if one body, like the Commons, were to possess substantially greater institutional rights, that body and the interests dominant within it would necessarily overawe the others (1994c, 43).

"But," Hume sardonically observed, "in this opinion, experience shows [that Cicero and Tacitus] would have been mistaken" (1994c, 44). In Britain, the Commons' institutional prerogatives clearly violated the principles just described. "The share of power, allotted by our constitution to the house of commons, is so great, that it absolutely commands all the other parts of the government" (44). The royal veto had little practical weight. And the Commons' budgetary privilege put the executive under its thumb. The division of powers was a descriptive failure. Yet Britain was no tyranny.

Hume was more sanguine about Britain's constitution than Bolingbroke was. But he shared the following view: Britain's politics were defined by the executive's advantage in orchestrating collective action. What kept the Commons from infringing on other bodies and opening the doors for tyranny? "I answer, that the interest of the body is here restrained by that of individuals, and that the house of commons stretches not its power, because such usurpation would be contrary to the interest of the majority of its members" (Hume 1994c, 45). In other words, contra the division-of-powers theory, the members of the Commons did not act as a coherent group, a group motivated by a common portfolio of interests. They acted as individuals, beset by problems of coordination and conflicting interest. And like Bolingbroke, Hume picked out the executive as the institution capable of solving these problems. "The Crown," Hume continued, "has so many offices at its disposal, that, when assisted by the honest and disinterested part of the house, it will always command the resolutions of the whole so far, at least to preserve the ancient constitution from danger" (1994c, 45). For Hume, the Crown's capacity to conduct collective action within the legislative branch was an attractive feature of the constitution.

Hume's standard for assessing a constitution was its capacity to "remedy mal-administration." The canonical method for achieving that end—the division of powers—was not available to the British. Like Bolingbroke, Hume suggested that the system required a "proper counterbalance," and he defended a moderate version of Bolingbroke's own solution. This chapter begins with evidence from "Idea of a Perfect Commonwealth" illustrating how Hume's famous distaste for factions did not entail the repudiation of legitimate opposition; a perfect commonwealth would feature regulated rivalry but lack factions.

The essay "That Politics May Be Reduced to a Science" concludes with a characteristic assault on factional zealotry. Hume reproaches supporters and defenders of leading ministers for exaggerating the faults of the other and the dangers they pose. Yet Hume does not champion a nonoppositional, collaborative mode of politics. Instead, he suggests that the remedy to "mal-administration" would amount to a moderate system of opposition. Power seekers would not paint the incumbent ministers as threats to the constitution when they were not. In turn, the ministry would accept that "a change in ministry" ought not be a source of existential anxiety. Turnover, Hume claimed, "is essential to such a constitution, in every ministry, both to preserve itself from violation, and to prevent all enormities in the administration" (1994d, 28–30).

Reading Hume's essays, it is difficult to accept that he did not see the value of legitimate opposition. It is therefore difficult not to see those essays as standing in contradiction to the orthodox understanding of opposition. Hume rejected factionalism and extremism, but even in a polity where moderation was the rule, he counseled that "the *country-party* might still assert that our constitution, though excellent will admit of mal-administration to a certain degree; and therefore, if the minister be bad, it is proper to oppose him with a *suitable* degree of zeal" (1994d, 30–31). Similarly, "the *court-party* may be allowed, upon the supposition that the minister were good, to defend, and with *some* zeal too, his administration" (31). In other words, a moderate regime in which the executive stimulated legislative action would feature a regular and constant opposition, if not partisanship or factionalism.

To be clear, my claim here is not that Hume and Bolingbroke agreed about political ends or even the value of executive influence. Surely, they did not. But both figures recognized that the Crown's capacities were a bedrock reality of British constitutional life. Both recognized that this reality was not covered by standard, clockwork constitutional principles. And both recognized that the appropriate character of a system of opposition turned on that reality. Hume's and Bolingbroke's common reading of the political terrain gains credibility, I believe, because they agreed about so little. And, as I will show, Edmund Burke defended a similar position in the most famous contribution to the theory of political partisanship.

Burkean Opposition

Edmund Burke's embrace of partisan activity is sometimes treated as a pivotal moment in the intellectual understanding of political parties, organized competition for power, and party government (Mansfield 1965). Breaking from his predecessors in the political canon, he offers a less equivocal defense of partisanship. "Party," he famously contended, "is a body of men united, for promoting by their joint endeavors the national interest, upon some particular principle in which they are all agreed" (1981b, 317). The originality of this position has come under sustained assault.[12] What matters here is the intellectual isthmus connecting Burke to his predecessors Bolingbroke and Hume.

Burke's best-known statement on matters of party and legitimate opposition is "Thoughts on the Cause of the Present Discontents" (1770). Unlike Bolingbroke, Burke accepted that Parliament should have a role in governance. But his argument otherwise shares the same basic structure as those already canvassed. "Every good political institution must have a preventive operation as well as a remedial," Burke famously remarked. "It ought to have a natural tendency to exclude bad men from Government, and not to trust for the safety of the State to subsequent punishment alone" (1981b, 279). In principle, fulfilling this task was the Commons' role, which "was originally supposed to be *no part of the standing Government of this country*. It was considered as a *controul*, issuing immediately from the people" (279). Before the accession of George III, Britain's system of opposition had turned out multiple leaders. But with George III's rise, Burke argued, the Commons' capacity to exclude men from government was under pressure. The new king's cabinet had tipped the scales of influence against the Commons, crippling the distinctive institutional character of Britain's constitutional monarchy. The new form of politics threatened to make Parliament "subservient to a system, by which it was to be degraded from the dignity of a national council, into a mere member of the Court, it must be greatly changed from its original character" (291). And if Parliament was blocked from exercising control, then Britain's system of legitimate opposition, the adversarial mechanism for impacting political outcomes, would be blocked too.

The Wilkes affair, for instance, illustrated that the government was willing to disrupt that system of opposition. John Wilkes had ferociously inveighed against the king's ministries. As a result, he had been subject to a general warrant and charges of libel and seditious libel. He was expelled from Parliament. Reelected, he was expelled again. Burke shared Wilkes's antipathy for the king's advisers, especially Lord Bute. And Burke argued, plausibly, that Wilkes's punishment had been constitutionally troubling. Putting "into the power of the House of Commons to disable any person disagreeable to them from sitting in Parliament, without any other rule than their own pleasure," posed a fundamental challenge to the Commons' character and to the capacity of the people to elect candidates (1981b, 295). Threatened with political ostracism, politicians would not cultivate the character required to defend the constitution but "an indolent and submissive disposition; a disposition to think charitably of all actions of men in power, and to live in a mutual intercourse of favours with them" (296).

The power to exclude ill-mannered MPs and frustrate their supporters was hardly the only weapon in the new king's arsenal. Executive influence loomed even larger. "The power of the Crown, almost dead and rotten as Prerogative, has grown up anew, with much more strength, and far less odium, under the name of Influence" (Burke 1981b, 258). Places and positions, Burke claimed, were more effective than legal powers; they "operated without noise and without violence; an influence which converted the very antagonist into an instrument of power" (258). Unlike other sources of control, the effectiveness of which might wane, Burke claimed that the force of influence was rooted deeply since "the interest of active men in the State is a foundation perpetual and infallible" (258).

Of course, Burke was a Whig. And Robert Walpole and his followers had been Whigs. And they were the great masters of influence, almost impossibly skilled in its deployment. Burke's critique of executive influence made him a target for a charge of gross hypocrisy. Burke self-consciously skipped past this problem, directly addressing this inconvenient history. "Since the

Revolution," Burke contended, "until the period we are speaking of, the influence of the Crown had always been employed in supporting the Ministers of States" (1981b, 269). But Burke judged that those ministers, like Walpole, had channeled that influence for the public's benefit. They were men of "popular weight and character" (259). With the accession of a new king, George III, a king independent of the Whigs, the Crown began to use its influence to loosen its reliance on any given Parliamentary figures including the ministry. Rather than using its influence to support a strong Parliamentary cabinet and divide the opposition, the Crown now sought to build support for itself and divide any political counterweight. Blocking figures whose own influence came from either "popular opinion" or "party connection," the Court faction aimed to "so thoroughly disunite every party and even every family, that *no concert, order, or effect, might appear in any future opposition*" (266; emphasis in the original).

"Thoughts on the Cause of the Present Discontents" does not offer an explicit justification of a system of political opposition. The essay *presumes* that system's acceptance. For instance, Burke's discussion of Wilkes is meant to shift debate from Wilkes's troubling character to questions of accepted principle; his argument requires his audience to have rejected the idea that an elected official's "opposition to acts of power was to be marked by a kind of civil proscription" (1981b, 298). Rather than establishing the bona fides of opposition *tout court*, Burke contends that given the cause of the present discontents—the activities of the Court—the only mode of opposition that will be effective is one that is coordinated and consistent, the kind of opposition spearheaded by his sponsor, Lord Rockingham.

Burke evaluates and discards two alternative strategies. The first was institutional: holding more frequent elections and limiting the ability of the executive to add representatives to Parliament at will—the so-called placemen (Burke 1981b, 308).

These were more ineffective clockwork solutions to a problem created by a clockwork view of the constitution, Burke concluded. More frequent elections would not limit the executive. They would provide it greater opportunity to use its influence. The removal of placemen would merely shift the ministry's target—from placemen to other members of Parliament. The underlying thought here is sound. The problem was not the design of British institutions. The problem was the way the cabinet's influence warped that design. Novel institutional solutions would not stop the cabinet from exercising influence. Those institutions would merely channel that influence in novel and invidious directions.

The second solution was an alternative oppositional strategy, one identified with William Pitt. Pitt, on Burke's reading, was overly concerned with the ethics of partisanship, preferring an independent and selective course. Competitive opposition, on this view, should be fought on the terrain of policy, not personality, on specific issues rather than the ministry itself. Burke rejected this approach as the manifestation of a superficial, self-indulgent political morality. Pitt confused the way opposition might be carried out under ideal conditions with the way it should be shouldered in the real world. In the face of the Court's influence, an independent member and his constituents would possess little chance of affecting policy, unable to build support for a cause. "The unfortunate independent member has nothing to offer but harsh refusal, or pitiful excuse or despondent representation of an hopeless interest," Burke contended (1981b, 299). "No man, who is not inflamed by vainglory into enthusiasm, can flatter himself that his single, unsupported, desultory, unsystematic endeavors are of power to defeat the subtle designs and united Cabals of ambitious men" (315). Independent opposition was self-defeating, an oxymoron. "It is surely no very rational account of a man's life, that he has always acted right; but taken special care, to act in such a manner that his endeavors could not possibly be productive of any consequence" (315).

As with Bolingbroke and Hume, Burke's argument is premised on the acceptability of a system of legitimate opposition and the failure of the division of powers. With the rise of the state, unformed opposition was ineffective. In an important sense, it undermined the whole point of a system of opposition. Accordingly, Burke argued that a system allowing space for formed opposition provided resources that a clockwork constitutional solution would not. "Whilst men are linked, they easily and speedily communicate the alarm of any evil design. They are enabled to fathom it with common counsel, and to oppose it with united strength. . . . In a connexion, the most inconsiderable man, by adding to the weight of the whole, has his value, and his use" (1981b, 314).

Assessing the Case for a System of Formed Opposition

Before proceeding, it is worth meeting potential concerns. The balance of power was a critical trope of eighteenth-century British political thought, especially the Whiggish strain. Did the authors I have discussed appeal to the trope because they believed that British institutions were failing to conform to the theory? Or did they merely use the trope to justify what would otherwise be aberrant political action (Skinner 1974)? In the latter case, we should place little weight on their (and my) claims. We have two significant reasons not to be moved by such doubts.

First, David Hume did not occupy the same political space as his colleagues. Hume had little reason to be biased, little strategic reason to claim that the division of powers had failed as a descriptive constitutional theory. Unlike Bolingbroke and

Burke, the groups Hume favored were in office at the time he wrote his essays. Hume's analysis cannot allay concerns about the purity of Burke's or Bolingbroke's intentions. But since he concurs with their assessment, his contributions lend credibility to their contentions.

Second, and more importantly, the British state *did* rapidly expand in the eighteenth century, powered by its foreign entanglements (Brewer 1989). And resources and bureaucratic positions *were* put to use by increasingly formal ministerial governments to manage Parliamentary politics and make life difficult for members of the opposition (Namier 1952; Plumb 1967; Brewer 1976). The existence of this system of patronage and its use to influence legislative politics did not barricade the government from *any* need to engage in persuasion or protect it from *any* form of challenge; Britain featured a system of opposition despite these executive advantages (Owen 1972). Yet consistent with the claims of the three authors I have discussed, that advantage shaped the activities of those who sought power. As the historian Lewis Namier observed in 1952, "those who enjoyed the favour of the Crown, and coalesced with the Court party, were naturally less of a party-forming element than those in disfavour, or uncertain of royal support, who had therefore to rely primarily on parliament and seek to form their following into a coherent party" (27).

Britain's constitutional system has changed since Burke's time. And the government's capacity to use offices as political capital has been reduced. Yet the advantages enjoyed by the leading executive figure, the prime minister, have not diminished (Cox 1987). The administrative requirements of the social-welfare state have vastly increased the executive's influence. And the role of the executive in shaping legislation remains fundamental. As a result, Britain's system of electoral and Parliamentary competition, its system of legitimate opposition, remains, self-evidently, a more important constitutional principle than the division of powers is.

Suppose you accept my thesis: the failure of clockwork constitutional institutions incited opponents of the government to establish the modern form of opposition. You might still suspect that this story only applies to Britain, a famous constitutional outlier.[13] Traditionally, scholars treat the emergence of legitimate opposition as a binational story, involving not just Britain but the United States as well.[14] But the political logic outlined by Bolingbroke et al. has no intrinsically national limitations. Just consider the US case.

James Madison decried factions in Federalist 10 (1961a). But in the same essay, he conceded their inevitability, advocating for a political system in which individuals competed for power, that is, a system of opposition. Sometimes it is claimed that elections during this period were forms of acclamation, rather than modes of regulating competition (Levinson and Pildes 2006, 2318). But political processes at the founding were diverse, and competition was well known (Beeman 1992). And the acclamatory view of elections is difficult to square with Federalist 10. In the famed essay, Madison claims that a large republic would make it more difficult for "unworthy candidates to practice with success the vicious arts by which elections are too often carried" (1961a, 63). If elections were a form of acclamation, why would anyone employ "vicious arts" to win them? And why would Madison offer the reduction of the effectiveness of the "vicious arts" as a justification for a large republic if elections were known to be mostly formal and uncompetitive processes?

Even George Washington, the famous scold of parties and an advocate of unanimity, engaged in robust competition for office before the Revolution. His early elections featured multiple candidates. And, according to Richard Beeman, an expert on eighteenth-century Virginia politics, after an early defeat, Washington's first victory came by coordinating support among local influentials and providing liquid thanks to his supporters: "28 gallons of rum, 50 gallons and one hogshead of rum punch, 34 gallons of wine, 46 gallons of 'strong beer,' and 2 gallons of cider" (1992, 417). "In all free governments," Washington later admitted, "contention in elections will take place" (1797). In other words, once we distinguish between a system of legitimate opposition and a system of legitimate opposition in which parties play the leading role, we can see that the latter was accepted in the United States even when political parties were not.

Did the United States, despite its famed tripartite constitutional division, feature an executive branch with an interest in legislative outcomes? Absolutely. Madison famously hoped that political life under the new constitution would be defined by a contestatory balance between its branches (1961b). But among the structural factors that drove Jefferson and Madison to build the United States' first formed opposition were Alexander Hamilton's political stratagems and his deployment of the growing state to advance his ends.[15] That is the exact same phenomenon that I discussed earlier. And Madison and Jefferson explicitly associated this style of politics with England. Jefferson explains this in two 1792 letters to Washington:

> [Hamilton's] system flowed from principles adverse to liberty, and was calculated to undermine and demolish the republic, by creating an influence of his department over the members of the legislature. I saw this influence actually produced, and it's first fruits to be the establishment of the great outlines of his project by the votes of the very persons who, having swallowed his bait were laying themselves out to profit by his plans: and that had these

persons withdrawn, as those interested in a question ever should, the vote of the disinterested majority was clearly the reverse of what they made it.
(1792b, qtd. in Aldrich and Grant 1993, 309–10)

Faced with a similar problem as Bolingbroke and Burke,
Jefferson and Madison devised a similar solution. They aimed
to elect a representative majority that was opposed, in principle,
to Hamilton's policies. Just as importantly, those representatives
would be organized. Only then would they forgo the inducements wielded by a modern executive.[16] Jefferson's explicit aim
was that "the great mass [of newly elected officials] will form
an accession to the republican party" (1792a). Madison and
Jefferson, like their British counterparts, understood that the
solution to the unanticipated influence of the executive in
the legislative branch, of the failure of clockwork constitutionalism, was to build a formed group that would provide an advantage within the larger system of regulated, regular political
contestation.

The was the context for Washington's famed broadside
against political parties, the 1796 farewell address he wrote with
Hamilton. The address allows that "in governments of a monarchical cast," like Britain, "patriotism may look with indul-
gence, if not with favor, upon the spirit of party." In other words,
Washington specifically acknowledges the organizational logic
I have identified in this chapter. But Washington claimed that
logic did not apply in the United States: "in [governments] of
the popular character, in governments purely elective, it is a
spirit not to be encouraged."

On my view, Washington was not inveighing against the
principle of legitimate opposition—the idea that power would
be competed for via a rule-based system—but against the idea
that parties would be essential protagonists in that competitive

system. The trick, of course, was that those who were opposed to Hamilton (and Washington) believed that he was advancing an English-style political system that would allow him to exert influence over the political system without creating a party. Washington's speech was thus understood as a partisan broadside, one that counseled his adversaries to unilaterally cease their efforts mobilizing collective action—to give up on the idea of effective opposition—just as incumbent governments in Britain had decried similar organizational efforts (Wilentz 2016, 6–7). As in Britain, the incipient partisans failed to heed this self-serving advice. And, as in Britain, the US political system never functioned as a clockwork set of institutions, reflecting instead a contest among parties, organizations that allow the executive to reach across ostensible institutional barriers (Levinson and Pildes 2006; Posner and Vermeule 2010). The United States' constitutional division of powers is hardly defunct, but its present-day working is incomprehensible without accounting for the country's partisan system of legitimate opposition.

Youngstown Sheet & Tube v. Sawyer (1952) is arguably the most important Supreme Court ruling on executive power. In a famed concurring opinion, Justice Robert Jackson captured the unanticipated character of the US division of powers: "[The] rise of the party system has made a significant extraconstitutional supplement to real executive power. No appraisal of his necessities is realistic which overlooks that he heads a political system as well as a legal system. Party loyalties and interests, sometimes more binding than law, extend his effective control into branches of government other than his own."[17] The executive in the United States simply is not bound, in some neat sense, by institutional barriers, Jackson concluded. For our purposes, this influential reading of the Constitution confirms that the simple political logic of opposition outlined earlier applies in the constitutional system of the United States, as it does in Britain.

Orthodox treatments of the intellectual origins of legitimate opposition have focused on the increasingly warm embrace of political parties offered by Bolingbroke, Hume, and Burke. Through their arguments, we can see the changing intellectual fortunes of parties: from temporary sufferance to grudging acceptance to positive estimation. I have argued that this orthodox narrative turns on the assumption that the only form of legitimate opposition worthy of the name is partisan opposition. Once we have dropped that faulty assumption, we can reassess opposition's character. In particular, I have claimed that the arguments of each of these authors are joined by five simple claims:

1. Regular, ruled-based political competition was legitimate.
2. Executives predictably used the resources of the modern state to advance their political ends.
3. A formalistic constitutional principle for limiting the government's political ambit—the division of powers—could not withstand the pressures imposed by the growth of the modern state.
4. The appropriate response to that failure was political organization.
5. Therefore, organized competitors, perhaps including partisan competitors, should be recognized as acceptable and even valuable elements of a system of legitimate opposition.

I believe that these claims are intuitive, logical, and plausible. They suggest that states' capacity to organize political action warrants groups playing a central role in a system of legitimate opposition. States make legitimate opposition into a constitutional principle of fundamental import. Still, formalistic, clockwork-style institutional proposals remain the bread and butter of contemporary political theory. Many such proposals would get rid of opposition altogether; others call for a reformed, virtuous version of the practice. These accounts rarely take the state seriously as a political resource. And, I believe, this limitation starves their conclusions of practical weight. The next section demonstrates this, returning to the influential, clockwork-style alternative to organized opposition outlined in J. S. Mill's *Representative Government*.

Millian Collegial Rivalry: Legitimate Opposition as Clockwork Constitutionalism

Like the authors previously discussed, J. S. Mill rejected the attractiveness of pure division-of-powers theories. But this did not cause him to fall back on the constitutional principle I have explored in this chapter: mere organized, adversarial opposition. Rejecting both the division of powers and out-and-out competition, *Representative Government* proposes an intricate, deliberative system of legitimate opposition. That system would capture the benefits of legitimate opposition without incurring the obvious costs of the existing, fiercely competitive examples of the practice. Mill did not reject competition outright. He imagined that this competition could be reformed so that it would focus on ideas and arguments rather than mere numbers and organizations. It was to be a contest of ideas. And that is what I mean by "collegial rivalry."

Mill's approach has inspired generations of political theorists. Indeed, in the recent book *Political Political Theory*, Jeremy Waldron judges, I believe accurately, Mill's *Considerations on Representative Government* to be the "best book on democracy in the canon of political theory" (2016, 79). In the same chapter, Waldron rates Hume's Court of Competitors, the proposal discussed in the introduction of this chapter, as "daft" (89). *Representative Government* has evident virtues, tackling many of the puzzles still vexing democratic theorists (e.g., what is the value of one person, one vote). Yet, as I will show, Mill's proposal is a classic instance of clockwork constitutionalism. And this section illustrates why Mill's treatment of legitimate opposition is at least as daft as Hume's proposal and lacks Hume's enviable intellectual consistency—that is, Hume's proposal was *self-consciously* unrealistic.

Nancy Rosenblum notes in her encyclopedic study of the political theory of parties that a superficial familiarity with Mill's writings could lead a reader to conclude that Mill would be a committed defender of bare-knuckled group competition (2008, 149). Mill offered explicit grounds for valuing contestation and the instability it generates. "No community has ever long continued progressive," he claimed, "but while a conflict was going on between the strongest power in the community and some rival power" (2008a, 315). This was the secret powering Jewish achievement. Jewish society, Mill held, was progressive because it lacked a centralized authority, resulting in "the antagonism of influences which is the only real security of improvement" (235). Clearly, this vision impelled his argument in *On Liberty* and drives his judgment that even a regime governed by an enlightened bureaucracy would, as a result of its inherent stability, lose its impulse toward progress (Mill 2008a, 291; 2008b).

Mill was sympathetic to the general aims of the division of powers but skeptical of its efficacy. He famously saw individual freedom as a necessary condition for well-being and improvement; and that condition required political institutions to block the domination of any single class (assuming the relevant citizens had reached the necessary level of development). "There should be, in every polity," he argued, "a centre of resistance to the predominant power in the Constitution—and in a democratic constitution, therefore, a nucleus of resistance to the democracy" (2008a, 386). But Mill regarded as impotent the traditional institutional schemes for combating this threat: "The power of final control is as essentially single, in a mixed and balanced government, as in pure monarchy or democracy. This is the position of truth in the opinion of the ancients, revived by the great authorities that a balanced constitution is impossible" (269). Any incipient balance depended not on clever institutional schemes but on the distribution of "active powers out of doors" (270). And that active power depended in part on numbers but also, and more deeply, on "organization" (214).

Mill also understood parliamentary politics and grasped the influence wielded by executives within the legislative branch. He knew the mechanisms supporting this relationship. *Representative Government* is riddled with negative allusions to "place-hunters" and the corrupting influence of the "mere struggle for office" (2008a, 266, 268). Moreover, formal institutional powers aside, a modern executive was not on par with the other branches: "In every country, the executive is the branch of the government which wields the immediate power, and is in direct contact with the public; to it, principally, the hopes and fears of individuals are directed, and by it both the benefits, and the terror and prestige of government, are mainly represented to the public eye" (258).

Finally, Mill was confident that individuals would use institutions to advance their ends. They would behave strategically, potentially frustrating the attractive plans dreamed up by institutional schemers. Throughout *Representative Government*, he punctures naive proposals, rejecting the view that political actors behave like inanimate clock elements. Consider his assessment of two-stage voting. In that system, voters select electors who then elect representatives. Mill concludes that this institution will fail utterly to temper popular passions, fail to pick out enlightened representatives. Why? Because individuals will simply identify electors who will vote for the flawed representatives they prefer (Mill 2008a, 348). Mill embraced open ballot voting for similar reasons. Voters could be moved to more reliably serve the common interest, but not without developing an external pressure or incentive to do so. Mill could be an unsentimental institutional realist. Government had to reflect the true capacities of the people. And institutional designers had to accept second-best institutions: "For if the country does not choose to pursue the right ends by a regular system directly leading to them, it must be content with an irregular makeshift, as being greatly preferable to a system free from irregularities, but regularly adapted to wrong ends, or in which some ends equally necessary with the others have been left out" (339).

In the hands of the authors previously discussed, these four intellectual ingredients were used to cook up the case for a system of legitimate opposition featuring organized competitors, that is, formed opposition. Mill was familiar with such arguments; he knew the recipe. But he did not accept it. He favored collegial competition, rejecting adversarial rancor and unthinking loyalty to a political group (Rosenblum 2008, 150; Mill 2008a, 203).

In lieu of merely embracing a system of organized opposition, Mill developed a complex scheme focused on legislative deliberation. His proposal aimed to allow widespread participation and improvements in the quality of a regime's decision-making and laws (Thompson 1976). That improvement would be achieved, in part, by providing points of resistance ("*points d'appui*") to the majority (Mill 2008a, 316). Following Mill's proposals, one could leave aside the baser methods of organizing collective action. Instead, Mill defended a reworked representative system that would not "allow any of the various sectional interests to be so powerful as to be capable of prevailing against truth and justice and the other sectional interests combined" (Mill 2008a, 301).

How would this be achieved? In part by Thomas Hare's single transferable vote system, a proportional mechanism for electing representatives. This system would, according to Mill, provide for the representation of a wider range of citizens than first-past-the-post systems, mitigating the dominance of the traditional parties. The legislature would become "a place where every interest and shade of opinion in the country can have its cause even passionately pleaded, in the face of the government and of all other interests and opinions, can compel them to listen" (Mill 2008a, 283). The forces compelling the majority's representatives to listen? Deference and respect for intellectual authority. "The instructed minority would, in the actual voting, count only for their numbers, but as a moral power they would count for much more, in virtue of their knowledge, and of the influence it would give them over the rest. An arrangement better adapted to keep popular opinion within reason and justice, and to guard it from the various deteriorating influences which assail the weak side of democracy, could scarcely by human ingenuity be devised" (317). These institutions would be competitive, a system of opposition, because it was electoral. Yet the competition would not be driven by numbers or organization; it would be driven by ideas and concern for the common good. It is this restrained, intellectual, almost apolitical variant of regulated competition that exemplifies collegial rivalry.

Mill asks the reader to accept the following two thoughts. First, a popular majority poses a substantial threat to the well-being of a polity's citizens. This majority will be unversed and unconcerned with the ideas, interests, and opinions of others, especially the enlightened. Special protections must therefore be established to stanch its power. Second, representatives of this dangerous majority will simply yield and heed the advice of an enlightened minority, when those views are presented in a representative body.

Perhaps even Mill doubted the irresistibility of enlightened opinion. He famously proposed to extend additional votes to the mentally superior. "The distinction in favour of education," he contended, was "right in itself." But it was "further recommended by its preserving the educated from the class legislation of the uneducated" (2008a, 337).

Critically, Mill did not intend for the enlightened themselves to dominate; they were not assumed to elect the majority of representatives. But this just means that Mill's extra-vote maneuver would not patch the yawning hole in his argument. If he is right about the threat posed by the majority, granting the enlightened additional votes will not temper that threat. If granting additional votes to the enlightened *does* temper the threat, because representatives of the majority can be moved by better arguments or simply because they are unlikely to act in lockstep with one another, then Mill's concerns about the majority seem unfounded.

The preceding institutional measures would, on Mill's account, obviate the need for resistance *between* different political branches of government. Each class would no longer require control of its own branch. Presumably, however, these institutions would not obviate the import of the organizational practices and competitive disposition recommended by Bolingbroke, Hume, and Burke. Even with proportional representation, extra votes for the enlightened, and a deliberative representative body, the majority might use its control over the executive to sustain itself, exerting control over Parliament and the electoral system more generally. Mill was aware of the precise contours of this problem. He decried the practice whereby ministers used positions "for the sake of gaining support or disarming opposition in the representative body" (2008a, 399). He recognized how politicization of the executive encouraged political contestation to focus on organization rather than ideas.

Mill devised an additional mechanism to keep the various springs and gears in his institutional design working: he called for separating the representative body from the state. In other words, Mill understood the basic logic outlined in the previous sections, but he drew a different conclusion. Rather than accept that in a modern state, vigorous competition among groups would be the dominating logic of legitimate opposition, why not simply keep the state from being used to impact political life? To ensure the deliberative character of representative politics and the promulgation of wise policy formulated by experts, to ensure that individuals responded to reasons and did not become solely focused on advancing the cause of their own group, Mill defended a sharp, functional, and institutional break between representing and governing. Given the import of this idea to my argument, I quote Mill at length:

> Instead of the function of governing, for which it is radically unfit, the proper office of a representative assembly is to watch and control the government: to throw the light of publicity on its acts: to compel a full exposition and justification of all of them which any one considers questionable; to censure them if found condemnable, and, if the men who compose the government abuse their trust, or fulfill it in a manner which conflicts with the deliberate sense of the nation, to expel them from office, and either expressly or virtually appoint their successors. . . . There are no means of combining these benefits except by separating the functions which

guarantee the one from those which essentially require the other; by disjoining the office of control
and criticism from the actual conduct of affairs,
and devolving the former on the representatives of
the Many, while securing for the latter, under strict
responsibility to the nation, the acquired knowledge and practised intelligence of a specially trained
and experienced Few. (2008a, 282–84)

Mill painted a thick institutional line between the state
and its representative bodies. This would block the exploitation
of executive advantage and the incentive it created for oppositional organization. Separated from the state and from the
exercise of power, elected officials would no longer engage in
or be encouraged to engage in the politicking characteristic of
modern opposition—for example, expelling and elevating
ministries on the basis of their political designs, deploying
patronage to enlarge their majority, and motivating their voters
by disparaging unjustifiably their rivals (Mill 2008a, 292).
One can see a similar logic in the designs of present-day
democratic theorists who defend the attractiveness of largely
deliberative representative bodies marked, fundamentally, by
intellectual competition (Christiano 1996; Goodin 2008). And,
as in Mill's account, these works typically simply assume that
clockwork institutional barriers protecting a system defined
by intellectual competition will hold. In William Selinger's
excellent and insightful work *Parliamentarism: From Burke to
Weber*, the author heaps praise on Mill's alchemical transmuta-
tion of legitimate opposition from bare-knuckled competition
into intellectual rivalry: "In *Considerations on Representative
Government*, Mill showed how it was possible to maintain the
supremacy of Parliament and preserve Parliament's capacity to
deliberate and hold executive officials responsible, even as

Parliament was elected through mass suffrage and guided by trained experts" (2019, 189).

I believe, however, that Selinger's praise for Mill's alchemy is too credulous. In fact, Mill provides little reason to believe in the effectiveness of his proposed bulwark between the executive and legislator (the bulwark against the use of patronage and low politicking).[18] Would legislators with the power to remove ministries and choose legislation abstain from encroaching on executive activities? Would ministers refrain from advancing their political fortunes by organizing support in the legislature or among the electorate? The answer to these questions must surely be negative. And all the relevant players would have acted as if the answers were negative.

Mill's defense of this division does not even meet baseline expectations of internal consistency. It is incompatible with his own realistic approach to political institutions. Recall his low regard for two-step elections and private voting. If his concerns about those institutions are plausible, then it is implausible that representatives or members of the bureaucracy would not seek political aggrandizement. Mill's barrier separating the executive from the legislative may be unnecessary, because individuals will not act strategically or in their own narrow self-interest. Or that barrier is implausibly flimsy, its normative justification dependent on modes of behavior that are inconsistent with its analysis of the problem to be solved. And if that is right, then the ostensible advantages of Mill's deliberative system over an avowedly adversarial system would, at best, be lost, since opponents of the government would have to organize and act as partisans in response to the government's efforts (at worst, the lack of recognition that the system would be marked by executive encroachment and formed opposition might lead to a lack of rules and regulation that could, in principle, be aimed at tempering these practices). In sum, we should be skeptical of

Mill's division of state and lawmaking. And we should therefore be skeptical of his attempt to reform legitimate opposition as a constitutional principle. We should, in sum, be skeptical of collegial rivalry.

Why does this matter? It matters partly because Mill's theory, his embrace of idea-based competition and his mode of ameliorative institutional analysis, still reverberates through democratic theory (think of the number of works proposing attractive alternatives to competitive, partisan opposition). And it also matters partly because Mill's criticism of the executive's capacity to shape collective action with and beyond the legislature throws into relief the theoretical wages of ignoring that capacity: what is offered as a plausible mechanism for reducing opposition to intellectual combat is obviously ill matched to a defining attribute of modern politics, that is, the state.

Organized opposition is not a fixed feature of legitimate government. But, if my arguments are persuasive, we can draw several clear implications. First, proposals to replace this constitutional principle should offer some plausible explanation of the way rivals to organized opposition would function in a world in which states exist (i.e., a world in which the resources of states could be used to advance governing groups' political ends). Second, proposals like Mill's, proposals that aim to reform the practice, reducing it to a form of intellectual competition, should also consider how those proposals will be impacted by the existence of the state. Finally, we should also assess alternative principles, like the separation of powers, in the light of organized opposition's role in the modern state (Levinson and Pildes 2006). This does not mean that the separation of powers will not function but that its character will be fundamentally affected by the play of opposition.

Beyond those institutional considerations, we can draw additional implications. Consider the following familiar claim:

official oppositions should offer full platforms of realistic policies, rather than merely criticizing the government for its unpopular positions and opportunistically focusing on popular but unrealistic policy changes (Hofstadter 1969, 5; Goodin 2008, 213–14; Waldron 2016, 102). This is a modern reformulation of a traditional idea: that truly *legitimate* opposition focuses on measures, not men. Though it is rarely stated explicitly, I believe that those who make such arguments assume, like Mill, that the state will not be used to shape collective action, that "the opposition" and "the government" are in positions of relative equality. On this common view, those who control governments are inevitably forced to address issues that make them look bad. And they face trade-offs when making difficult policy choices. Accordingly, to advance citizens' moral interests in governing themselves, oppositions ought to offer a fully worked-out platform (Goodin 2008, 213–14). Doing so, they offer voters a clear choice. And they ought to do so, even at the cost of their own potential political success.

But what if the playing field is systematically tilted toward the incumbent (as I have suggested)? Under these circumstances, members of the opposition will face a basic dilemma: offer a full-fledged, realistic platform or make salient the attractive parts of their platform in ways that the incumbent cannot. Where the opposition justifiably believes that the incumbent poses a threat to the common good and the incumbent possesses a state-based advantage over the opposition, members of the opposition may actually have a duty to offer the most attractive, if unrealistic, set of proposals. Why? Because a strategy that ensures the ineffectiveness of an opposition will undercut citizens' interest in governing themselves.

The implication here is not that the opposition should always act opportunistically. My claim is that some, perhaps most, of the ostensible duties of a "responsible opposition" are dependent on the character of the political system and the advantages enjoyed by the executive. This conclusion echoes, not surprisingly, the arguments of Bolingbroke, Hume, and Burke. And it implies that when political theorists assess the responsibilities of political competitors and the nature of opposition more generally, they should account for executive influence.

Conclusion

This chapter reconsiders the invention of partisan opposition in light of the existence of ancient opposition. That shift in perspective underlines the state's import for the modern, organized practice. States make legitimate opposition a preeminent constitutional principle. And I have argued that those who offer alternatives to competitive opposition, like J. S. Mill, ignore the state at the cost of generating proposals of questionable relevance.

Mill was fully aware of the arguments I have raised against his proposal. *Considerations* commences with a defense of blue-sky institutional theorizing and the importance of reasoned choice in the formation of political institutions. There is no abstract reason to accept the futility of political reform. If a theorist proposes a novel institutional reform, that reform might well gain the support necessary to win establishment, Mill argued (2008a, 215–16). A modern follower of Mill, of which there are many, might point out that my argument assumes that an adversarial, us-versus-them ethos is a fixed feature of modern political life. Perhaps a more collaborative, more Millian alternative to opposition would be successful. The problem is how to get our hands around this kind of claim. That is the work of chapter 7. I consider what the French Revolutionary experience can tell us about the possibility of establishing a democracy without opposition.

7

Democracy without Opposition
Condorcet, Sieyès, and the French Revolution

Without doubt, it would be superfluous proving that opposition between two parties is anything but an illusory fortification for liberty, and that agreement, not the struggle for political power, is the end of a rational constitution.

—Condorcet, 1790

"In England, the government is a subject of perpetual combat between the ministry and the aristocracy in opposition," observed Emmanuel-Joseph Sieyès (Abbé Sieyès) in his pamphlet *Views of the Executive Means Available to the Representatives of France in 1789.*[1] For Sieyès, a political regime defined by a system of legitimate opposition was normatively defective. In 1789, as I discussed in chapter 6, British politics did not feature modern political parties. But it did feature regular competition for influence and office.[2] It featured the practice of legitimate opposition. Forgoing cooperation inspired by the collective good, Sieyès observed, the English treated politics as "gladiatorial combat." Sieyès's objection to that system was not merely the well-worn concern with parties, partisanship, or factionalism but more deeply with competition and adversarial action—social action aimed to advance one's ends, even public-minded ends, at the potential costs of cooperation, compromise, and candor. Those activities fractured a polity needlessly. They created a situation in which "the Nation suspects both the stronger and weaker party" (Sieyès 2003b, 131). Adversarial rivalry was not the necessary consequence of political liberty. It was a peculiar outgrowth of peculiar institutions. Breaking from the English model, France could set its own institutional course, establishing a collaborative system better suited to French exigencies, better suited to holding the polity together, a system unspoiled by vigorous competition.

Sieyès was hardly the only political philosopher of his generation to reject opposition's attractions. The same skepticism marks the writing of some of the most influential political theorists of his period, including Marie Jean Antoine Nicolas de Caritat, the Marquis de Condorcet. Condorcet's defense of democratic representation and the epistemic promise of democracy make him, along with Sieyès, one of the most influential theoreticians of democracy's value (Goodin and Spiekermann 2012; Landemore 2013).[3]

Scholars like Nadia Urbinati and Lisa Disch have argued persuasively that Sieyès and Condorcet set out distinctive and imaginative ways of solving a thorny theoretical puzzle: how to combine democracy and representation (Urbinati 2006; Disch 2011). Part of the Revolutionary theorists' strategy was to imagine a democratic form of government free from opposition. Opposition, on this view, would increase the difficulty of uniting a new French republic, of bridging distinctions of status, wealth, faith, and geography.[4]

In this book, I have targeted the democratic conception of legitimate opposition, developing an account of opposition's value that does not depend on the simple amalgamation of it with democracy. Sieyès and Condorcet too would have rejected the blithe conflation of these practices. As both clearly understood, competitive regimes are not merely distinct from political theorists' collaborative visions of democracy. Competitive regimes can be rival to those ideals. Adversarial competition would systematically block the achievement of legitimate outcomes, on their view. Determining the relative attractiveness of collaborative and competitive systems, we face numerous questions, many of which I have treated in earlier chapters. In this chapter, I consider a different question: Can ostensibly attractive plans like those formulated by Sieyès and Condorcet suppress the competitive impulse without undue cost? If not, we have yet another reason to embrace opposition even while acknowledging its frequent distance from democracy.

Questions of this sort are by no means novel. James Madison famously structured Federalist 10 around the *assertion* that political factionalism and competition could only be stemmed by suppressing liberty. He rejected that strategy (Madison 1961a).[5] Yet Madison's claim that freedom and factionalism are necessarily intertwined is just that: a claim.[6] And it is a claim that contemporary lottery-focused and deliberative diehards would find unpersuasive—just as Condorcet and Sieyès were unmoved by similar claims. They might ask, What if a people actually established a popular regime designed specifically to thwart rivalrous action? How can we know it would not succeed? Indeed, this was a line of argument advanced by J. S. Mill in defending his proposals in *Considerations on Representative Government* (2008a, 207). Madison certainly provided no evidence to meet this challenge. Short of actually establishing a noncompetitive regime, it seems there is no obvious way to test Madison's conjecture. The tenuous character of claims about the essentially competitive character of political life explains, in part, political theorists' perennial

efforts to advance alternatives to mere opposition and competition. Beyond the specific focus of this chapter on Sieyès and
Condorcet, it tackles this long-standing challenge to legitimate
opposition, providing forceful support for Madison's conjecture.
Doing so, the chapter provides additional support for the adversarial conception of legitimate opposition.

Authors of idealistic institutional proposals sometimes
defend their efforts by referring to the possibility of an institutional or intellectual revolution, a political turn allowing the
realization of their ideals.[7] Unlike more recent democratic theorists, Sieyès and Condorcet got the chance. They witnessed and
played important roles in the institutional life of France's early
Revolutionary regime (1789–91). That period and its institutions
were defined by a widespread distaste for regulated, entrenched
political competition. Accordingly, the Revolution provides a
uniquely valuable perspective for assessing the relation between
competition and political liberty. And it provides a uniquely
valuable perspective for assessing a belief that undergirds almost
all proposals for popular forms of government free from opposition: that popular politics could be free of competition *if
only* institutions did not treat adversarial rivalry as a brute fact
of political life.[8] Of course, the kind of rivalry we are concerned
with here is not the public-good-generating collegial contestation
that all democratic theorists endorse but authentic rivalry, the
kind that creates winners *and* losers. The French Revolution has
long been the subject of theoretical investigation (Burke 1987;
Arendt 1963). Still, political theorists and philosophers have not
given sufficient weight to the Revolutionary experience for our
understanding of popular alternatives to legitimate opposition.

Presumably, most readers expect a defense of legitimate
opposition to use the Reign of Terror to impugn radical, potentially illiberal, notions of democracy. But deploying this tired
argument is not my aim or method.[9] My focus is on theorists

whose ideas remain guiding stars for liberal democratic thinking. And I hope to show that their approach to the design of
popular institutions comes up short. It comes up short not
because it caused the Terror but because it failed to grasp the
basic adversarial character of popular politics in a regime divided by questions of economic interest, identity, geography,
and religion. Revolutionary measures aimed to block competition were a spectacular failure. Rivalrous action emerged immediately once a measure of political freedom was granted, and
it exploded with the establishment of truly popular institutions.
The Revolutionary experience therefore provides strong support
for Madison's conjecture. And because competition's value was
not recognized and fostered, its costs, unregulated, came to the
fore. Rather than creating a system of legitimate opposition, a
regulated system of political rivalry, the Revolution unleashed
a competitive process that was disorganized, unfair, and often
violent. Discomfort with opposition had evident implications
for French citizens' capacity to exercise their political agency.
The toll of that orientation ought to be weighed by any who
believe that adversarial rivalry and struggle should not be
premises of institutional design.

Idealistic institutional proposals are often criticized for
their unfeasibility. And the character of this critique has recently been subject to profitable exploration (Gilabert and
Lawford-Smith 2012). Feasibility is not the source of my concern. The French Revolution shows that dramatic institutional
change is within our reach. The question addressed here is not
the possibility of institutional change. It is the character of the
institutions achieved.

Condorcet did not survive the Revolution. Sieyès did. The
experience reoriented his understanding of the nature and
value of opposition. "The existence of two parties similar or
analogous to those known elsewhere as the ministerial party

and the party of the opposition is inseparable from any type of representative system," Sieyès admitted in 1795, just six years after he published the pamphlet from which this chapter's epigraph comes. "Speaking the truth," he continued, "they are found everywhere, no matter the form of government". Opposition would flourish wherever groups could "make full use of their right to speak and write" (2014, 167, qtd. in Sonenscher 2003, xxxiii).[10] Ignoring that reality would leave institutional entrepreneurs adrift, unmoored from political life.

This chapter develops over seven sections. The first two very briefly describe the reservoir of anti-opposition thought that existed before the Revolution. The next two treat the constitutional proposals and theories of Condorcet and Sieyès. These sections illustrate their entirely familiar aversion to opposition. That aversion took institutional form with the establishment of the Estates General in 1789, as I show in the fifth section, which examines the electoral and representative systems of 1789–91. That section also describes the failure of these institutional mechanisms to keep quotidian forms of competition at bay. That failure may have been uncommonly violent. Its sources were completely conventional and enduring. The sixth section draws out the theoretical implications of my argument, reassessing Condorcet's and Sieyès's influential proposals in light of Madison's conjecture. The final section considers two objections to my argument.

Anticipating Revolutionary Opposition to Opposition: The Monarchists

Book 11 of Montesquieu's *Spirit of the Laws* provides political philosophy's most influential endorsement of England's constitution. Montesquieu concisely summarizes what he took to be the animating principle of the English regime: "All would be lost if the same man or the same body of principal men, either of nobles, or of the people, exercised these three powers: that of making the laws, that of executing public resolutions, and that of judging the crimes or the disputes of individuals" (1989, 157).

Montesquieu's embrace of English institutions is well known. It is less frequently acknowledged that book 19 of the same work returns to English shores. In the later chapter, Montesquieu's estimation of the English constitution is decidedly less favorable: "I have spoken in Book 11 of a free people, and I have given the principles of their constitution." Having picked out England, Montesquieu continues, "let us see the effects that had to follow, the character that is formed from it, and the manners that result from it" (1989, 325). Here he draws a grimmer and perhaps more realistic portrait of the same polity.

Like many contemporaneous observers of the English system, Montesquieu does not neatly distinguish the conflicts sparked by the division of powers from the conflicts triggered by England's emergent system of opposition (it is unlikely that this distinction could be readily drawn even had he tried). He nonetheless concludes that the distinctively English cocktail of freedom and competition—in this case, between the king's followers and the opposition in Parliament—generated two unattractive results. First, it splintered the population. "Most people," Montesquieu observes, "have more affection for one of these powers [the government and its opponents in Parliament] than for the other, as the multitude is ordinarily not fair or sensible enough to have equal affection for both of them." As a result of these fractures, "all the passions are free there, hatred, envy, jealousy, and the ardor for enriching and distinguishing oneself would appear to their full extent" (1989, 325). The second consequence followed from the first. The laws and policies generated by the English constitution failed the test of good government; shaped by passion and propelled by self-interest, they were unreasonable. "This nation, always heated, could more easily be led by its passions than by reason, which never produces great effects on the spirit of men, and it would be easy for those who governed it to make it undertake enterprises against its true interests" (327).

Montesquieu's twin concerns—a divided people and unreasonable laws—became hallmarks of Ancien Régime critiques of England's system of organized adversarial rivalry—whether those critiques were advanced by monarchists or republicans.

For instance, England was harshly judged by those who wrote within the penumbra of the Physiocratic movement—an influential, pastiche ideology that emphasized nature, the divine character of human reason, and the import of agriculture to the economy. It would be deeply surprising had the Physiocrats embraced England's political system or the modes of rivalry it fomented. Ensuring that new laws were reasonable, consistent with the laws of nature, they believed, would advance the economy and the monarch's rule (Vardi 2012). Pierre-Paul Lemercier de la Rivière, a prominent Physiocrat, precisely expressed the problem of opposition or counterforce, holding that "power and authority inhere in their evidence; thus counterforces can have no place. If on the contrary these principles are not evident, the establishment of counterforces is a useless procedure" (qtd. in Acomb 1950, 43). Justifying decisions required evidence that they were consistent with natural order (Vardi 2012, 138). Lacking such evidence, they were not justified at all. And Lemercier de la Rivière could not fathom why allowing outsiders to attack and embarrass the monarch's government would result in more reasonable policy. The legitimacy of opposition therefore required two things to be true: the government's course would have to be unreasonable, and the opposition's actions would have to result in better policy. Lemercier de la Rivière doubted the likelihood of the latter proposition. Accordingly, embracing opposition as a motivating principle entailed choosing "a blind man to lead another blind man" (qtd. in Acomb 1950, 43).[11]

Anne-Robert-Jacques Turgot echoed the same skepticism about the epistemic quality of outcomes generated via opposition. Turgot served as controller-general in the administration of Louis XVI from 1774 to 1776. English opposition eroded the state's capacity to impose intelligent policy, Turgot claimed: "because a republican constitution sometimes opposes obstacles to the reformation of certain abuses when these abuses can be corrected only by an authority whose exercise, however, advantageous to the public, always excites its distrust" (1913, 601–2). Here the problem is not the existence of checks on the executive. It is how the system marshaled conflict and stimulated suspicion.

To achieve epistemically rigorous rule without inciting rivalrous divisions, Turgot proposed a tiered, uncompetitive system of assemblies in his *Mémoire sur les municipalités*, a work drafted by his adjutant, Pierre-Samuel Dupont de Nemours.[12] The elaborate system would, it was hoped, provide the monarch's government with crucial information about the state of the polity, bind its diverse population, and facilitate the collection of taxes. It would do so without offering constituents a chance to challenge the government or exercise political agency meaningfully. At the village or municipal level, assemblies would assess taxes, guide local public projects, manage relations with neighboring assemblies, and undertake poor relief. Assembly members, a mix of wealthy property holders and of delegates elected by less-wealthy property holders, would not represent a particular group, like their estate. They would seek to forge policy in common. "The village assemblies," Gerald Cavanaugh, a historian of France, observes, "were to be small gatherings whose deliberations would be calm and whose decisions, one might expect, would usually be approved unanimously" (1969, 34). This end was to be advanced by requiring members to possess sufficient wealth or property. One step up from the local assemblies were the Assemblées Municipales des Élections. Each of these bodies would be made up of representatives, selected by the subordinate assemblies, which it would oversee. Above these assemblies would be an Assemblée Provinciale, supervising no more than thirty Assemblées Municipales des Élections. And, finally, the Grande Muncipalité Générale would sit at the top of this elaborate hierarchy, overseeing the other assemblies, assessing taxes, deliberating over expenditures, and debating matters of public interest. Turgot's proposal is a shining example of clockwork-style alternatives to opposition. Reading it, it is extremely difficult to imagine that it would have run how Turgot imagined: either competition would have reared its head, or stronger measures would be required to keep it at bay.

Like present-day representative assemblies in autocratic regimes, it was clear that these bodies' influence would be comparatively limited; the system was intended to refine the workings of the monarch's government, not provide a mechanism through which it could be disputed. These bodies would not, for instance, possess the power to legislate or check the powers of the ruler. Instead, they would have some responsibility for energizing the government's fiscal aspirations, distributing rents, and educating citizens, sparking, it was theorized, widespread commitment to the regime and to the common good. And via the deliberations of these bodies' propertied participants, they would generate information that the monarch, not the people, could put to use making rational decisions. Turgot's constrained, nonpolitical, uncompetitive system evidently influenced Condorcet, who wrote a biography of Turgot and whose own thinking about political representation continues to influence democratic theory today.

Because Turgot's proposal made some limited space for the ambitious to pursue influence, a reader might regard it as a system of opposition, a limited system to be sure, but a system of opposition nonetheless. Allowing individuals to exercise their agency, collectively or individually, however, was not the target of this proposal. This was well understood. Indeed, Alexis de Tocqueville ridiculed this element of Turgot's approach—all the more notable given Tocqueville's esteem for Turgot, whom he called "a great soul and rare genius" (2011, 145). Turgot's proposal, on Tocqueville's view, clashed with the "spirit of one's time." The imagined representative body "would concern itself solely with administration and never with government, and offer its opinions rather than express its will. In fact, its sole mission would be to discuss laws rather than make them." Ultimately, Tocqueville concluded that the plan would "give the people the shadow of liberty without its substance" (132). It is difficult to argue with Tocqueville's apt judgment. Even Turgot predicted that the characteristic by-products of free, political competition, "the confusion, the intrigues, the rival spirits, the animosities, the prejudices between the orders," would be entirely absent from this system, a system that would "neither provoke nor generate aggravations among society's orders" (Turgot 1922, 619; qtd. in Cavanaugh 1969, 37). In sum, Turgot imagined a representative system without competition, a representative system without politics, one that would place an autocratic regime on the firm footing of public devotion and epistemically sound policy.

Anticipating Revolutionary Opposition to Opposition: The Republicans and Rousseau

Committed advocates of a reformed and enlightened monarchy rejected organized political contestation. This is unsurprising, deeply so. Skepticism about the value of adversarial competition was also widespread among republican critics of monarchy. Perhaps this too was predictable. They also saw the great value of enlightened rule and the import of binding the polity together.

Contestation, at least on the English model, catalyzed dissensus and division—a suspicion affirmed by the trajectory of leading political players in England's political drama like John Wilkes, who fled from England to the Continent (Acomb 1950, 31).

A conversation I discussed in chapter 3, one reported to have been carried out between Wilkes and the academician Jean-Baptiste-Antoine Suard, nicely captures the ingredients of republican unease with legitimate opposition. On Wilkes's account, permanent opposition, the institutionalized threat of political loss, induced governments to justify their actions and reduced the payoff of endangering liberty. "The freest of nations is never sure enough of its liberty, which is a fortress constantly under siege: The ramparts must be manned, even when the firing has stopped" (Garat 1821, 94, qtd. in Baker 1990, 199). Wilkes provided the traditional, liberal, instrumental defense of the practice. But arguments of this sort presume that individuals do not share interlocking commitments to liberty and the common good. Or at least this was the view advanced by Wilkes's interlocutor, Suard. If people shared such commitments, however, concord would be within reach, leaving little reason to praise competition and certainly not to institutionalize adversarial rivalry and its constant companion, discord. Opposition, Suard argued, induced "alarms where there are neither dangers, storms, nor clouds. ... The agreement of opinions alone gives the springs of public order a mild and easy force. Once this agreement is found, obedience anticipates the law, and the political spheres are subject to harmony, just like the celestial spheres" (Garat 1821, 94–95, qtd. in Baker 1990, 197).

Like Turgot, Suard did not object to fierce debate and discussion. He welcomed contests of ideas in pursuit of a reasoned policy. Such debates no more required parties and the other paraphernalia of competition than did efforts to solve chess or mathematical puzzles. "Even for those who know neither the rules of the game, nor the rules of mathematical solutions, the solution and the outcome of the game become facts which only have to be attested. For that, parties are unnecessary" (Garat 1821, 95). What competition entailed was the replacement of one end—the common good—with another—political power. "Could it be possible," Suard wondered, whether "in all these discussions there is only one dispute: that the ministry is really at issue when it is a question (and one speaks the language) of the interests of the country and of humanity?" (95). Conflict on this view was not merely the motivation or cause of political rivalry but its avoidable product. Other thinkers, like the Spinozist philosophe Paul-Henri Thiry d'Holbach and the Abbé Mably, held a similarly dim view of England's adversarial system, defined by competition, riven with conflict (Acomb 1950, 36–38).

Jean-Jacques Rousseau is, undoubtedly, the best-known pre-Revolutionary republican. And it seems clear that the activities of the sovereign, as described in *The Social Contract*, would not be defined by legitimate opposition. At least two related pieces of evidence support this claim. The first is simply the character of the general will, the will of the sovereign. If the will is general, it advances a common interest, one shared by all members of the society. Accordingly, where law accurately reflects the general will, individuals would have no claim to oppose it. Of course, for Rousseau, identifying the general will was of signal import. This concern provides the second piece of evidence for classing Rousseau as a foe of opposition. He inveighed against the threat of factions. "When factions arise, small associations at the expense of the large association, the will of each one of these associations becomes general in relation to its members and particular in relation to the State; there can then no longer be said to be as many voters as there are men, but only as many as there are associations. The differences become less numerous and yield a less general result" (1997b,

60). Distinguishing healthy disagreement from factionalism, Rousseau cites Machiavelli: "In truth, says Machiavelli, some divisions harm Republics, and some benefit them; harmful are those that are accompanied by factions and parties; beneficial are those that do not give rise to factions and parties. Therefore, since the founder of a Republic cannot prevent enmities, he must make the best provision possible against factions" (60). The fix for factional strife was simple. Individuals should avoid acting in concert. An "adequately informed people" ought to arrive at a decision with "no communication among themselves" (60). Oppositional systems, as Rousseau rightly understood, regularly violate both of these criteria: giving space to faction, thriving on communication and group action.

Was Rousseau an unstinting opponent of opposition? The case cannot only stand on the passages just cited. Rousseau is sometimes pigeonholed as a direct democrat who abjured any political organizations. But he distinguished carefully between the role of the sovereign in making laws and the role of the government applying those laws to particular situations and particular people (Garsten 2010). Sovereigns could not be represented legitimately. But legitimate governments could take a number of different forms including direct democracy, aristocracy, monarchy, and mixed forms. And Rousseau evinced sustained skepticism that the workings of government could be walled off from self-interest. "A people which would always govern well," he famously observed, "would not need to be governed" (1997b, 91). Since governments would inevitably reflect partial interests, what mattered was that governments not inculcate, to the degree possible, those interests in the sovereign. The distinction drawn between the sovereign and the government means that we cannot simply assume that a governmental system featuring opposition would, necessarily, be illegitimate. *The Social Contract* provides evidence that Rousseau

might have objected to opposition. Still, the lack of detail provided about the institutions of government requires a level of
tentativeness in this verdict.

Rousseau's *Considerations on the Government of Poland*, I
think, provides the fortification necessary to buttress that verdict, illustrating Rousseau's anti-opposition bona fides. That
work chides the English Parliament for disqualifying Wilkes.
And Rousseau embraces a form of competition to fill political
positions. Still, I believe, he did not conceive the proposed,
constrained system of competition as a system of legitimate
opposition in the English vein. Public servants *would* have the
chance to contest for the honor and the esteem of their fellow
citizens. Opportunities to exercise political agency were nevertheless tightly restricted. What would achieve these seemingly
incompatible ends? A highly idealized reworking of the Roman
cursus honorum, the fixed ladder of political offices and positions that aspiring Roman leaders climbed as they sought
higher office and greater influence.

Rousseau's proposal is jammed with elections—highly
restricted elections, limiting, not facilitating, the exercise of
agency. There is nothing paradoxical about this. Recall that
today, many autocracies hold elections that do not advance
anyone but the rulers' agency. The core of Rousseau's vision was
occupied by local councils: Dietines. Membership would be
determined via a public apprenticeship lasting at least three
years. Candidates would then be assessed on the basis of "their
merit, their ability, their accuracy, and above all their integrity"
(Rousseau 1997a, 240). From their membership, they would
elect delegates to the lawmaking Diet, a higher-level body. Having served three terms in the Diet, one was eligible to be
elected as a member of the Senate. And having served three
terms in the Senate, one was eligible to be elected to the highest
offices including the king. In practice, this electoral system might

have fostered a system of real political rivalry. It was not intended to do so. The aim was to identify individuals on the
basis of merit, rather than allowing individuals to collectively
advance their political projects.

For instance, Rousseau hoped that the identities of the
deputies would have little effect on the policies chosen by the
Diet. Overlapping mechanisms would be deployed to achieve
this end. Deputies would be blocked from serving consecutive
terms. They would be forced to carry out the instructions of
their Dietines. And they would be subjected to scrutiny in the
aftermath of their term in office. "This scrutiny is of the utmost
importance. . . . The Deputy must, with every word he speaks
in the Diet, with every action he takes, anticipate himself under
the scrutiny of his constituents, and sense the influence their
judgment will have on his projects for advancement as well as
on the esteem of his fellow citizens." Discouraged from acting
on their "private sentiment," the deputies would "declare the
wills of the Nation" (Rousseau 1997a, 202).

A different mechanism would inhibit politicos from competing for senatorial office. Elections for the Senate would be
voted on by members of the Diet. Yet there would be no campaigns, no statements of position, no organization. Deputies
would cast their ballot solely on the basis of the known virtues
of the candidates. Of course, one might expect candidates to
compete despite these limitations. Rousseau did too. He proposed the following gambit: potential candidates for the Senate
would only become public on the night before the vote. As
Rousseau suggests, this method of choosing would constrain
the familiar theatrics of political rivalry; it would be "so simple
that without any argument or noise the entire Senate would
easily be filled in a single session" (Rousseau 1997a, 210).

Rousseau's design for the selection of the monarch confirms his low estimation of legitimate opposition. Rejecting a

hereditary system as an invitation to corruption, Rousseau called for the election of the king. Members of the Diet would choose one of three candidates. But as with the Senate, Rousseau devised an institutional wrinkle to keep individuals from jockeying and contesting: the three candidates for election would be determined by lot. After the names of candidates were chosen, members of the Diet would, without delay, select the candidate via a vote. The method, Rousseau asserts, would block adversarial competition; it "checks the factions" and keeps individuals from actively seeking power: "for who among them would go to the trouble of securing for himself a preference that does not depend on men, and sacrifice his fortune for the sake of an outcome with so many odds of failing for one of succeeding?" (1997a, 251). In sum, the institutions proposed by Rousseau in *Considerations* confirm the suspicion earlier elaborated: like many others, he rejected the value of legitimate opposition and sought ways of avoiding its emergence.

Condorcet's Epistemic Democracy and the Absence of Opposition

Before 1789, aversion to opposition crossed the French political spectrum. Yet the aim of this chapter is to illustrate the fate of that aversion in the run-up to the Revolution. This section and the next one show that opposition to legitimate opposition persisted among key actors in the Revolutionary era and influenced the institutions adopted during the period's constitutional conventions.

Consider Condorcet's reaction to the machinations of the members of the Estates General after they had transformed that body into a National Assembly in 1789. Condorcet worried that the members of the Assembly had already developed an overly uncooperative relationship with each other and with the monarch and his ministers. "Why seek to create, using English example, a ministerial party and a party of opposition? That struggle is not between liberty and power, but between two plotters both seeking power. It is on the one hand, hypocritical patriotism, on the other, corruption reduced to a system" (Condorcet 1847e, 33). Condorcet's concerns anticipated the whole-sale rejection of institutions thought to be too redolent of England's rivalrous system—like allowing government ministers to hold seats in the National Assembly.

Political institutions, on Condorcet's view, were established for the good of those who were subject to them. Institutions advanced that end to the degree that their decisions tracked justice and truth. Accepting that capable citizens had a claim to participate in political life, he regarded structures that would foreseeably enable individuals to undermine the common interest as the definition of unreason. Systems of legitimate opposition like the one on display in England were, on this view, unacceptable. "Man," he had argued in 1788, "did not enter into society to be crushed between opposing powers, becoming their victim in times of unity as well as dissent, but to enjoy peacefully all his rights under one authority created specifically to uphold them, and which, with no power to infringe them, does not have to be counterbalanced by another power" (1847a, 658; trans. in Williams 2004, 188).

What institutional contrivances would allow individuals to play a part in political life, advance their welfare, and avoid slipping into oppressive adversarialism? Condorcet's elaborate scheme can be streamlined into three elements. A legitimate regime would feature a declaration of rights, though he does not explicitly describe how such a document would actually limit the purview of the state. He favored a radical reformation of the educational system, allowing individuals to reliably pursue the common interest. And he envisaged a system of representative bodies, given fullest expression in his *Essai sur la constitution et les fonctions des assemblées provinciales*, a work providing the inspiration for the constitution he proposed to the National Assembly in 1793 (Condorcet 1847a, 1847c). In that work, Condorcet outlined an alternative to opposition. It is my focus here.

Condorcet proposed a now-familiar tiered system of representation, with local, provincial, and national bodies. The system's multilevel design was conventional, reflecting, in part, the influence of his mentor, Turgot (Baker 1990, 240). Additionally, Condorcet developed a moderate position on citizen participation, between equal manhood suffrage and a highly restrictive system. Broadly inclusive direct elections would be employed, but only for local assemblies. Members of higher-level assemblies would be selected by elected members of a lower assembly. In this limited respect, this would be a system of legitimate opposition. Still, as in Rousseau's plan for Poland, Condorcet's scheme contained multiple, overlapping mechanisms aimed at stanching the competitive impulse.

For instance, Condorcet proposed dividing policy making and candidate selection. Directly elected intermediate bodies charged with electing members to provincial and national assemblies would be given no legal or policy-making role. Alternative local assemblies, also directly elected, would guide local policy but would have no hand in elections. This feature would restrict the clout of local policy makers, ensuring that only the policy-minded would seek those positions. In turn, since members of the intermediate electoral bodies would not make substantive political decisions, the self-regarding appeal of these positions would be limited, as would candidates' capacity to appeal to their policy-based interests. Partitioning elections and policy, Condorcet sought to thwart rivalrous designs, ensuring that elections turned solely on candidates' "sense, probity and good intentions" (Condorcet 1847a, 147).

Condorcet's preferred method of selecting candidates provided a different impediment to the eruption of competition. Insights into voting procedures have assured Condorcet's fame, but the polymath did not endorse what is now known as "Condorcet voting" in his essay on provincial assemblies, admitting that it would be too cumbersome and time-consuming. Still, he endeavored to preserve the epistemic independence of individual voters. He proposed that for a given position, "each elector would make a list of 20 candidates he believes would be most worthy of the post" (Condorcet 1847a, 199).[13] Positions would be filled by the candidate on the most lists, assuming that that candidate was listed on more than half of the lists. Forcing voters to identify a large number of candidates would increase the costs of successfully coordinating around a single candidate. The mechanism would stunt strategic behavior, rendering competition unappealing as a political strategy. As the benefits of rivalrous action would be significantly diminished, parties would be defanged, if not eradicated, reduced to groups of individuals who happened to agree with one another (Condorcet 1847a, 200; see also 1847b, 400). Here competitors would not check each other. Those individuals would not engage in competitive behavior at all.

The most striking manifestation of Condorcet's aversion to regulated rivalry was his proposal to hold elections without campaigns, an institutional device that we also saw in Rousseau's proposed Polish constitution (Condorcet 1847a, 193–211). Potential candidates would be revealed just before voting occurred. Delays in the electoral process, Condorcet feared, would merely encourage individuals to ferret out others' positions and seek to influence them, creating the pressure to, as he put it, engage in "intrigue" (200). Engaging in intrigue would necessarily undermine voters' independence and cause them to support inferior candidates for strategic reasons. With little time to coordinate their actions, Condorcet's electors would base their choices on their knowledge of candidates' personal fitness. Elections, on this view, were not mechanisms for selecting representatives. They were mechanisms for identifying the elect (135, 194). Ideally, Condorcet contended, voters need not meet or discuss the election. Instead, they would simply send their list of favored candidates to an electoral board after receiving a list of potential candidates. The practical difficulties of persuading and coordinating voters would subvert competition and ensure that votes only reflected voters' "true feelings" (202). These defensive mechanisms would thwart those who were interested in advancing their own interests, block damaging coalitions, and cordon off legislative bodies from electoral intrigue.

Finally, Condorcet suggested that legislative assemblies themselves could be designed to limit the play of opposition. In this and other respects, Condorcet's proposals anticipate Mill's. In Condorcet's assemblies, deliberations would be highly structured. There would be time for open debate. *Intellectual* adversarialism had its place. But actual decision-making would be orchestrated by a small council of delegates. Those delegates would break down decisions into a series of propositions (e.g., Is crime a problem? Should that problem be addressed via a policy change? Should that policy change be policy X?) or a series of distinct but logical propositions allowing members to vote yes or no. Structuring decisions in this way, the committee would ensure, to the degree possible, the reasonableness of the outcome. Condorcet assumed that the officials orchestrating legislative decisions would not be politicized and would not politicize the work of the assembly. The defining feature of this elaborate system was not opposition but choreographed cooperation.

In a 1789 essay, "Sur la forme des élections," Condorcet recapitulated his views on organizing an electoral system. In doing so, he gave further insight into the motivation for his designs. Those who had malign aims were simply more effective at organizing, at adversarial action, than those who pursued the good. Condorcet's objective was to tip the balance of advantage from strategy to numbers, laundering strategic considerations out of the political process, so that "honest men can campaign for a common goal without having to make pacts amongst themselves." A rational system of decision-making would not require a system of legitimate opposition; it would allow each to "follow his reason and his conscience." This, he concluded, "should be the aim of every method of decision-making or election" (Condorcet 1847d, 330; trans. in Condorcet 1989, 188–89).

Was Condorcet simply being naive in thinking that competition could be edited out of political life? It is worth noting that in *On the Constitution and the Functions of Provincial Assemblies*, he insisted that his system of election and deliberation, like any good institutional design, required only "mediocre enlightenment and common decency." Rules "requiring great talent or heroic virtue," he advised, "are dangerous and cannot be useful over the longer term" (Condorcet 1847a, 206). Optimistic proposals could be dangerous, but Condorcet did not think his alternative to legitimate opposition was subject to this fear. Starting in section 6 of this chapter, I consider the accuracy of this claim's two parts, confirming the first, rejecting the latter. Before undertaking that work, however, I turn to Sieyès.

Sieyès's Representative Design for a World without Opposition

Emmanuel Joseph Sieyès is best known for pressing two arguments in the run-up to the Revolution. Most famously, Sieyès distinguished the capacity and right to make the constitution from the capacity and right to make law under that constitution: *pouvoirs constituant* and *constitué* (Sieyès 2003b, 143). Sieyès saw wisdom in driving a wedge between these activities, both theoretically and institutionally. Second, and more importantly for my analysis, Sieyès argued that representation and democracy could be reconciled—that representation and well-designed representative institutions were a necessary element of legitimate lawmaking in a polity of any size. Though he rejected important elements of Rousseau's theoretical and institutional legacy, Sieyès embraced the idea that political institutions ought to identify a will common to all. He regarded representative institutions as *the* indispensable mechanism for identifying that general will, for binding the polity together. Opposition was antithetical to that goal.

Societies, on Sieyès view, were not masses of individuals or groups defined into Aristotelian sections; they were political associations united by common aims. Political regimes fell into disorder when their laws and political institutions expressed partial wills, "intentions contrary to the general interest of the associates." Where that occurred, "there would be no more association, no more society" (Sieyès 2003a, 49).

The primary solvent of legitimate government, according to Sieyès, was not people's self-interest but their tendency to join forces to pursue it, that is, their tendency to act strategically. Sieyès divvied up people's many interests into three broad groups: common interest, self-interest, and factional interest. Common interest, of course, occupied a privileged position as a source of law. Bowing in the direction of reality, Sieyès admitted that political actors would be unable to still their self-interest. But "self-interest is not to be feared. It is isolated. Everyone has his own." Striking an optimistic, Madisonian note, Sieyès concluded, "[self-interest's] variety is its own solution" (2003b, 154). On the Abbé's view, if citizens were kept separate, their capacity for strategic action would be contained and de-fused. This is the source of his confidence, one seemingly shared by Condorcet, that under the right institutional conditions, self-interest would launder self-interest, leaving only common interest to motivate law and policy. What could thwart this happy outcome? The strategic pressure people faced to join with others to advance their interests. "The real problem thus arises from that interest by which one citizen combines with no more than a small number of others. It is this interest that makes for combination and leagues. It is the source of projects that are a danger to the community. It is the cradle of the most redoubtable public enemies. History is full of evidence of this sad truth" (154).

The combinations that Sieyès feared most were those among aristocrats or members of the clergy—the populations represented by the first and second estates. But his arguments were perfectly general. And they led him to reject systems of opposition, as well as the best-known justifications advanced on their behalf. For Sieyès, the value of England's oppositional politics and its balance of powers was their capacity to deter power holders from pursuing harmful courses. But limiting harm was far too low a bar for legitimate political institutions.

Rejecting the inevitability of a deficient state of affairs, Sieyès claimed that political theorists should endeavor to show how deficient conditions might be overcome. Like others, he concluded that legitimate rule could be achieved not via adver-sarial contestation but through a graduated system of repre-sentation and an appropriately deliberative legislative body. "If, instead of leaving the management of its affairs as a prize in this gladiatorial combat, the people decided to take them in hand by way of genuine representatives, can it, in all good faith, not be believed that all the importance presently attached to the *balance* of powers would not fall away, along with the order of arrangements that alone was what made it necessary?" (Sieyès 2003b, 131).

The Abbé prescribed an array of devices aimed at making space for "genuine" representatives to engage in "genuine" representation, institutions aimed at making space for liberty without setting loose people's interest in combination and competition. These devices included special legislative committees, short terms for those who were charged with presiding over legislative bodies, parliamentary immunity, and restrictions on who could vote and on the possibility of reelection. Delegates would openly debate questions—potentially divided into smaller groups or chambers—so that each might have the opportunity to speak and hear others. Once all views were heard and the main options were revealed, a vote would be held using majority rule. Witnessing a process aimed to identify the common will, association members would share a duty to obey its outcomes (Sieyès 2003b).

Representatives' freedom from constituent instructions was the linchpin of this deliberative system (a position that distinguished Sieyès from Rousseau). Sieyès feared that delegates, employed as "mere vote carriers," would be unable to find common ground. And because instructions thwart real deliberation, they would block the path to the common will, effectively sundering the association. "By trying to keep the use of its will under direct control, the general mass of associates has actually deprived itself of the ability to use its will at all" (Sieyès 2003a, 12). Citizens had absolutely no claim to have their partial interests represented in the legislature; "the right to be *represented* belongs to citizens only in respect to what they have in common and not to what serves to differentiate them" (Sieyès 2003b, 155). Loosening the bonds on representatives, Sieyès contended, would allow them to represent the interest of the nation as a whole, not of their particular locale (2003a, 37).

It is worth weighing Sieyès's stand against instructions. The position betrays the ardency of Sieyès's institutional faith. "A good constitution," he argued in the months before the meeting of the Estates General, "can give and guarantee citizens the enjoyment of their natural and social rights, can confer stability on everything that may be done for the good and can progressively extinguish all that has been done for the bad" (Sieyès 2003a, 5). Legitimate government was within reach. Escaping the bonds of suspicion, individuals should reject a system of opposition and embrace institutions allowing them "to join their individual wills together to form a common will that should be synonymous with the public interest" (Sieyès 2003b, 153).

A Regrettable Achievement: France's Uncompetitive Democracy

Contemporary political theorists might reject various elements of Condorcet's and Sieyès's views on democracy. They were, for instance, more skeptical about universal suffrage than most are today. Still, their demonstrated misgivings about political competition remain constituent features of much democratic theory, as is their faith that institutional ingenuity could divine a path to a popular form of government unracked by adversarial opposition. Focusing on the first two years of the Revolutionary era (1789 to 1791), this section considers the fate of the most famous actual attempt to establish an uncompetitive form of popular rule. The conclusions arrived at are consistent with the adversarial conception of legitimate opposition: opposition may not be intrinsically democratic, but it is valuable nonetheless.

In the last part of the twentieth century, it became increasingly common for historians to pin the French Revolution's failure on participants' disdain for bare, rule-based, popular contestation and liberal government more generally—a thesis closely associated with the historian François Furet (Furet 1981). This famed thesis is consistent with my argument. I will not defend it. Since it was offered, it has been subject to challenge (Tackett 2015, 14). And I am not in a position to arbitrate that debate. Instead, I provide evidence for a simpler and hardier thesis: 1789 was as likely a moment for the establishment of a popular form of government without a system of opposition as one can reasonably expect. Nonetheless, political actors still engaged in costly contestation, an outcome that should give considerable pause to theoreticians who recommend clock-work-style alternatives to contestatory institutions on the assumption that adversarial rivalry and uncooperative behavior can be suppressed without excessive moral cost.

Condorcet and Sieyès clearly took the view that opposition was avoidable and undesirable. But as I have shown, they were hardly alone in that view. Indeed, the norm against the base elements of popular politics, like campaigns and strategic maneuvering, held force well beyond the intellectual contributors I have discussed—it was a defining feature of political life prior to 1789 (Tackett 1996, 96; Crook 1996, 8). As the historian Lynn Hunt has argued, at the time of the Revolution, "politics and politicking were consistently identified with narrowness, meanness, divisiveness, factionalism, opportunism, egotism, and selfishness" (1984, 3).[14]

This powerful norm took clear institutional expression in 1789. In that year, the administration of King Louis XVI was weighed down by debts and financial commitments. Yielding to financial reality, the king called a meeting of the Estates General—a traditional representative body—which he hoped would help secure the necessary funds. The call for the Estates General constituted a considerable widening of the aperture for political activity in France, a dramatic, if notoriously temporary, increase in political liberty. The Estates General would be constituted by elected members from three estates: the clergy, aristocrats, and other members of society. Local assemblies were established to select representatives to the Estates General. Within just a few months, the body would transform itself into a National Constituent Assembly, a process in which Sieyès played a substantial role.

Despite Condorcet's and Sieyès's status as institutional grandees, they never saw their institutional designs fully realized during the Revolution. But Revolutionary institutions still reflected opposition to opposition. This is perhaps most apparent in the National Assembly's famous debates over a royal veto, the possibility of a multiple-chamber legislature, and the wisdom of allowing government ministers to simultaneously hold seats in the legislature, as they do in the United Kingdom. Each of these institutional mechanisms raised distinct concerns. Yet they were joined by their accepted connection to British politics and the practice of opposition. And they were collectively judged inconsistent with the cooperative, unitary conceptions of popular sovereignty widely held at the time.

Democratic resistance to competitive opposition was not only expressed in high-level constitutional battles. It impacted the basic details of political life. For instance, votes in local assemblies were made publicly, on the theory that this would increase the incentive to comply with norms against rivalry and intrigue (Crook 1996, 20). And the assemblies were charged with providing deputies with lists of concerns (*cahiers de doléance*) to convey to the king. Sieyès had rejected such mechanisms. But the practice was consistent with an aversion to competition, keeping delegates from exercising their own judgment or pursuing strategic courses. In principle, the practice undercut the import of selecting any individual candidate, blunting the designs of the ambitious. Why engage in that activity if the role of a representative was simply to transmit or relay the concerns of the electorate? Neither public voting nor instructions survived long in the Revolutionary era. A variety of other measures in the same vein did.

Most impressively, Revolutionary elections rarely featured either official candidates or campaigns.[15] Participants were simply presumed to know who would make a good candidate for election, regardless of that candidate's views or commitments. This may seem a bizarre, an obviously unworkable method of selection. Yet the practice, as I discussed in treating the proposals of Rousseau and Condorcet, was consistent with treating election as a mark of esteem, reflecting the intrinsic merit of the elevated (Crook 1996, 20). In addition, elections to the legislative bodies were staged. Electors were selected, and then those electors chose the actual representatives. Property requirements limited the pool of those who could serve as electors, ostensibly increasing the likelihood that they could not be moved by inducements. Per Condorcet's reflections, the relatively wide geographical area of the secondary electoral assemblies would increase the difficulty of forging alliances. Electing a member to the legislative assembly would require coordination across multiple local districts. Shielded from candidates and organized campaigns, the electors could focus on the merits of potential representatives. And selected in this manner, representatives would presumably not form competitive groups once they arrived at the legislature. In sum, French institutions were insulated by impressive normative and institutional levees protecting the political process against the surge of political competition.

How long did these levees hold? Not long. France's first elections in 1789 already featured systematic attempts to influence electoral outcomes. Events were held to convince voters to cast ballots for particular candidates. Arms were twisted, meals were served, and lists of favored candidates were distributed (Tackett 1996, 95). Malcolm Crook, a historian, quotes the following report from Le Puy-en-Velay, a town in central France: "Supporters of Mathieu Bernard esquire, a merchant, posted several persons at various vantage points along the roads into town in order to persuade delegates to vote for him; they distributed handbills and then, during the days that followed, they went into the hostelries where deputies were staying to continue their canvassing. All this intrigue was accompanied by a pack of lies concerning those whom the public seemed likely to appoint as deputies" (1996, 27).

These early setbacks did not discourage institutional re-formers, who introduced new rules intended to better structure and control elections, reinforcing limits on competitive action. For instance, new positions were created that would allow officers to preside over the electoral processes (the *bureau*). Yet the selection of the officers immediately became a site of contestation— that is, partisans worked to elect confederates as representatives *and* as officers in the *bureaux* (Crook 1996, 52, 146).

In 1789, France boasted no parties—institutionalized groups established to flourish under competitive conditions. If one's goal is to establish an uncompetitive popular regime, it is a noteworthy advantage to begin that quest unburdened by such groups (Masket 2016). In spite of this decided advantage, participants in Revolutionary politics almost immediately divided along lines of interest and ideology, an outcome that makes sense given the stakes involved. As early as 1790, ideological groups formed to coordinate support of like-minded politicians, and, at least in Paris, the norm against public discussion of "candidates" had already flatlined (Crook 1996, 179). "The two parties (conservative and reformist)," a leading Revolutionary figure and historian, Jean-Paul Rabaut Saint-Étienne, commented, "had already formed" even before the Estates General were called into existence. Those parties, he claimed, would shape France's new constitution (Tackett 1996, 94; Rabaut 1793, 63).

Consistent with Rabaut's observation, new political associations, if not modern political parties, burst into the space
opened by the call for the Estates General. Given the potential
activities of one's foes, acting together was simply the best way
to advance one's own projects, interests, and security (M. Kennedy 1982, 10). Of the groups that formed after 1789, the most
famous is certainly the Society of the Friends of the Constitution,
commonly known as the Jacobin Club (Doyle 1989, 142). Though
it survived just three years, its best-known English-language
chronicler, Michael Kennedy, claims that it became the coordinating hub of political life in Paris, and "its affiliates enveloped the
nation like the tentacles of a colossal sea creature" (1982, viii). As
Kennedy's florid description indicates, the clubs were not merely local organizations but national bodies facilitating national
action. Other groups would eventually rival and challenge the
Jacobins, including the radical Cordelier Club; the conservative
Monarchical Club; and the Feuillants, who split from the Jacobins
and supported a constitutional monarchy (Walton 2015, 364).

As we would expect, the groups sought to influence both
policy and elections. And, as we would expect, that competition
was self-reinforcing, propelling the players to deepen their
commitment to their rivalry, extending their activities to more
localities, forcing political participants to choose sides at the
risk of becoming politically impotent, and engaging in increasingly brazen, if totally familiar, efforts at electioneering—for
example, clubs would publish slates of approved candidates (M.
Kennedy 1982, 214–20; Tackett 2015, 148).

So much for political life out of doors. Were Revolutionary assemblies walled deliberative gardens protected by an
ostensibly nonadversarial electoral process from the scourge
of out-and-out contestation? They were not. Consider the
Breton Club. Originally it was a group of Estates General delegates from Bretagne who agreed to meet with one another and

coordinate their efforts. They met for the first time before the convocation of the Estates General. Quickly members from other provinces began attending the meetings. Augmenting their collective influence, members resolved to decide questions by majority vote, agreeing to support group decisions as a bloc. For similar reasons, members sought to influence the Estates' working groups (Tackett 1996, 125–26). Notwithstanding Sieyès's clear position on the crippling disease of factionalism, he was affiliated with the Breton Group. He shared its aversion to noble privilege. And membership offered the best way to advance that project.

The efforts of the reformers, their success in moving the body and selecting officials for various bodies, seeded the formation of a rival group: the Monarchiens, who were concerned about law and order and opposed the speed of political reform. In contrast to their rivals, the Monarchiens sat on the right side of the assembly. To gain an advantage, they organized themselves hierarchically. They created a small central committee, which would distribute instructions to subcommittees and to its members. Members would whip votes; Timothy Tackett cites the report of a delegate who claimed that a Monarchien "is to be seen every corner of the hall, pleading, speaking, shouting, spying to see who is for and against" (1996, 186–87). Though neither the Breton Group nor the Monarchiens survived the elections under the constitution of 1791 (no members of the Estates General were allowed to seek reelection), the new constitution was no more successful at bridling competitive impulses. The Legislative Assembly of 1791 was organized along similar lines: with two dominant groups, now the Jacobins and Feuillants (Tackett 2015, 149). Throughout the Revolutionary period, many delegates would never join a formal group. But after 1789, these formal groups flourished, and they would be dominant elements of Revolutionary politics until they were outlawed.

Despite a widespread distaste for political competition, it emerged weed-like in soil made fertile by new opportunities to exercise political agency. Opposition was not desired or considered legitimate, but it emerged nonetheless. The conditions for its emergence were minimal. Opposition and competition arose after 1789, the great historian François Furet once dryly explained, because "there was power to be had and people willing to fight for it" (1981, 43).

The Implications of Madison's Fork

Will rivalrous behavior persist even after a nation establishes a popular regime designed specifically to thwart it? Ought we assume that legitimate popular regimes will always feature some form of opposition? These were the questions I proposed at the beginning of this chapter. They bear directly on the question of opposition's value: if alternatives are unattractive, we have weightier reasons to embrace legitimate opposition. France's Revolutionary experience provides a clear answer to the first question, demonstrating the intellectual error marring the proposals of both Condorcet and Sieyès. The second question probably cannot be answered without reservations. But the French case suggests that it is misleading to declare that one's conception of popular rule simply will not feature adversarial rivalry.

Of course, one might imagine that the French Revolution was sui generis, comparable to no other situation. It was marked by surprising and unpredictable turns, unique ideological allegiances, and flights of immoderate violence. Yet for the period's ostensible world-historical originality, the source of its competitive politics was strikingly banal. Basic forms of political action were no longer penalized or less likely to be punished. The gains to rivalrous action were obvious. It was undertaken by some people, and that activity encouraged similar action by others. The banality is what counts here. It is the sheer ordinariness of this chain of actions that should give us new confidence in Madison's claim that "the latent causes of faction are thus sown in the nature of man" and might only be controlled "by destroying the liberty which is essential to its existence liberty" (1961a, 58). Contemporary theorists who follow in Sieyès's and Condorcet's footsteps face a fork outlined by Madison: stifle contestation by limiting liberty or accept its pervasiveness. Either choice, I believe, enhances the comparative attractiveness of systems of legitimate opposition.

Consider, for instance, a proposed deliberative setup that assumes that individuals will not act as rivals. A candid account of such a proposal will describe the measures needed to reliably limit the ambit of strategic action. Unless a persuasive explanation is provided, we should, following Madison, treat such theories as recommending measures that we know to be effective—that is, restrictions on political liberties. History has shown such restrictions to be a potent salve to the ostensible discomforts of regulated rivalry. Contemporary regimes like Venezuela and Russia have pursued just this course. But a hangnail can also be cured by lopping off an arm. The difficulty of justifying that course does not turn on its effectiveness; it turns on the proportionality and the character of its costs. The challenge, a considerable one, is to justify why those costs are warranted, why the form of popular government that survives such restrictions is one we have reason to value.

Certainly, this admission would not flatter the epistemic and deliberative proposals of Condorcet and Sieyès. Condorcet defended the import of a bill of rights to keep the government from impinging on citizens' liberties. If citizens were fearful of being punished for expressing their views or for supporting a candidate, the capacity of the political system to generate outcomes that reliably tracked the truth would be crippled.[16] A similar analysis applies to Sieyès's uncompetitive designs. Restrictions on political liberty would block citizens from selecting "genuine" representatives and thwart "genuine" representatives from deliberatively identifying a common will. In sum, our reasons for preferring these alternatives to legitimate opposition are undercut by the measures required to block competition.

A more sensible approach to Madison's fork would be to concede that one's ostensibly uncompetitive proposal will actually feature rivalry, rivalry of the adversarial sort. Yet making this admission would require ceding the claimed advantage that cooperative systems have over oppositional systems. Condorcet's system for selecting candidates and making decisions depends on the independence, diversity, and quality of the voters. That system would not reliably achieve its ends if individuals purposefully voted for less preferred options or grouped together. Similarly, Sieyès's deliberative system would no longer reliably achieve its end if individuals did not cooperatively pursue the common good via deliberation, engaging instead in strategic arguments or group tactics aimed at winning a vote. That acknowledging competition would lessen the appeal of these theories should not be surprising; the theories were explicitly premised on the rejection of opposition.

More deeply, as both Condorcet and Sieyès argued, systems defined by opposition are not lesser versions of cooperative forms of popular government. They are normatively distinct. Our assessment of what constitutes valuable political activity will differ between them. As I argued in chapter 2 of this book, where individuals can be expected to avoid rivalrous action, we might reasonably expect different parties to offer fully differentiated policy proposals even at the cost of any individual group's success. This expectation makes sense because all parties will avoid tailoring their proposals just to advance their ends. Where we expect individuals to behave as rivals, however, it might be unreasonable and self-defeating for a party to unilaterally forgo strategic considerations, offering policies that prioritize differentiation over victory, a victory that members of the party might plausibly think will advance the cause of justice. Given these distinct expectations, intelligent design of institutions will necessarily differ. And if the French example is relevant, where we have reason to believe contestation will be a prominent feature of life, we will have reason to concentrate on the question of how to manage, not escape, it. In other words, we will have reason to institutionalize opposition.

Of course, regimes defined by opposition share institutional characteristics with largely imaginary noncompetitive democracies. And one might hold out hope that oppositional regimes will develop into cooperative polities. Yet there is little evidence supporting a belief in such a transformation. Just as horses are unlikely to become unicorns, oppositional systems are not reasonably treated as steps on the way to cooperative ideals. In sum, choosing the second branch of Madison's fork not only implies an acknowledgment of the relative value of opposition (the central claim of the adversarial conception) but also raises questions about how noncompetitive institutional schemes function as institutional ideals.

Two Objections

A critic might respond to this argument in the following fashion: conceding that competition is likely to emerge under conditions of political liberty does not imply that one should seek to positively entrench and incentivize it. Acknowledging the pervasive character of competition in political life does not imply that institutional designers should embrace a system of legitimate opposition. That requires a more positive argument. Historians frequently refer to the regulatory vacuum that characterized politics during the first years of the French Revolution (Gueniffey 1989, 35). Is there any reason to think creating institutions aimed at regulating competition would be preferable to that vacuum? If not, then there may be little harm in attempting to institute cooperative institutions even if they are unlikely to succeed.

The French Revolutionary experience suggests at least two reasons to reject this conjecture. It therefore provides two reasons to acknowledge the comparative value of regulated opposition. First, in the French case, failing to create institutions to regulate competitive politics and coordinate citizens' activities generated results that were unreasonable and plausibly self-defeating, outcomes that would be difficult to defend on any theory of democracy's value. The lack of regulation did not successfully block the emergence of competition. But that regulatory lacuna was "self-defeating" because it actually made it more difficult for individuals to exercise their agency: the political system kept them from advancing their goals and made it more challenging for those who lacked resources to organize and engage politically. For instance, the lack of regulation around campaigns contributed to their irregularity, confusing voters, who had difficulty determining who might win or what the candidate would do if elected. And it significantly increased the length of the electoral process, because so many candidates would get votes in the first rounds. The longer the process went, the more costly it was to participate, the fewer the number who participated (Crook 1996, 67–78). Limiting participation is not rejected by all theories of legitimate government. But making individuals wait days and days to make their choices seems difficult to justify on any theory of political legitimacy. Of course, one might propose different uncompetitive institutions than those selected during the Revolution—Condorcet and Sieyès certainly did. But the early Revolution suggests that there may be high, potentially devastating, costs for establishing institutions divorced completely from the way individuals will behave. And it suggests that those costs will not be borne evenly. In sum, ill-fitted procedures can inhibit rather than advance the achievement of normative ideals.

Here is a second reason to acknowledge competition and institutionalize opposition. The value of competitive processes turns substantially on their capacity to generate valuable by-products—outcomes that are not the principal aim of the competitors (Elster 1986). For instance, we might think political candidates seek elected office to satisfy their ambition. By-products of that competition might be public policies that plausibly advance the well-being of the majority or the sense that one is not being manipulated politically. Yet competitors also face incentives to engage in activities that increase their likelihood of winning while limiting the capacity of the process to generate valuable by-products. For instance, competitors might try to win by stuffing the ballot box instead of offering attractive policies. One aim of institutional design is to keep contestants from undermining the practice. By failing to institute mechanisms to shape political rivalry, by failing to create mechanisms encouraging the competitors to stay in specific bounds, French institutional designs increased the likelihood that Revolutionary competition would become an untempered race to the bottom.

At first, for example, there were no sanctions for engaging in electoral violence or intimidation. There were no rules concerning how political clubs and organizations could seek to influence political outcomes. An unbounded competitive process fueled a culture of political calumny and demonization—a culture that arguably contributed to violence and to the destruction of competitive politics (Walton 2015). For Americans, efforts to police electoral combat and speech may seem intuitively objectionable. But numerous countries have judged that political rhetoric can generate unwarranted political instability and use such rules to temper competition, for example India and Israel. And since political figures in eighteenth-century France were particularly concerned about threats to their honor, the absence of regulation aggravated a contentious situation, fueling a process in which political players, even former allies, came to view each other as mortal enemies (Tackett 2015, 158). My aim here is not to defend particular regulations, such as limitations on calumny. Instead, I am emphasizing reasons to reject the complete absence of competition-reinforcing regulations. In sum, barring plausible proposals to thwart Madison's conjecture, it seems reasonable to conclude, as Sieyès eventually did, that where political liberty is protected, political competition will emerge. And where it emerges, it should be accepted and planned for.

A critic might be uncomfortable with the weight I am willing to place on a single case (though political theory is rife with single cases being used to support larger theoretical arguments, e.g., the Mytilene Debate, the failure of the Weimar Republic, and so forth). In particular, someone might worry that the background conditions in eighteenth-century France were sufficiently unfavorable to undermine any putative lessons about the liberty-competition connection. As Condorcet offered his constitutional proposal to the Convention in 1793, he expressed his own doubts: "Never before, however, have the upheavals caused by a more complete revolution, the passions aroused by a more rapid movement of ideas, the burden of a more dangerous war, and the greater difficulties in the state of public affairs seemed to present greater obstacles to the establishment of a constitution" (1847b, 335–36; trans. in Condorcet 1976, 144). Condorcet's summary does not capture many other disadvantages: French citizens, by today's standards, were not well educated; the country featured grave forms of social and economic inequality; and the citizenry had no extended experience with popular government.

On the basis of just a single case, one certainly cannot conclude that conditions were sufficiently favorable to establish a popular regime free of legitimate opposition. And given the dearth of contemporary examples, it may have been reasonable for Condorcet and Sieyès to wager on the success of popular institutions whose function depended on consistent cooperation and nonstrategic interactions. The same, however, cannot be said of present-day political theorists. We now possess two centuries' worth of experience with popular politics and the likelihood of political competition. It seems reasonable to conclude that those who laud a noncompetitive politics should bear the burden of describing what conditions would be necessary to establish and sustain it, how those conditions might be achieved, and what the costs involved would be.

I have claimed that France provides a uniquely attractive case to consider because the norm against competitive politics was widespread and because partisan institutions and identities were not already entrenched. As Condorcet emphasized in the speech just cited, "Never before has a people freer from prejudices and more liberated from the yoke of ancient institutions presented a greater opportunity for the creation of its laws in firm accordance with general principles consecrated by reason" (1847b, 335). If the advantages enjoyed by France at the end of the Ancien Régime were not sufficient to foster a competitionless form of politics, then the conditions that would be required are likely to be onerous and the number of candidate polities insignificant. And where those conditions are not met, we might regard attempts to actually institute noncompetitive institutions as self-defeating and plausibly dangerous.

Conclusion

This chapter extends the adversarial conception of legitimate opposition, shedding additional light on the relative value of legitimate opposition, on precisely what is lost when the practice is undermined. To do so, it has considered whether attractive institutional designs, like those devised by Condorcet and Sieyès, might stanch the competitive impulse, thereby reaping the benefits of democratic cooperation without undermining political liberty. Providing a unique and underappreciated test of uncompetitive popular institutions, the Revolution suggests that this common premise is flawed. And if that premise is flawed, so are the cooperative democratic institutional designs it supports.

The historical section of this book has taken aim at the democratic conception and the assumptions on which it is constructed—for example, that opposition is essentially democratic or that cooperative alternatives to opposition are easily achieved or even attractive given current political conditions. My goal via these analyses has been twofold: to better understand legitimate opposition's character and history and to gain a better grip on its value relative to its competitors. Chapter 8, the conclusion, pulls the strands of my argument together.

8
Conclusion

"I didn't think I'd say this, I'm going to say it, and I hate to say it." Of course, Donald Trump said it. On October 9, 2016, at a debate in St. Louis, the future president of the United States said, "If I win, I am going to instruct my attorney general to get a special prosecutor to look into your situation, because there has never been so many lies, so much deception. There has never been anything like it, and we're going to have a special prosecutor." Trump's rival, Hillary Clinton, responded by claiming that it was good news that Trump would never be president. "Because you'd be in jail," the future president shot back (*New York Times* 2016).

Trump's threats to imprison his political rival returned the idea of the legitimacy of opposition to political prominence. His refusal to accept his defeat in 2020 and the attack on the US Capitol make plain that the questions raised in this book are not merely academic. And the practice of legitimate opposition is not just in question in the United States. Poland, Hungary, Turkey, Venezuela, and Brazil have all been impacted by challenges to the practice. Even in contemporary France and Germany, where forces antagonistic to opposition have not been victorious, governments and citizens must still grapple with the way to respond to those who might reject the practice.

It is likely that some readers expected this work to rebuke politicians, like Trump, who have labored to cut opposition down, carefully demonstrating why their actions are inconsistent with the ethics or principles of opposition. A classic approach would be to outline the rules that would characterize opposition in a true democracy, a political system in which people had equal status and fellow citizens treated one another with mutual respect. I have not offered that account. Trump's actions are blatantly inconsistent with the practice of legitimate opposition. Coming to that conclusion did not require reading this book (or writing it).

In fact, this book was conceived before Trump instigated the siege of the US Capitol or even set foot in the Oval Office. The intellectual case for investigating legitimate opposition and for considering its relation to democracy does not rest on the frankly disorienting events of 2020 and 2021. Nor does it rest solely on the experience of the United States. Even if you disagree with my conclusions, I hope you accept that these developments dramatically illustrate the necessity of debating what legitimate opposition is, whether we should value it, and why.

Of course, a defender of the orthodox approach to opposition, the democratic conception, might hold out hope that current challenges to opposition will fade, making the democratic conception of opposition great again. The January 6 attack on the US Capitol was, for instance, preceded by Trump's defeat. Perhaps that election augurs a return to a deeper commitment to a democratic form of opposition.

That comforting view is, I think, a mistake. I live in North Carolina. It is pleasant enough. But when a Democratic candidate narrowly ousted a Republican governor, the Republican-controlled legislature stripped the incoming governor of various powers, undercutting the election outcome. We have highly gerrymandered electoral districts, both federal and state, that are designed to ensure that one party holds onto power. A federal court found that a previous redistricting plan specifically targeted African American voters. Those who devised that plan suffered no appreciable consequence. North Carolinians have little reason to be confident that their fellow citizens exercise power in ways that treat them as political equals. The challenges to achieving true democracy in North Carolina preceded the rise of Donald Trump—by several centuries. And the opponents of democracy and opposition in North Carolina owe little to him, ideologically or politically.

Were Trump to disappear unexpectedly, to simply evanesce, much of the challenge would remain. The legislature would be no less likely to engage in gerrymandering. And the work that people are doing right now to protect and extend the state's system of opposition would still require doing. Had Donald Trump sat out the 2016 election, keeping his attention fixed on real estate, reality television, and the golf links, I am not sure what would be different here. These conclusions also hold in other states. And they are certainly true in all of the other polities where opposition is menaced by populists and authoritarians. These may strike you as banal observations. It would be no small thing if our theoretical frameworks could handle them. The adversarial conception of legitimate opposition can do so.

Legitimate opposition is valuable because it is respectful of citizens' agency, allowing a range of individuals and groups to pursue political change peacefully. It can serve this end under a remarkably wide array of political conditions. It is easy to mistake this flexibility for a flaw—to believe that an alternative set of institutions would somehow elude all the objectionable and disheartening realities that bend systems of opposition into form. But I believe this flexibility is an element of opposition's virtue.

Most regimes shaped by opposition fall far short of democratic ideals, not least because many stakeholders are threatened by those ideals and work to thwart their attainment. This observation is especially likely to hold in the polities where legitimate opposition is in peril. The adversarial conception of legitimate opposition makes sense of this state of affairs. My goal has been to develop an account fitting with the long, varied history of the practice, one that applies broadly, to the diverse polities where opposition is put to work. If successful, I have offered a credible, historically enriched account of opposition's value. Legitimate opposition is an achievement, one that warrants active, concerted, even militant defense.

Notes

1
Introduction

1. In November 2018, Florida voters approved a state-constitutional amendment enfranchising former felons who had been barred from voting. The legislature soon passed rules circumscribing the effect of the amendment, stipulating, among other things, that former felons would have to pay all fees associated with their sentence in order to vote. Yet Florida established no systematic mechanisms allowing those former felons to determine how much they owed. In many cases, officials themselves were unsure how this information could be obtained. To vote, former felons must attest that they have paid all of their fines. Yet if their attestation is incorrect, and if they still owe money, they will have committed an additional felony. As a result of this uncertainty, many choose not to vote (Gardner and Rozsa 2020).

2. In a blog post, Philip Pettit (2013) comes to a similar conclusion: "Just as there is no no democracy without other institutions, then—no democracy without free speech, legitimate opposition, judicial independence and property rights—so it is impossible to have such institutions in any proper sense without democracy. The inseparability runs both ways."

3. In practice, substantial movement away from true democracy would be very likely to precede the failure of opposition.

4. In an essay on the US approach to loyal opposition, Heather Gerken also promotes a nontraditional, nonideological conception of the practice, one centered on federalism. See Gerken 2014.

5. For an excellent analysis of these issues see Wiens 2016.

6. Another, depressing example of the problem of the second best comes from university economics departments. Efforts to approximate an ideal of equal treatment by allowing professors of all genders to take family leave actually increased the gap in tenure rates between men and women (Antecol, Bedard, and Stearns 2018).

7. For a compelling, alternative take on Schumpeter see Piano 2019.

8. More recently, for instance, Przeworski has developed a somewhat less minimalist, somewhat more hopeful account of democracy's value: "For in the end, democracy is but a framework within which somewhat equal, somewhat effective and somewhat free people can struggle peacefully to improve the world according to the different visions, values and interests" (2010, 16). I think Przeworski has here provided a good explanation of the value of legitimate opposition. But I do not think he offers a credible explanation of why we should call systems that suffer all the ails he describes as democracies. And I do not think he offers a sufficiently persuasive theory for why we should value systems like this relative to systems that lack opposition (systems that may allow individuals to pursue their visions and values outside the political system). A central aim of this work is to provide that theory. The more minimal view is embraced again in Przeworski 2015.

9. In contrast to Przeworski, Huntington, like Dahl, regarded full participation as a prerequisite for minimal democracy (polyarchy, in Dahl's terms). But like Dahl, Huntington's treatment of opposition still revolved around his conception of democracy (Dahl 1971; Huntington 1991, 33).

10. I am not the first to trip over this argument. In a Twitter exchange with the political theorist Corey Robin, Ziblatt suggests that he does not think the United States was a democracy before 1965 ("Fully agree america was NOT a democracy pre 1965" [Ziblatt 2018]). That claim, however, is inconsistent with his book's argument. In the book, Levitsky and Ziblatt refer to the United States as "one of the world's oldest and most successful democracies" (2018, 2). Presumably, they are not referring to a democracy that was founded in 1965 as one of the "oldest democracies." The view that the United States only became a democracy in 1965 is inconsistent with their claim that Americans' acceptance of opposition and political restraint "undergirded American democracy for most of the twentieth century" (9). The whole rhetorical force of the gravely titled *How Democracies Die* is that basic, long-standing American values are under attack. Finally, Levitsky and Ziblatt's claims about the Civil War are not a one-off. They argue that after the two parties' "undemocratic" abandonment of Black civil and political rights in the nineteenth century, "polarization gradually declined, giving rise to the kind of politics that would characterize American democracy for the decades that followed" (125). *How Democracies Die* exemplifies how the traditional conflation of democracy and opposition leads systematically to conceptual confusion, to the kind of situation in which a justifiably renowned scholar of popular politics, like Ziblatt, finds it necessary to disavow a claim at the center of his own book.

11. This project is modeled on Bernard Manin's classic work *The Principles of Representative Government* (1997). Other works that also served as models include Schwartzberg 2007; and Urbinati 2006.

2

Opposition's Value

1. My account of individuals' interest in agency is informed by Annie Stilz's influential arguments about the value of self-determination, e.g., Stilz 2016.

2. Thanks to Jeff Spinner-Halev for suggesting that I address this question.

3. For an especially powerful argument centered on the instrumental advantages of competition, see Bagg 2018.

4. In a variety of ways, my account of opposition's value echoes Eric Beerbohm's account of the ethics of democratic action in *In Our Name: The Ethics of Democracy* (2012). Beerbohm's argument turns on the moral import of individual contributions to collective outcomes. And the notion of moral relations at the heart of his account is closely related to the idea of respect for agency at the heart of my account.

5. One might be concerned that Sen's example (and the argument to come) mislead. Perhaps our intuitive assessment of these cases still actually turns on their outcomes. One can stop fasting. But, presumably, one cannot stop starving. And that may color our judgment. So imagine the limiting cases: both the fasting person and the starving person die of hunger. Does the example still work? I think it does. I am still liable to treat the instance of starvation as worse just because it was not chosen, just because it was not the product of that person's agency. Is this thought still dependent on outcomes? To be sure, I suspect that those who starve themselves will, in some sense, suffer less, psychologically speaking, than those who are starved. But this difference turns on the mere fact that the outcome is the product of someone's agency, a conclusion that adds force to the claim that agency matters. Thanks to Shmulik Nili for raising this concern.

6. My account is informed by a long-running philosophical debate about the nature of self-governance. The literature on the topic is extensive, but two of the classic works are Frankfurt 1971; and Watson 1975.

7. My account of these conditions draws on the description of the conditions of democratic authority and the import of political equality outlined in Thomas Christiano's *The Constitution of Equality* (2008).

8. In *The Rule of the Many* (1996), Tom Christiano develops a defense of multiparty democracy that shares many features with Goodin's account. The key difference is over the way the number of parties facilitates or inhibits a full choice.

9. With respect to the possibility of collective agency, accounts such as Dworkin's have gained in plausibility with the growth of the philosophical literature precisely delineating the contours and conditions of group agency (Kutz 2000; Bratman 2014). Where before the assertion of collective agency could reasonably be treated as a kind of intellectual fudge, these accounts,

distinct though they are, indicate how the coordinated activity of individuals can result in actions and decisions that can justifiably, and sometimes only, be attributed to a group. It is, of course, a separate question what implications can be assigned to the mere fact that political activity is something that can be done collectively—i.e., how this conclusion shapes questions concerning a putative duty to vote. On issues of this sort see Stilz 2009; Beerbohm 2012; and Brennan and Sayre-McCord 2015.

10. Przeworski has argued that in a democracy, the parties "know what winning or losing can mean to them, and they know how likely they are to win or lose, but they do know if they will lose or win. Hence democracy is a system of ruled open-endedness, or organized uncertainty" (1991, 13). On this view, even if we are quite sure of an outcome, because individuals *could* change the outcome by changing their behavior, the outcome is uncertain. I think this is not an intuitive way of thinking about uncertainty. I think it is better to say that the outcome may be certain, but the system remains competitive. I am grateful to Claudio López-Guerra and the participants at Princeton's University Center for Human Values Workshop for helping me think this through.

11. In *On the Side of Angels* (2008), Nancy Rosenblum comes to a similar conclusion about the limits of Edmund Burke's defense of parties (121).

12. Shapiro argues that his understanding of opposition is Millian, but he does not address the implications of Mill's embrace of a depoliticized, collaborative, collegial set of political institutions in *Considerations on Representative Government*.

13. My analysis of Shapiro's conception of domination may not apply to the influential neorepublican theory outlined by Philip Pettit. In *On the People's Terms* (2012), Pettit's theory does not turn on the harm to someone's well-being caused by domination, as does Shapiro's, but on the wrongful status or unfreedom implied by "exposure to another's power of uncontrolled interference" (28). On this view, a citizen in Polity B would be dominated and unfree, notwithstanding the efforts by the regime to track its citizens' interests. On the other hand, if Polity A is like most flawed, real-world regimes marked by opposition, then citizens of Polity A are probably also dominated by elites on Pettit's robust account of republican freedom and its extensive institutional requirements. Discussing Schumpeter, Pettit concludes that systems in which people exercise influence but not control over elected elites (i.e., most existing oppositional systems) "would not enable them to enjoy freedom as non-domination in their relationship with the government" (23). So citizens in both regimes are probably dominated on this account. What would be lost if a real-world system were to be undermined on Pettit's account? It is difficult to say. The upshot is that Pettit's elegant theory of republican democracy and justice may not provide a fully satisfying account

of what is lost just in case opposition is undermined in the real world. And that is why I have not put that theory at the center of my analysis. Moreover, I suspect that Pettit's account would also fail to offer resources to distinguish the system of noncompetitive accountability that I describe from a system featuring electoral competition. This is another reason to focus on agency in order to understand the distinctive value of opposition.

3
Opposition under Attack

1. There is, of course, an impressively broad literature on populism. Examples include Laclau 2005; and Urbinati 1998.

2. Some movements claim to be populist, but if they do not embrace an exclusive conception of the people, they are not actual populists, on Müller's account.

4
Rethinking Opposition's Boundaries

1. These are the organizations the American founders famously feared. Previous generations of scholars variously treated Athens's classes, informal groupings, and social associations, such as the *heiratai*, as parties (Whibley 1889). Contemporary scholars reject the view that these informal or not primarily political associations bear a strong resemblance to modern parties. That conclusion is well founded, and I accept it in this chapter. For further analysis of this question and of the character of political competition in Athens, see Connor 1971 5–9; Strauss 1987, 15–31; Hansen 1991, 277–87; Cartledge 2000.

2. On the development of the modern conception of legitimate opposition, see Robbins 1958; Foord 1964; Mansfield 1965; Skinner 1974; Aldrich and Grant 1993; Leonard 2002; Engel 2011; J. Selinger 2012.

3. See Dicey 2009, 150–56; Fontana 2009; Gerken 2014, 1964.

4. There are, of course, many recent works on militant democracy, including Malkopoulou and Norman 2018; Malkopoulou and Kirshner 2019; Schupmann 2017.

5. See Lessig 2011; and Fishkin and Forbath 2014.

6. To be sure, under the democracy, the well-off faced special political and fiscal responsibilities, like liturgies. But carrying out these special responsibilities actually increased their status and influence among their fellow citizens. See Rhodes 2000, 469–71.

7. To my knowledge, Aristotle is actually the first author to employ the term "monopoly." Aristotle 1996b, 1259a15–35. See also De Roover 1951.

8. Ober makes the same point when he discusses the use of a lottery to select archons and other magistrates (Ober 1989, 76).

9. Even Antony Andrewes, who is skeptical of Plutarch's interpretation, admits that this element of Plutarch's account is plausible. See Raubitschek 1960; and Andrewes 1978.

10. As noted earlier, Thucydides, son of Melesias (i.e., not the historian), was ostracized. But it appears that the ostracism occurred well after Thucydides forced Perikles to defend his spending. Raubitschek 1960, 94–95; Strauss 1987, 27.

11. This conclusion is additionally supported by Demosthenes's repeated efforts to change his fellow citizens' minds concerning the threat paused by Phillip of Macedonia. See Demosthenes 1926.

12. In theory, one could bring actions against political actors (as opposed to military figures) if they misled the people. Based on the evidence for the fifth century, it appears that this was rarely or never undertaken, and rules of this sort did not limit political practice in the city (Hansen 1974).

13. There is considerable debate about the date when ostracism was introduced. The main line of scholars now agree that ostracism was introduced at the same time as the other Kleisthenic reforms (D. Kagan 1961; Ostwald 1988; De Ste. Croix 2004, 182; Forsdyke 2005, 282–83; Missiou 2011, 36).

14. There is an extensive debate about the intended use of ostracism. See Ostwald 1988; Hansen 1991; Ober 1989, 74; De Ste. Croix 2004; Forsdyke 2005; Ober 2008, 160–61. The author of an illuminating monograph about ostracism, Sarah Forsdyke, offers an important alternative to the interpretation I defend. She contends that the practice was largely symbolic, a pantomime institution, epitomizing the people's power and reason (Forsdyke 2005, chap. 4). A full treatment of Forsdyke's thought-provoking book would not be appropriate here. But it is worth noting that Forsdyke's interpretation is finely balanced on two a priori claims (Forsdyke 2005, 149). The first claim is that the infrequency of ostracisms illustrates their intentionally symbolic character (no ostracisms were held after 415, though votes whether to ostracize someone continued to take place). Forsdyke's second claim is that the expulsion of a single actor could not have protected the regime from a substantial threat. Despite the persuasiveness of much of Forsdyke's analysis, I believe these deductive arguments cannot sustain the argumentative weight placed on them.

15. There is a disagreement concerning the figure of six thousand: some scholars believe that six thousand votes were needed in total, in order to reach a kind of quorum; others contend that to be ostracized required six thousand votes for a particular person. Most scholars now tend to favor the former interpretation over the latter.

16. On the biases of Aristotle and Plutarch, see Ober 1989, 50; Hansen 1991, 15.

17. My account of this rivalry is primarily drawn from Aristotle's account in *The Athenian Constitution* (1996a) and Plutarch's essays on Kimon and Perikles (1914b, 1916).

18. On the historical support for this tale, see Forsdyke 2005, 148.

19. The literature on the Supreme Court's campaign-finance jurisprudence is predictably immense. Good reviews include E. Kagan 1996; K. Sullivan 1997; and Hasen 2011. At one point, the Court ruled that the state had a strong interest in ensuring that the political process was not overly distorted by the political capacities of large organizations, like corporations and unions. See Austin v. Mich. Chamber of Comm., 494 U.S. 652 (1990). That view echoes the Athenian approach to legitimate opposition. But the antidistortion principle has now been set aside by the Court (Citizens United v. Federal Election Commission, 558 U.S. 310 (2010)), and it was never as potent as political reformers had hoped (Hasen 2011).

5

Opposition without Democracy

1. There is a tradition of thought, associated with Fergus Millar, claiming that, in fact, the people, broadly considered, exercised sovereignty in Rome (Millar 1984, 1986, 1998). These claims have been subjected to substantial challenge by classicists. For my purposes, it is merely worth observing that Millar's definition of democracy, one focused on a certain kind of popular sovereignty, is inconsistent with the egalitarian notion I employ in this work. His definition would treat as democratic a political system in which men had ten votes and women one concerning who was elected to political office. That system would be democratic because "the people" in such a political system would have control over elected officials. On my view, such a system would be too distant from egalitarian values to be democratic.

2. Thanks to Jed Atkins for emphasizing to me the multisource character of Roman institutional life. See also Straumann 2016, esp. chap. 1.

3. In this case, I have used Lintott's translation (Lintott 1999a, 57). After consulting with scholars with a better sense of Latin, they confirm that Lintott's translation of these remarks is more consistent with the force of Cicero's claim than that found in the Loeb edition.

4. I relied on the new translation of this work (Q. Cicero 2012). Thanks to Jed Atkins for pointing me to it.

5. There is a substantial academic debate about the democratic character of these reforms. Erich Gruen, for instance, claims that Cicero and Plutarch overstated the degree to which these reforms ran counter to the interests of the higher orders (Gruen 1991). Notwithstanding the existence of the debate

concerning the beneficiaries of that legislation, the passage of this legislation, the import it played in Rome's public political culture, and the fact that it withstood the test of time suggest that these reforms were responses to serious institutional shortcomings.

6. There are many accounts of the life and death of Tiberius. See Plutarch 1921, *Tiberius and Gaius Gracchus*. I rely on Mackay 2009; and Flower 2010.

7. These examples are drawn from Lintott 1999b; and Mackay 2009.

8. Alternative versions of this story can be found in Appian 1913, 1.4.28; Livy 1959, *Periochae* 69; Plutarch 1920, *Pyrrhus and Gaius Marius* 29.

9. I believe the analysis in this section would also apply to Hélène Landemore's recent work (2020).

6
It's the State, Not Parties

1. There is a long-standing debate about the exact character of Hume's contribution to the Founders' views on parties (Adair 1957; Morgan 1986; Spencer 2002).

2. The claim is not wholly unknown to political theorists. Harvey Mansfield usefully distinguishes partisan practices from opposition in his *Statesmanship and Party Government* (1965, 112–119), though he does not place the same emphasis on the role of the state in shaping the relationship between the two practices. In *Bolingbroke and His Circle* (1968), Isaac Kramnick, like Dahl and Hofstadter, tends to conflate partisan conflict and opposition. Historians have generally been more sensitive to this distinction (e.g., Clark 1980).

3. Hume's sketch was avowedly informed by his reading of Harrington 1992. As I note later, Jeremy Waldron discusses Hume's proposal in his book *Political Political Theory* (2016, 101).

4. Jeremy Waldron refers to legitimate opposition as a constitutional principle in his essay on loyal opposition (2016, 105).

5. Darryl Levinson and Richard Pildes make a similar argument in a 2006 essay. But they claim that the Founders' focus on the division of powers must be reconsidered in light of the rise of parties. I argue that the pure theory of the division of powers never held water; it was the state, not parties, that rendered it fanciful. But I think Levinson and Pildes are correct that an impure theory of the separation of powers, one that acknowledges how it will be impacted by the practice of opposition, merits development.

6. As one of the anonymous readers of this book noted, Woodrow Wilson famously critiqued the American Founders' institutional approach to the division of powers as a product of a flawed, "Newtonian" worldview, in which institutional designers' mechanistic plans for political life would reliably guide

real-world behavior. The function of governmental institutions, for Wilson, was to work together. This meant that members of the government would seek to cooperate notwithstanding mechanical efforts to separate powers. The result was a political system that did not match the Founders' designs and functioned inefficiently because it was ill suited to its actual purpose (Wilson 1908, 57). My own view echoes Wilson's skepticism of proposals that rely on overly mechanical understandings of political institutions. But I do not accept Wilson's functionalist, Darwin-inspired alternative. Wilson, for instance, argued in favor of particular institutional alternatives in light of his functionalist approach. I do not defend a particular institutional scheme, and my argument is not functionalist. Instead, I show that important players in the history of political thought recognized that state-based resources would be used by the government to compromise institutional barriers. Contemporary students of politics, including defenders of the separation of powers, should weigh this concern. Taking it into account, I believe, strengthens the comparative case for a system of organized political opposition. My account of Wilson draws from Tulis 1987, 117–44.

7. Steven Klein's penetrating efforts to reconceptualize the democratic state and democratic action share several themes with my argument here, especially with respect to the way political activity is shaped by and reshapes the state, a topic too often overlooked by democratic theorists (Klein 2020).

8. For an excellent, alternative perspective on Bolingbroke, one that suggests that Bolingbroke was more sanguine about parties than the traditional view suggests, see Skjönsberg 2016. This conclusion, I believe, fits nicely with the argumentative tack I take in this chapter.

9. I emphasize "formed" here because as I indicate later in this chapter, Bolingbroke's attack on party nonetheless left space for a limited, "team of rivals" version of opposition. "Team of rivals" opposition is to the recognizable benefit of both the opposition and the opposed.

10. Following the ascension of George I, publications suspected of Jacobite allegiances were frequently shut down, numerous Tories were pursued legally, and some lost office. Opposition to the king—to the regime, in other words—was not accepted. But this, in itself, is not an indication that opposition is not accepted. Why not? Because many regimes defined by regulated, rule-based competition place limits on participation, in particular participation aimed at changing the regime. Consider the case of modern Germany. It restricts the activities of antidemocratic parties, but it clearly features the practice of opposition, i.e., a regular, peaceful, and regulated competition for political power.

11. Just a few years later, David Hume would publish *A Treatise of Human Nature* (1739), containing several different allusions to this problem.

12. On this dispute, see Brewer 1971.

13. Parliamentary regimes, like Germany, have explicitly formulated opposition as a constitutional practice. The Basic Law outlines the role of parties and the formal powers of opposition groups.

14. Beyond Hofstadter's great work (1969), there is a growing literature on this topic: Leonard 2002; Engel 2011; J. Selinger 2012, 2016.

15. For a fuller account of the politics of this period and its implications for the development of parties, see Aldrich and Grant 1993. See also Ceaser 1979.

16. See also Jefferson's 1795 "Notes on the Letter of Christoph Daniel Ebeling." In those notes, Jefferson echoed this analysis of the state-party connection:

> Hence the anti-republicans appeared a considerable majority in both houses of Congress. They pressed forward the plan therefore of strengthening all the features of the government which gave it resemblance to an English constitution, of adopting the English forms and principles of administration, and of forming like them a monied interest, by means of a funding system, not calculated to pay the public debt, but to render it perpetual, and to make it an engine in the hands of the Executive branch of government which added to the great patronage it possessed in the disposal of public offices, might enable it to assume by degrees a kingly authority. . . . Still however it is inevitable that the Senate will at length be formed to the republican model of the people, and the two houses of the legislature, once brought to act on the true principles of the Constitution, backed by the people, will be able to defeat the plan of sliding us into monarchy, and to keep the Executive within republican bounds, notwithstanding the immense patronage it possesses in the disposal of public offices, notwithstanding it has been able to draw into this vortex the judiciary branch of the government and by their expectancy of sharing the other offices in the Executive gift to make them auxiliary to the Executive in all its views instead of forming a balance between that and the legislature as it was originally intended and notwithstanding the funding phalanx which a respect for public faith must protect, tho it was engaged by false brethren. Two parties then do exist within the US. (2004, 506–10)

17. Youngstown Sheet & Tube Co. v. Sawyer, 343 U.S. 579, 654 (1952). Quoted in Levinson and Pildes 2006, 2315.

18. Carl Schmitt also found Mill's treatment of the state lacking. The Nazi legal theorist did not conclude, as I do, that Mill's failure strengthened the case for legitimate opposition (Schmitt 1988).

7

Democracy without Opposition

1. I have been opportunistic in my use of English translations in this chapter. Where credible translations have existed and been close at hand, I have used them. Where this was not the case, I have translated the material myself.

2. The position of prime minister existed in all but name by 1789.

3. A full historical survey of opposition to opposition in Revolutionary France would surely discuss the writings and speeches of figures like Robespierre. But my critical concerns are with contemporary liberal democratic theory. Accordingly, I have chosen figures whose thought continues to exert significant influence over that body of work.

4. Thanks to Geneviève Rousselière for correctly emphasizing the extent to which concerns about political stability drove these theorists' rejection of opposition.

5. Such ideas were a common assumption of eighteenth-century treatments of factions and parties. Hume makes similar claims, and Burke notes, "Party divisions, whether on the whole operating for good or evil, are things inseparable from free government (1981a, 109; Hume 1994b, 56). On the common character of this claim, see Brewer 1971, 492.

6. As Robert Dahl emphasized this was true of much of Madison's theoretical edifice (Dahl 1956).

7. There is no reason to assume that this is a new stratagem. In "Idea of a Perfect Commonwealth," David Hume suggested that consideration of the best regime, beyond its intrinsic value, was justified by the possibility that in some "future age, an opportunity might be afforded of reducing the theory to practice, either by dissolution of some old government, or by the combination of men to form a new one, in some distant part of the world" (1994a, 513).

8. *Parties* were also regarded with suspicion in the newly created United States. But its new constitution made clear space for rivalrous action and regulated competition among different groups. It would be impossible to make sense of the new polity's electoral system were this not the case.

9. Dan Edelstein briefly contends in his excellent *The Terror of Natural Right: Republicanism, the Cult of Nature, and the French Revolution* (2009) that the rejection of opposition is unlikely to explain the Terror. The founders of the American republic, he contends, rejected opposition too (132). And they did not carry out their own Terror. I hope by now it is clear that Edelstein's deduction teeters precariously on the orthodox, democratic conception of opposition. It should now be clear that the Americans rejected *partisan* opposition, but unlike their French counterparts, they *accepted* opposition. With respect to opposition, the intellectual breach between the American and the French Revolutionaries remains unbridged. By implication, Edelstein's

clever effort to disqualify opposition to opposition as a potential cause of Revolutionary violence does not hold.

10. The development of Sieyès's thought did not stop in 1795. He was a major player during the Directory period and played a key, if self-defeating, role in the rise of Napoleon. On the intricacies of his political theory, see Pasquino 1998.

11. On the place of "counterforces" in French political thought, see Rosanvallon 2008.

12. I am treating the *Mémoire sur les municipalités* as a reflection of Turgot's ideas, though the project was drafted by the economist Dupont de Nemours. On this choice, see Cavanaugh 1969; Baker 1978. Liana Vardi argues that the work reflects the views of Dupont de Nemours (2012, 248). I am not well positioned to arbitrate that dispute. But Turgot was in favor of a system of assemblies that did not provide a forum for exercise of political agency, and the larger *Mémoire* reflects that view. I do not believe my argument hangs on who is the rightful author of that text.

13. The number twenty was illustrative. The number should be large enough to keep voters from only including their personal favorites. If there were two positions at stake, he recommended a list of twenty-one, and so on.

14. Opposition to opposition was dominant but not uniform. Some individuals viewed England as a model to be emulated. And allowing executive ministers to hold a position in the legislative assembly was even proposed. But that proposal and others like it were almost uniformly unsuccessful. See Gunn 2009, 28–32; Gooch 1960.

15. With the exception of the 1797 election, Year V, candidates were simply not a feature of the many elections held during the Revolutionary period (Gueniffey 1993b, 92). See also M. Edelstein 2014; Gueniffey 1993a.

16. On this, see Ladha 1992.

References

Acemoglu, Daron, and James A. Robinson. 2006. *Economic Origins of Dictatorship and Democracy*. Cambridge: Cambridge University Press.

———. 2012. *Why Nations Fail: The Origins of Power, Prosperity and Poverty*. London: Profile.

Ackerman, Bruce, and Ian Ayres. 2002. *Voting with Dollars*. New Haven, CT: Yale University Press.

Acomb, Frances Dorothy. 1950. *Anglophobia in France, 1763–1789: An Essay in the History of Constitutionalism and Nationalism*. Durham, NC: Duke University Press.

Adair, Douglass. 1957. " 'That Politics May Be Reduced to a Science': David Hume, James Madison, and the Tenth Federalist." *Huntington Library Quarterly* 20 (4): 343–60.

Aldrich, John H. 1995. *Why Parties? The Origin and Transformation of Political Parties in America*. Chicago: University of Chicago Press.

Aldrich, John H., and Ruth W Grant. 1993. "The Antifederalists, the First Congress, and the First Parties." *Journal of Politics* 55 (2): 295–326.

Amar, Akhil Reed. 2005. *America's Constitution: A Biography*. New York: Random House.

Anastaplo, George. 2003. "Loyal Opposition in a Modern Democracy." *Loyola University Chicago Law Journal* 35 (4): 1009–20.

Anderson, Elizabeth S. 1999. "What Is the Point of Equality?" *Ethics* 109 (2): 287–337.

Andrewes, Antony. 1978. "The Opposition to Perikles." *Journal of Hellenic Studies* 98:1–8.

Antecol, Heather, Kelly Bedard, and Jenna Stearns. 2018. "Equal but Inequitable: Who Benefits from Gender-Neutral Tenure Clock Stopping Policies?" *American Economic Review* 108 (9): 2420–41.

Appian. 1913. *Roman History*. Vol. 3, *The Civil Wars, Books 1–3.26*. Translated by Horace White. Loeb Classical Library 4. Cambridge, MA: Harvard University Press.

Arditi, Benjamin. 2004. "Populism as a Spectre of Democracy: A Response to Canovan." *Political Studies* 52 (1): 135–43.

Arena, Valentina. 2012. *Libertas and the Practice of Politics in the Late Roman Republic*. Cambridge: Cambridge University Press.

Arendt, Hannah. 1963. *On Revolution*. New York: Penguin.

Aristotle. 1996a. *The Constitution of Athens*. In *"The Politics" and "The Constitution of Athens,"* edited by S. Everson, 209–64. Cambridge: Cambridge University Press.

———. 1996b. *The Politics*. In *"The Politics" and "The Constitution of Athens,"* edited by S. Everson, 9–208. Cambridge: Cambridge University Press.

Arneson, Richard. 1993. "Democratic Rights at National and Workplace Levels." In *The Idea of Democracy*, edited by D. Copp, J. Hampton, and J. E. Roemer, 118–48. Cambridge: Cambridge University Press.

———. 2004. "Democracy Is Not Intrinsically Just." In *Justice and Democracy: Essays for Brian Barry*, edited by K. Dowding, R. E. Goodin, and C. Pateman, 40–58. Cambridge: Cambridge University Press.

Arrow, Kenneth Joseph. 1963. *Social Choice and Individual Values*. 2d ed. New York: Wiley.

Asconius Pedianus, Quintus. 2006. *Commentaries on Speeches of Cicero*. Translated by R. G. Lewis. Oxford: Oxford University Press.

Bagg, Samuel. 2018. "The Power of the Multitude: Answering Epistemic Challenges to Democracy." *American Political Science Review* 112 (4): 891–904.

Baker, Keith Michael. 1978. "French Political Thought at the Accession of Louis XVI." *Journal of Modern History* 50 (2): 279–303.

———. 1990. *Inventing the French Revolution: Essays on French Political Culture in the Eighteenth Century*. Cambridge: Cambridge University Press.

Balot, Ryan K. 2004. "Free Speech, Courage, and Democratic Deliberation." In *Free Speech in Classical Antiquity*, edited by I. Sluiter and R. Rosen, 233–59. Leiden: Brill.

Bandura, Albert. 2006. "Toward a Psychology of Human Agency." *Perspectives on Psychological Science* 1 (2): 164–80.

———. 2018. "Toward a Psychology of Human Agency: Pathways and Reflections." *Perspectives on Psychological Science* 13 (2): 130–36.

Beeman, Richard R. 1992. "Deference, Republicanism, and the Emergence of Popular Politics in Eighteenth-Century America." *William and Mary Quarterly* 49 (3): 401–30.

Beerbohm, Eric Anthony. 2012. *In Our Name: The Ethics of Democracy*. Princeton, NJ: Princeton University Press.

Boix, Carles. 1999. "Setting the Rules of the Game: The Choice of Electoral Systems in Advanced Democracies." *American Political Science Review* 93 (3): 609–24.

———. 2003. *Democracy and Redistribution*. Cambridge: Cambridge University Press.

Bolingbroke, Henry St. John. 1841a. "The Idea of a Patriot King." In *The Works of Lord Bolingbroke, with a Life*, vol. 2, 372–429. Philadelphia: Carey and Hart.

———. 1841b. "A Letter on the Spirit of Patriotism." In *The Works of Lord Bolingbroke, with a Life*, vol. 2, 352–71. Philadelphia: Carey and Hart.

Bonotti, Matteo. 2017. *Partisanship and Political Liberalism in Diverse Societies*. Oxford: Oxford University Press.

Bratman, Michael. 2014. *Shared Agency: A Planning Theory of Acting Together*. New York: Oxford University Press.

Brennan, Geoffrey, and Geoffrey Sayre-McCord. 2015. "Voting and Causal Responsibility." In *Oxford Studies in Political Philosophy*, vol. 1, edited by D. Sobel, P. Vallentyne, and S. Wall, 36–60. Oxford: Oxford University Press.

Brettschneider, Corey. 2010. "When the State Speaks, What Should It Say?" *Perspectives on Politics* 8:1–39.

Brewer, John. 1971. "Party and the Double Cabinet: Two Facets of Burke's Thought." *Historical Journal* 14 (3): 479–501.

———. 1976. *Party Ideology and Popular Politics at the Accession of George III*. Cambridge: Cambridge University Press.

———. 1989. *The Sinews of Power: War, Money and the English State, 1688–1783*. New York: Knopf.

Bronner, Laura, and Nathaniel Rakich. 2021. "Advantage, GOP: Why Democrats Have to Win Large Majorities in Order to Govern While Republicans Don't Need Majorities at All." *FiveThirtyEight*, April 29, 2021.

Brunt, P. A. 1988. *The Fall of the Roman Republic and Related Essays*. Oxford, UK: Clarendon.

Buchanan, Allen. 2002. "Political Legitimacy and Democracy." *Ethics* 112 (4): 689–719.

Burke, Edmund. 1981a. "Observations on a Late State of the Nation." In *The Writings and Speeches of Edmund Burke*, vol. 2, *Party, Parliament, and the American Crisis, 1766–1774*, edited by P. Langford and W. B. Todd, 102–218. Oxford, UK: Clarendon.

———. 1981b. "Thoughts on the Cause of the Present Discontents." In *The Writings and Speeches of Edmund Burke*, vol. 2, *Party, Parliament, and the American Crisis, 1766–1774*, edited by P. Langford and W. B. Todd, 241–322. Oxford, UK: Clarendon.

———. 1987. *Reflections on the Revolution in France*. Indianapolis: Hackett.

Card, David, and Thomas Lemieux. 2001. "Going to College to Avoid the Draft: The Unintended Legacy of the Vietnam War." *American Economic Review* 91 (2): 97–102.

Cartledge, Paul. 2000. "Greek Political Thought: The Historical Context." In *The Cambridge History of Greek and Roman Political Thought*, edited by C. J. Rowe and M. Schofield, 11–22. Cambridge: Cambridge University Press.

Casey, Nicholas. 2018. "Venezuela Delays Presidential Vote, but Opposition Still Plans a Boycott." *New York Times*, March 1, 2018.

Cavanaugh, Gerald J. 1969. "Turgot: The Rejection of Enlightened Despotism." *French Historical Studies* 6 (1): 31–58.

Ceaser, James W. 1979. *Presidential Selection: Theory and Development*. Princeton, NJ: Princeton University Press.

Christiano, Thomas. 1996. *The Rule of the Many: Fundamental Issues in Democratic Theory*. Boulder, CO: Westview.

———. 2008. *The Constitution of Equality*. Oxford: Oxford University Press.

Cicero. 1923. *On Old Age. On Friendship. On Divination*. Translated by W. A. Falconer. Loeb Classical Library 154. Cambridge, MA: Harvard University Press.

———. 1928. *On the Republic. On the Laws*. Translated by Clinton W. Keyes. Loeb Classical Library 213. Cambridge, MA: Harvard University Press.

———. 1931. *Pro Milone. In Pisonem. Pro Scauro. Pro Fonteio. Pro Rabirio Postumo. Pro Marcello. Pro Ligario. Pro Rege Deiotaro*. Translated by N. H. Watts. Loeb Classical Library 252. Cambridge, MA: Harvard University Press.

———. 1954. *Rhetorica ad Herennium*. Translated by Harry Caplan. Loeb Classical Library 403. Cambridge, MA: Harvard University Press.

———. 1958. *Pro Sestio. In Vatinium*. Translated by R. Gardner. Loeb Classical Library 309. Cambridge, MA: Harvard University Press.

———. 1976. *In Catilinam 1–4. Pro Murena. Pro Sulla. Pro Flacco*. Translated by C. Macdonald. Loeb Classical Library 324. Cambridge, MA: Harvard University Press.

———. 2010. *Philippics 1–6*. Edited and translated by D. R. Shackleton Bailey. Revised by John T. Ramsey, Gesine Manuwald. Loeb Classical Library 189. Cambridge, MA: Harvard University Press.

Cicero, Quintus Tullius. 2012. *How to Win an Election: An Ancient Guide for Modern Politicians*. Translated by P. Freeman. Princeton, NJ: Princeton University Press.

Clark, Jonathan C. D. 1980. "A General Theory of Party, Opposition and Government, 1688–1832." *Historical Journal* 23 (2): 295–325.

Cohen, G. A. 2008. *Rescuing Justice and Equality*. Cambridge, MA: Harvard University Press.

Cohen, Joshua. 2009. "Money, Politics, Political Equality." In *Philosophy, Politics, Democracy: Selected Essays*, 268–302. Cambridge, MA: Harvard University Press.

Condorcet, Jean-Antoine-Nicolas de Caritat. 1847a. *Essai sur la constitution et les fonctions des assemblées provinciales*. In *Œuvres de Condorcet*, vol. 8, edited by F. Arago and A. O'Connor, 115–659. Paris: F. Didot Frères.

————. 1847b. "Exposition des principes et des motifs du plan de constitution." In *Œuvres de Condorcet*, vol. 12, edited by F. Arago and A. O'Connor, 335–416. Paris: F. Didot Frères.

————. 1847c. "Projet de constitution française." In *Œuvres de Condorcet*, vol. 12, edited by F. Arago and A. O'Connor, 423–502. Paris: F. Didot Frères.

————. 1847d. "Sur la forme des élections." In *Œuvres de Condorcet*, vol. 9, edited by F. Arago and A. O'Connor, 285–330. Paris: F. Didot Frères.

————. 1847e. "Sur l'étendue des pouvoirs de l'Assemblée nationale." In *Œuvres de Condorcet*, vol. 10, edited by F. Arago and A. O'Connor, 23–34. Paris: F. Didot Frères.

————. 1976. "On the Principles of the Constitutional Plan Presented to the National Convention." In *Condorcet: Selected Writings*, edited by K. M. Baker, 143–82. Indianapolis: Bobbs-Merrill.

————. 1989. *The Political Theory of Condorcet*. Translated by F. Sommerlad and I. McLean. Oxford: University of Oxford, Faculty of Social Studies.

Connor, W. Robert. 1971. *The New Politicians of Fifth-Century Athens*. Princeton, NJ: Princeton University Press.

Constant, Benjamin. 1988. "The Liberty of the Ancients Compared with that of the Moderns." In *Political Writings*, edited by B. Fontana, 309–27. Cambridge: Cambridge University Press.

Cox, Gary W. 1987. *The Efficient Secret: The Cabinet and the Development of Political Parties in Victorian England*. Cambridge: Cambridge University Press.

Crook, Malcolm. 1996. *Elections in the French Revolution: An Apprenticeship in Democracy, 1789–1799*. Cambridge: Cambridge University Press.

Dahl, Robert. 1956. *A Preface to Democratic Theory*. Chicago: University of Chicago Press.

————. 1966. Preface to *Political Oppositions in Western Democracies*, edited by R. A. Dahl, xiii–xxi. New Haven, CT: Yale University Press.

————. 1971. *Polyarchy: Participation and Opposition*. New Haven, CT: Yale University Press.

Demosthenes. 1926. "Olynthiacs." In *Demosthenes Orations*, vol. 1, 4–66. Loeb Classical Library 238. London: Heinemann.

De Roover, Raymond. 1951. "Monopoly Theory Prior to Adam Smith: A Revision." *Quarterly Journal of Economics* 65 (4): 492–524.

De Ste. Croix, Geoffrey E. M. 2004. *Athenian Democratic Origins and Other Essays*. Edited by D. Harvey, R. Parker, and P. Thonemann. Oxford: Oxford University Press.

Dicey, Albert Venn. 2009. *General Characteristics of English Constitutionalism: Six Unpublished Lectures*. New York: Peter Lang.

Disch, Lisa. 2011. "Toward a Mobilization Conception of Democratic Representation." *American Political Science Review* 105 (1): 100–114.

Doyle, William. 1989. *The Oxford History of the French Revolution*. Oxford, UK: Clarendon.

Dworkin, Ronald. 1997. *Freedom's Law: The Moral Reading of the American Constitution*. Cambridge, MA: Harvard University Press.

———. 2000. *Sovereign Virtue: The Theory and Practice of Equality*. Cambridge, MA: Harvard University Press.

———. 2006a. *Is Democracy Possible Here? Principles for a New Political Debate*. Princeton, NJ: Princeton University Press.

———. 2006b. "The Right to Ridicule." *New York Review of Books*, March 23, 2006.

———. 2009. Foreword to *Extreme Speech and Democracy*, edited by I. Hare and J. Weinstein, v–ix. Oxford: Oxford University Press.

Economist. 2020. "Why So Many Singaporeans Voted for the Opposition: Though Not Enough to Boot Out the Ruling Party." July 18, 2020. https://www.economist.com/asia/2020/07/18/why-so-many-singaporeans-voted-for-the-opposition.

Edelstein, Dan. 2009. *The Terror of Natural Right: Republicanism, the Cult of Nature, and the French Revolution*. Chicago: University of Chicago Press.

Edelstein, Melvin. 2014. *The French Revolution and the Birth of Electoral Democracy*. New York: Routledge.

Elster, Jon. 1986. "The Market and the Forum: Three Varieties of Political Theory." In *Foundations of Social Choice Theory*, edited by J. Elster and A. Hylland, 103–32. Cambridge: Cambridge University Press.

———. 1998. Introduction to *Deliberative Democracy*, edited by J. Elster, 1–18. Cambridge: Cambridge University Press.

Engel, Stephen M. 2011. *American Politicians Confront the Court: Opposition Politics and Changing Responses to Judicial Power*. New York: Cambridge University Press.

Estlund, David. 2008. *Democratic Authority: A Philosophical Framework*. Princeton, NJ: Princeton University Press.

Falcón, Henri. 2018. "Why I Am Running for President of Venezuela." *New York Times*, March 16, 2018.

Finlay, Robert. 1980. *Politics in Renaissance Venice*. New Brunswick, NJ: Rutgers University Press.

Fishkin, James S. 2009. *When the People Speak: Deliberative Democracy and Public Consultation*. Oxford: Oxford University Press.

Fishkin, Joseph, and William E. Forbath. 2014. "The Anti-Oligarchy Constitution." *Boston University Law Review* 94 (3): 669–96.

Flower, Harriet I. 2010. *Roman Republics*. Princeton, NJ: Princeton University Press.

Fontana, David. 2009. "Government in Opposition." *Yale Law Journal* 119 (3): 548–623.

Foord, Archibald S. 1964. *His Majesty's Opposition, 1714–1830*. Oxford, UK: Clarendon.

Forsdyke, Sara. 2005. *Exile, Ostracism, and Democracy: The Politics of Expulsion in Ancient Greece*. Princeton, NJ: Princeton University Press.

Frankfurt, Harry G. 1971. "Freedom of the Will and the Concept of a Person." *Journal of Philosophy* 68 (1): 5–20.

Freedom House. 2017. *Freedom in the World 2017: The Annual Survey of Political Rights and Civil Liberties—Methodology*. https://freedomhouse.org /report/methodology-freedom-world-2017.

Frost, Frank J. 1964. "Pericles, Thucydides, Son of Melesias, and Athenian Politics before the War." *Historia: Zeitschrift für Alte Geschichte* 13 (4): 385–99.

———. 1968. "Themistocles' Place in Athenian Politics." *California Studies in Classical Antiquity* 1:105–24.

Furet, François. 1981. *Interpreting the French Revolution*. New York: Cambridge University Press.

Gandhi, Jennifer. 2008. *Political Institutions under Dictatorship*. Cambridge: Cambridge University Press.

Gandhi, Jennifer, and Ellen Lust-Okar. 2009. "Elections under Authoritarianism." *Annual Review of Political Science* 12:403–22.

Garat, Dominique-Joseph. 1821. *Mémoires historiques sur le XVIIIe. siècle, et sur M. Suard*. 2 vols. Paris: A. Belin.

Gardner, Amy, and Lori Rozsa. 2020. "In Florida, Felons Must Pay Court Debts before They Can Vote. But with No System to Do So, Many Have Found It Impossible." *Washington Post*, May 13, 2020.

Garsten, Bryan. 2010. "Representative Government and Popular Sovereignty." In *Representation*, edited by I. Shapiro, S. Stokes, E. Wood, and A. Kirshner, 90–110. Cambridge: Cambridge University Press.

Gelzer, Matthias, and Matthias Gelzer. 1969. *The Roman Nobility*. Oxford, UK: Blackwell.

Gerken, Heather. 2014. "The Loyal Opposition." *Yale Law Journal* 123 (6): 1958–94.

Gilabert, Pablo, and Holly Lawford-Smith. 2012. "Political Feasibility: A Conceptual Exploration." *Political Studies* 60 (4): 809–25.

Gilbert, Margaret. 1990. "Walking Together: A Paradigmatic Social Phenomenon." *MidWest Studies in Philosophy* 15 (1): 1–14.

Gilens, Martin. 2012. *Affluence and Influence: Economic Inequality and Political Power in America*. Princeton, NJ: Princeton University Press.

Goldman, William. 2007. *The Princess Bride: S. Morgenstern's Classic Tale of True Love and High Adventure*. New York: Houghton Mifflin Harcourt.

Gooch, R. K. 1960. *Parliamentary Government in France: Revolutionary Origins, 1789–1791*. Ithaca, NY: Cornell University Press.

Goodin, Robert E. 2008. *Innovating Democracy: Democratic Theory and Practice after the Deliberative Turn*. Oxford: Oxford University Press.

Goodin, Robert E., and Kai Spiekermann. 2012. "Epistemic Aspects of Representative Government." *European Political Science Review* 4 (3): 1–23.

Goodwin, Doris Kearns. 2005. *Team of Rivals: The Political Genius of Abraham Lincoln*. New York: Simon and Schuster.

Gruen, Erich S. 1991. "Politics in Conflict: The Exercise of Power in the Roman Republic." In *City States in Classical Antiquity and Medieval Italy: Athens and Rome, Florence and Venice*, edited by A. Molho, K. A. Raaflaub, J. Emlen, and T. J. Watson Jr., 251–67. Stuttgart: F. Steiner.

Gueniffey, Patrice. 1989. "Elections." In *A Critical Dictionary of the French Revolution*, edited by F. O. Furet and M. Ozouf, 33–44. Cambridge, MA: Harvard University Press.

———. 1993a. *Le nombre et la raison: La Révolution française et les élections*. Paris: Editions de l'Ecole des hautes études en sciences sociales.

———. 1993b. "Revolutionary Democracy and the Elections." In *The French Revolution and the Meaning of Citizenship*, edited by R. E. Waldinger, P. Dawson, and I. Woloch, 89–103. Westport, CT: Greenwood.

Guerrero, Alexander A. 2014. "Against Elections: The Lottocratic Alternative." *Philosophy & Public Affairs* 42 (2): 135–78.

Gunn, J. A. W. 2009. *When the French Tried to Be British: Party, Opposition, and the Quest for Civil Disagreement, 1814–1848*. Montréal: McGill-Queen's University Press.

Habermas, Jürgen. 1998. *Between Facts and Norms: Contributions to a Discourse Theory of Law and Democracy*. Translated by W. Rehg. Cambridge, MA: MIT Press.

Hansen, Mogens Herman. 1974. *The Sovereignty of the People's Court in Athens in the Fourth Century B.C. and the Public Action against Unconstitutional Proposals*. Odense: Odense Universitetsforlag.

———. 1991. *The Athenian Democracy in the Age of Demosthenes: Structure, Principles, and Ideology*. Norman: University of Oklahoma Press.

Harrington, James. 1992. *The Commonwealth of Oceana*. Cambridge: Cambridge University Press.

Hasen, Richard L. 2011. "Citizens United and the Illusion of Coherence." *Michigan Law Review* 109 (4): 581–624.

Havel, Václav. 1985. "The Power of the Powerless." In *The Power of the Powerless: Citizens against the State in Central-Eastern Europe*, edited by J. Keane, 23–96. Armonk, NY: M. E. Sharpe.

Heath, Joseph. 2016. "On the Scalability of Cooperative Structures: Remarks on G. A. Cohen, Why Not Socialism?" Paper presented at Duke University, April 1, 2016.

Herman, Lise Esther. 2017. "Democratic Partisanship: From Theoretical Ideal to Empirical Standard." *American Political Science Review* 111 (4): 738–54.

Herman, Lise Esther, and Russell Muirhead. 2020. "Resisting Abusive Legalism: Electoral Fairness and the Partisan Commitment to Political Pluralism." *Representation*, April 8, 2020, 1–21.

Herodotus. 1987. *The History*. Translated by David Grene. Chicago: University of Chicago Press.

Hofstadter, Richard. 1969. *The Idea of a Party System: The Rise of Legitimate Opposition in the United States, 1780–1840*. Berkeley: University of California Press.

Hume, David. 1994a. "Idea of a Perfect Commonwealth." In *Essays, Moral, Political and Literary*, edited by E. F. Miller, 512–29. Indianapolis: Liberty Classics.

———. 1994b. "Of Parties in General." In *Essays, Moral, Political and Literary*, edited by E. F. Miller, 54–62. Indianapolis: Liberty Classics.

———. 1994c. "Of the Independency of Parliament." In *Essays, Moral, Political and Literary*, edited by E. F. Miller, 42–46. Indianapolis: Liberty Classics.

———. 1994d. "That Politics May Be Reduced to a Science." In *Essays, Moral, Political and Literary*, edited by E. F. Miller, 14–31. Indianapolis: Liberty Classics.

Hunt, Lynn. 1984. *Politics, Culture, and Class in the French Revolution*. Berkeley: University of California Press.

Huntington, Samuel P. 1991. *The Third Wave: Democratization in the Late Twentieth Century*. Norman: University of Oklahoma Press.

Hussain, Waheed. 2020. "Pitting People against Each Other." *Philosophy & Public Affairs* 48 (1): 79–113.

Issacharoff, Samuel, and Pamela S. Karlan. 1999. "The Hydraulics of Campaign Finance Reform." *Texas Law Review* 77:1705–38.

Jefferson, Thomas. 1792b. 1792a. "From Thomas Jefferson to George Washington, 23 May 1792." National Archives. Accessed at Founders Online.

———. "From Thomas Jefferson to George Washington, 9 September 1792." National Archives. Accessed at Founders Online.

———. 2000. "Notes on the Letter of Christoph Daniel Ebeling." In *The Papers of Thomas Jefferson*, vol. 28, *1 January 1794 to 29 February 1796*, edited by J. Catanzariti, 506–9. Princeton, NJ: Princeton University Press.

Kagan, Donald. 1961. "The Origin and Purposes of Ostracism." *Hesperia* 30 (4): 293–401.

Kagan, Elena. 1996. "Private Speech, Public Purpose: The Role of Governmental Motive in First Amendment Doctrine." *University of Chicago Law Review* 63 (2): 413–517.

Kasparov, Garry. 2017. "Did he also announce the results? Would save every-one a lot of time and effort." Twitter, December 6, 2017. https://twitter.com/Kasparov63/status/938431455146979329.

Kennedy, Joseph C. G. 1864. *Population of the United States in 1860: Compiled from the Original Returns of the Eighth Census under the Direction of the Secretary of the Interior.* Washington, DC: Bureau of the Census Library; Government Printing Office.

Kennedy, Michael L. 1982. *The Jacobin Clubs in the French Revolution: The First Years.* Princeton, NJ: Princeton University Press.

Kirshner, Alexander S. 2014. *A Theory of Militant Democracy: The Ethics of Combatting Political Extremism.* New Haven, CT: Yale University Press.

Kishlansky, Mark A. 1986. *Parliamentary Selection: Social and Political Choice in Early Modern England.* Cambridge: Cambridge University Press.

Klarman, Michael J. 2020. "The Degradation of American Democracy-and the Court." *Harvard Law Review* 134:4–264.

Klein, Steven. 2020. *The Work of Politics: Democratic Transformations in the Welfare State.* Cambridge: Cambridge University Press.

Kolodny, Niko. 2014a. "Rule over None I: What Justifies Democracy?" *Philosophy & Public Affairs* 42 (3): 195–229.

———. 2014b. "Rule over None II: Social Equality and the Justification of Democracy." *Philosophy & Public Affairs* 42 (4): 287–336.

Kramnick, Isaac. 1968. *Bolingbroke and His Circle: The Politics of Nostalgia in the Age of Walpole.* Cambridge, MA: Harvard University Press.

Krentz, Peter. 1984. "The Ostracism of Thoukydides, Son of Melesias." *Historia: Zeitschrift für Alte Geschichte* 33 (4): 499–504.

Kutz, Christopher. 2000. *Complicity: Ethics and Law for a Collective Age.* Cambridge: Cambridge University Press.

Laclau, Ernesto. 2005. *On Populist Reason.* London: Verso.

Ladha, Krishna K. 1992. "The Condorcet Jury Theorem, Free Speech, and Correlated Votes." *American Journal of Political Science* 36 (3): 617–34.

Lafont, Cristina. 2019. *Democracy without Shortcuts: A Participatory Conception of Deliberative Democracy.* Oxford: Oxford University Press.

Landa, Dimitri, and Ryan Pevnick. 2021. "Is Random Selection a Cure for the Ills of Electoral Representation?" *Journal of Political Philosophy* 29 (1): 46–72.

Landemore, Hélène. 2013. *Democratic Reason: Politics, Collective Intelligence, and the Rule of the Many.* Princeton, NJ: Princeton University Press.

———. 2020. *Open Democracy: Reinventing Popular Rule for the Twenty-First Century.* Princeton, NJ: Princeton University Press.

Lawrence, Charles R. 1990. "If He Hollers Let Him Go: Regulating Racist Speech on Campus." *Duke Law Journal* 1990 (3): 431–83.

Lefkowitz, David. 2007. "On a Moral Right to Civil Disobedience." *Ethics* 117 (2): 202–33.

Leonard, Gerald. 2002. *The Invention of Party Politics: Federalism, Popular Sovereignty, and Constitutional Development in Jacksonian Illinois.* Chapel Hill: University of North Carolina Press.

Lessig, Lawrence. 2011. *Republic, Lost: How Money Corrupts Congress—and a Plan to Stop It.* New York: Hachette.

Levinson, Daryl J., and Richard H. Pildes. 2006. "Separation of Parties, Not Powers." *Harvard Law Review* 119 (8): 2312–85.

Levitsky, Steven, and Daniel Ziblatt. 2018. *How Democracies Die.* New York: Crown.

Lintott, Andrew. 1990. "Electoral Bribery in the Roman Republic." *Journal of Roman Studies* 80:1–16.

———. 1999a. *The Constitution of the Roman Republic.* Oxford, UK: Clarendon.

———. 1999b. *Violence in Republican Rome.* Oxford: Oxford University Press.

Lipsey, R. G., and Kelvin Lancaster. 1956–57. "The General Theory of the Second Best." *Review of Economic Studies* 24 (1): 11–32.

Livy. 1959. *History of Rome.* Vol. 14, *Summaries. Fragments. Julius Obsequens. General Index.* Translated by Alfred C. Schlesinger. Index by Russel M. Geer. Loeb Classical Library 404. Cambridge, MA: Harvard University Press.

———. 2018a. *History of Rome.* Vol. 10, *Books 35–37.* Edited and translated by J. C. Yardley. Loeb Classical Library 301. Cambridge, MA: Harvard University Press.

———. 2018b. *History of Rome.* Vol. 11, *Books 38–40.* Edited and translated by J. C. Yardley. Loeb Classical Library 313. Cambridge, MA: Harvard University Press.

Loewenstein, Karl. 1937. "Militant Democracy and Fundamental Rights, I." *American Political Science Review* 31 (3):417–32.

López-Guerra, Claudio. 2011. "The Enfranchisement Lottery." *Politics Philosophy & Economics* 10 (2): 211–33.

———. 2014. *Democracy and Disenfranchisement: The Morality of Electoral Exclusions.* Oxford: Oxford University Press.

López-Guerra, Claudio, and Alexander S. Kirshner. 2020. "Donald Trump Can—and Should—Be Stopped from Running in 2024." *Guardian,* December 4, 2020.

MacFarquhar, Neil. 2017. "Russian Socialite Enters Race to Challenge President Putin." *New York Times,* October 18, 2017.

Mackay, Christopher S. 2004. *Ancient Rome: A Military and Political History.* Cambridge: Cambridge University Press.

———. 2009. *The Breakdown of the Roman Republic: From Oligarchy to Empire*. New York: Cambridge University Press.

Madison, James. 1961a. "Federalist 10." In *The Federalist*, edited by J. E. Cooke, 56–65. Middletown, CT: Wesleyan University Press.

———. 1961b. "Federalist 51." In *The Federalist*, edited by J. E. Cooke, 347–53. Middletown, CT: Wesleyan University Press.

Maguire, Marti. 2016. "North Carolina Republicans Try to Strip Powers from Incoming Democratic Governor." Reuters, December 15, 2016.

Malkopoulou, Anthoula, and Alexander S. Kirshner, eds. 2019. *Militant Democracy and Its Critics: Populism, Parties, Extremism*. Edinburgh: Edinburgh University Press.

Malkopoulou, Anthoula, and Ludvig Norman. 2018. "Three Models of Democratic Self-Defence: Militant Democracy and Its Alternatives." *Political Studies* 66 (2): 442–58.

Manin, Bernard. 1997. *The Principles of Representative Government*. Cambridge: Cambridge University Press.

Mansbridge, Jane J. 1980. *Beyond Adversary Democracy*. New York: Basic Books.

Mansfield, Harvey C. 1965. *Statesmanship and Party Government: A Study of Burke and Bolingbroke*. Chicago: University of Chicago Press.

Margalit, Avishai. 1983. "Ideals and Second Bests." In *Philosophy for Education 77*, edited by S. Fox, 77–89. Jerusalem: Van Leer Foundation.

Markovits, Daniel. 2004. "Democratic Disobedience." *Yale Law Journal* 114:1897–1952.

Marshall, Monty G., Ted Robert Gurr, and Keith Jaggers. 2017. "Polity IV: Political Regime Characteristics and Transitions, 1800–2016." Edited by C. F. S. Peace. George Mason University, Fairfax, VA.

Masket, Seth E. 2016. *The Inevitable Party: Why Attempts to Kill the Party System Fail and How They Weaken Democracy*. New York: Oxford University Press.

Matsuda, Mari J. 1989. "Public Response to Racist Speech: Considering the Victim's Story." *Michigan Law Review* 87 (8): 2320–81.

McCormick, John P. 2011. *Machiavellian Democracy*. New York: Cambridge University Press.

Medearis, John. 2009. *Joseph A. Schumpeter*. New York: Continuum.

Mill, John Stuart. 2008a. *Considerations on Representative Government*. In *"On Liberty" and Other Essays*, edited by J. Gray, 203–470. New York: Oxford University Press.

———. 2008b. "On Liberty." In *"On Liberty" and Other Essays*, edited by J. Gray, 5–130. New York: Oxford University Press.

Millar, Fergus. 1984. "The Political Character of the Classical Roman Republic, 200–151 BC." *Journal of Roman Studies* 74:1–19.

———. 1986. "Politics, Persuasion and the People before the Social War (150–90 BC)." *Journal of Roman Studies* 76:1–11.

———. 1998. *The Crowd in Rome in the Late Republic*. Ann Arbor: University of Michigan Press.

Missiou, Anna. 2011. *Literacy and Democracy in Fifth-Century Athens*. Cambridge: Cambridge University Press.

Mitchell, T. N. 1971. "Cicero and the Senatus 'consultum ultimum.'" *Historia: Zeitschrift für Alte Geschichte* 20 (1): 47–61.

Monoson, S. Sara. 1994. "Frank Speech, Democracy, and Philosophy: Plato's Debt to a Democratic Strategy of Civic Discourse." In *Athenian Political Thought and the Reconstruction of American Democracy*, edited by J. P. Euben, J. R. Wallach, and J. Ober, 172–97. Ithaca, NY: Cornell University Press.

Montesquieu, Charles de Secondat. 1965. *Considerations on the Causes of the Greatness of the Romans and Their Decline*. Translated by David Lowenthal. New York: Free Press.

———. 1989. *The Spirit of the Laws*. Translated by A. M. Cohler, B. C. Miller, and H. S. Stone. Cambridge: Cambridge University Press.

Morgan, Edmund S. 1986. "Safety in Numbers: Madison, Hume, and the Tenth 'Federalist.'" *Huntington Library Quarterly* 49 (2): 95–112.

Morstein-Marx, Robert. 2004. *Mass Oratory and Political Power in the Late Roman Republic*. Cambridge: Cambridge University Press.

Mouffe, Chantal. 2000. *The Democratic Paradox*. New York: Verso.

Mounk, Yascha. 2018. *The People vs. Democracy: Why Our Freedom Is in Danger and How to Save It*. Cambridge, MA: Harvard University Press.

Mouritsen, Henrik. 2001. *Plebs and Politics in the Late Roman Republic*. Cambridge: Cambridge University Press.

Mudde, Cas, and Cristóbal Rovira Kaltwasser. 2012. *Populism in Europe and the Americas: Threat or Corrective for Democracy?* Cambridge: Cambridge University Press.

Muirhead, Russell. 2014. *The Promise of Party in a Polarized Age*. Cambridge, MA: Harvard University Press.

Muirhead, Russell, and Nancy L. Rosenblum. 2020. "The Political Theory of Parties and Partisanship: Catching Up." *Annual Review of Political Science* 23:95–110.

Müller, Jan-Werner. 2016. *What Is Populism?* Philadelphia: University of Pennsylvania Press.

———. 2018. "Homo Orbánicus." *New York Review of Books*, April 5, 2018.

Münzer, Friedrich. 1999. *Roman Aristocratic Parties and Families*. Baltimore: Johns Hopkins University Press.

Namier, L. B. 1952. *Monarchy and the Party System*. Oxford, UK: Clarendon.

New York Times. 2016. "Transcript of the Second Debate." October 10, 2016.

North, John A. 1990. "Democratic Politics in Republican Rome." *Past & Present* 126:3–21.

Nozick, Robert. 1969. "Coercion." In *Philosophy, Science, and Method: Essays in Honor of Ernest Nagel*, edited by S. Morgenbesser, P. Suppes, and M. White, 440–72. New York: St. Martin's.

Ober, Josiah. 1989. *Mass and Elite in Democratic Athens: Rhetoric, Ideology, and the Power of the People*. Princeton, NJ: Princeton University Press.

———. 1998. *Political Dissent in Democratic Athens*. Princeton, NJ: Princeton University Press.

———. 2008. *Democracy and Knowledge: Innovation and Learning in Classical Athens*. Princeton, NJ: Princeton University Press.

Ostwald, Martin. 1955. "The Athenian Legislation against Tyranny and Subversion." *Transactions and Proceedings of the American Philological Association* 86:103–28.

———. 1988. "The Reform of the Athenian State by Cleisthenes." In *The Cambridge Ancient History*, edited by John Boardman, N. Hammond, D. M. Lewis, and M. Ostwald, 303–46. Cambridge: Cambridge University Press.

Owen, J. B. 1972. "Political Patronage in 18th Century England." In *The Triumph of Culture: 18th Century Perspectives*, edited by P. Fritz and D. Williams, 369–87. Toronto: A. M. Hakkert.

Pasquino, Pasquale. 1998. *Sieyès et l'invention de la constitution en France*. Paris: O. Jacob.

Pettit, Philip. 1997. *Republicanism: A Theory of Freedom and Government*. Oxford: Oxford University Press.

———. 2012. *On the People's Terms: A Republican Theory and Model of Democracy*. Cambridge: Cambridge University Press.

———. 2013. "A Response to Roger Scruton: No, Democracy Is Not Overrated." *Politics and Policy* (blog), August 24, 2013. http://blogs.lse.ac.uk/politicsandpolicy/a-response-to-roger-scruton-no-democracy-is-not-overrated/.

Piano, Natasha. 2019. "Revisiting Democratic Elitism: The Italian School of Elitism, American Political Science, and the Problem of Plutocracy." *Journal of Politics* 81 (2): 524–38.

Plato. 1981. *Five Dialogues: Euthyphro, Apology, Crito, Meno, Phaedo*. Translated by G. M. A. Grube. Indianapolis: Hackett.

Plumb, J. H. 1967. *The Origins of Political Stability, England, 1675–1725*. Boston: Houghton Mifflin.

Plutarch. 1914a. "Life of Aristeides." In *Plutarch's Lives*, vol. 2, translated by B. Perrin, 211–99. London: Heinemann.

———. 1914b. "Life of Kimon." In *Plutarch's Lives*, vol. 2, translated by B. Perrin, 405–68. London: Heinemann.

————. 1914c. "Life of Themistokles." in *Plutarch's Lives*, vol. 2, translated by B. Perrin, 1–92. London: Heinemann.

————. 1916. "Life of Perikles." In *Plutarch's Lives*, vol. 3, translated by B. Perrin, 3–91. London: Heinemann.

————. 1920. *Lives*. Vol. 9, *Demetrius and Antony. Pyrrhus and Gaius Marius*. Translated by B. Perrin. Loeb Classical Library 101. Cambridge, MA: Harvard University Press.

————. 1921. *Lives*. Vol. 10, *Agis and Cleomenes. Tiberius and Gaius Gracchus. Philopoemen and Flamininus*. Translated by B. Perrin. Loeb Classical Library 102. Cambridge, MA: Harvard University Press.

Pocock, J. G. A. 2003. *The Machiavellian Moment: Florentine Political Thought and the Atlantic Republican Tradition*. 2nd pbk. ed. Princeton, NJ: Princeton University Press.

Polybius. 2011. *The Histories*. Vol. 3, *Books 5–8*. Translated by W. R. Paton. Revised by F. W. Walbank and Christian Habicht. Loeb Classical Library 138. Cambridge, MA: Harvard University Press.

Posner, Daniel. 2004. "The Political Salience of Cultural Differences: Why Chewas and Tumbukas are Allies in Zambia and Adversaries in Malawi." *American Political Science Review* 98 (3): 529–45.

Posner, Eric A., and Adrian Vermeule. 2010. *The Executive Unbound: After the Madisonian Republic*. New York: Oxford University Press.

Przeworski, Adam. 1991. *Democracy and the Market: Political and Economic Reforms in Eastern Europe and Latin America*. Cambridge: Cambridge University Press.

————. 1999. "Minimalist Conception of Democracy: A Defense." In *Democracy's Value*, edited by I. Shapiro and C. Hacker-Cordón, 23–55. Cambridge: Cambridge University Press.

————. 2005. "Democracy as an Equilibrium." *Public Choice* 123:253–73.

————. 2010. *Democracy and the Limits of Self-Government*. New York: Cambridge University Press.

————. 2011. "Divided We Stand? Democracy as a Method of Processing Conflicts 1: The 2010 Johan Skytte Prize Lecture." *Scandinavian Political Studies* 34 (2): 168–82.

————. 2015. "Acquiring the Habit of Changing Governments through Elections." *Comparative Political Studies* 48 (1): 101–29.

————. 2019. *Crises of Democracy*. Cambridge: Cambridge University Press.

Putin, Vladimir. 2018. Speech at the inauguration ceremony as President of Russia. May 14, 2018. http://en.kremlin.ru/events/president/news/57416.

Quong, Jonathan. 2004. "The Rights of the Unreasonable Citizens." *Journal of Political Philosophy* 12 (3): 314–35.

Raaflaub, Kurt A. 2005. "From Protection and Defense to Offense and Participation: Stages in the Conflict of Orders." In *Social Struggles in Archaic*

Rome: New Perspectives on the Conflict of the Orders, edited by K. Raaflaub, 1–46. Malden, MA: Blackwell.

Rabaut, Jean-Paul. 1793. *The History of the Revolution in France, Translated . . . by James White, Esq.* London: J. Debrett.

Raubitschek, A. E. 1960. "Theopompos on Thucydides the Son of Melesias." *Phoenix* 14 (2): 81–95.

Raz, Joseph. 1986. *The Morality of Freedom.* Oxford: Oxford University Press.

Reuters. 2018. "Venezuela Opposition to Boycott 'Fraudulent' Presidential Vote." February 21, 2018.

Rhodes, Peter John. 1986. "Political Activity in Classical Athens." *Journal of Hellenic Studies* 106:132–44.

———. 2000. "Who Ran Democratic Athens?" In *Polis and Politics*, edited by P. Flensted-Jensen, T. H. Nielsen, and L. Rubinstein, 465–77. Aarhus, Denmark: Museum Tusculanum Press.

Robbins, Caroline. 1958. " 'Discordant Parties': A Study of the Acceptance of Party by Englishmen." *Political Science Quarterly* 73 (4): 505–29.

———. 1959. *The Eighteenth-Century Commonwealthman: Studies in the Transmission, Development, and Circumstance of English Liberal Thought from the Restoration of Charles II until the War with the Thirteen Colonies.* Cambridge, MA: Harvard University Press.

Rosanvallon, Pierre. 2008. *Counter-democracy: Politics in an Age of Distrust.* Translated by A. Goldhammer. Cambridge: Cambridge University Press.

Rosenblum, Nancy L. 2008. *On the Side of the Angels: An Appreciation of Parties and Partisanship.* Princeton, NJ: Princeton University Press.

Rosenbluth, Frances McCall, and Ian Shapiro. 2018. *Responsible Parties: Saving Democracy from Itself.* New Haven, CT: Yale University Press.

Rosenstein, Nathan. 1993. "Competition and Crisis in Mid-Republican Rome." *Phoenix* 47 (4): 313–38.

Rousseau, Jean-Jacques. 1997a. *Considerations on the Government of Poland.* In *"The Social Contract" and Other Later Political Writings*, edited by V. Gourevitch, 177–260. Cambridge: Cambridge University Press.

———. 1997b. *The Social Contract.* In *"The Social Contract" and Other Later Political Writings*, edited by V. Gourevitch, 39–152. Cambridge: Cambridge University Press.

Rovira Kaltwasser, Cristóbal. 2014. "The Responses of Populism to Dahl's Democratic Dilemmas." *Political Studies* 62 (3): 470–87.

Rovira Kaltwasser, Cristóbal, Paul A Taggart, Paulina Ochoa Espejo, and Pierre Ostiguy. 2017. *The Oxford Handbook of Populism.* Oxford: Oxford University Press.

Rubinstein, Nicolai. 1997. *The Government of Florence under the Medici (1434 to 1494).* 2nd ed. Oxford, UK: Clarendon.

Rummens, Stefan. 2017. "Populism as a Threat to Liberal Democracy." In *The Oxford Handbook of Populism*, edited by C. R. Kaltwasser, P. Taggart, P. O. Espejo, and P. Ostiguy, 571–89. Oxford: Oxford University Press.

Saez, Emmanuel, and Gabriel Zucman. 2014. "Wealth Inequality in the United States since 1913: Evidence from Capitalized Income Tax Data." Working Paper no. w20625. National Bureau of Economic Research, Cambridge, MA.

Sallust. 2013. *The War with Catiline; The War with Jugurtha*. Edited by J. T. Ramsey. Translated by J. C. Rolfe. Loeb Classical Library 116. Cambridge, MA: Harvard University Press.

Saxonhouse, Arlene W. 2006. *Free Speech and Democracy in Ancient Athens*. New York: Cambridge University Press.

Scanlon, Thomas. 1972. "A Theory of Freedom of Expression." *Philosophy & Public Affairs* 1 (2): 204–26.

———. 1986. "The Significance of Choice." *Tanner Lectures on Human Values* 7:149–216.

Schedler, Andreas. 2009. "Electoral Authoritarianism." In *The Sage Handbook of Comparative Politics*, edited by T. Landman and N. Robinson, 381–93. Thousand Oaks, CA: Sage.

———. 2020. "Democratic Reciprocity." *Journal of Political Philosophy* 29 (2): 252–78.

Schmitt, Carl. 1988. *The Crisis of Parliamentary Democracy*. Translated by E. Kennedy. Cambridge, MA: MIT Press.

Schumpeter, Joseph A. 1943. *Capitalism, Socialism, and Democracy*. Abingdon, UK: Routledge.

Schupmann, Benjamin A. 2017. *Carl Schmitt's State and Constitutional Theory: A Critical Analysis*. Oxford: Oxford University Press.

Schwartzberg, Melissa Ann. 2007. *Democracy and Legal Change*. Cambridge: Cambridge University Press.

Seelye, Katharine Q. 2004. "Cheney's Five Draft Deferments during the Vietnam Era Emerge as a Campaign Issue." *New York Times*, May 1, 2004.

Selinger, Jeffrey S. 2012. "Rethinking the Development of Legitimate Party Opposition in the United States, 1793–1828." *Political Science Quarterly* 127 (2): 263–87.

———. 2016. *Embracing Dissent: Political Violence and Party Development in the United States*. Philadelphia: University of Pennsylvania Press.

Selinger, William. 2019. *Parliamentarism: From Burke to Weber*. Cambridge: Cambridge University Press.

Sen, Amartya. 1992. *Inequality Reexamined*. New York; Cambridge, MA: Russell Sage Foundation; Harvard University Press.

Shackleton, Robert. 1949. "Montesquieu, Bolingbroke, and the Separation of Powers." *French Studies* 3 (1): 25–38.

Shapiro, Ian. 1999. *Democratic Justice*. New Haven, CT: Yale University Press.

—. 2016. *Politics against Domination*. Cambridge, MA: Harvard University Press.

Sherif, Muzafer. 1967. *Group Conflict and Co-operation: Their Social Psychology*. London: Routledge and K. Paul.

Sieyès, Emmanuel Joseph. 2003a. "Views on the Executive Means Available to the Representatives of France in 1789." In *Political Writings: Including the Debate between Sieyès and Tom Paine in 1791*, edited and translated by M. Sonenscher, 1–67. Indianapolis: Hackett.

—. 2003b. "What Is the Third Estate?" In *Political Writings: Including the Debate between Sieyès and Tom Paine in 1791*, edited and translated by M. Sonenscher, 92–162. Indianapolis: Hackett.

—. 2014. "Views Concerning Several Articles of Section IV and V of the Draft Constitution." In *Emmanuel Joseph Sieyès: The Essential Political Writings*, edited by O. W. Lembcke and F. Weber, 152–69. Leiden: Brill.

Simmel, Georg, Kurt H. Wolff, and Reinhard Bendix. 1955. *Conflict*. Glencoe, IL: Free Press.

Simpser, Alberto. 2013. *Why Governments and Parties Manipulate Elections: Theory, Practice, and Implications*. Cambridge: Cambridge University Press.

Sinclair, R. K. 1988. *Democracy and Participation in Athens*. Cambridge: Cambridge University Press.

Skinner, Quentin. 1974. "The Principles and Practice of Opposition: The Case of Bolingbroke versus Walpole." In *Historical Perspectives: Studies in English Thought and Society*, edited by N. McKendrick, 93–128. London: Europa.

Skjönsberg, Max. 2016. "Lord Bolingbroke's Theory of Party and Opposition." *Historical Journal* 59 (4): 947–73.

—. 2021. *The Persistence of Party: Ideas of Harmonious Discord in Eighteenth-Century Britain*. Cambridge: Cambridge University Press.

Smith, Mitch, and Monica Davey. 2018. "Wisconsin's Scott Walker Signs Bills Stripping Powers From Incoming Governor." *New York Times*, December 14, 2018.

Smith, Paul. 2020. " 'Use It or Lose It': The Problem of Purges from the Registration Rolls of Voters Who Don't Vote Regularly." *Human Rights Magazine* (American Bar Association) 45 (1). https://www.americanbar.org/groups/crsj/publications/human_rights_magazine_home/voting-rights/-use-it-or-lose-it---the-problem-of-purges-from-the-registration0/.

Snyder, Timothy. 2017. *On Tyranny: Twenty Lessons from the Twentieth Century*. New York: Tim Duggan Books.

Sonenscher, Michael. 2003. Introduction to *Political Writings: Including the Debate between Sieyès and Tom Paine in 1791*, by E. J. Sieyès, vii–lxiv. Indianapolis: Hackett.

Spencer, Mark G. 2002. "Hume and Madison on Faction." *William and Mary Quarterly* 59 (4): 869–96.

Stilz, Anna. 2009. *Liberal Loyalty: Freedom, Obligation, and the State*. Princeton, NJ: Princeton University Press.

———. 2016. "The Value of Self-Determination." In *Oxford Studies in Political Philosophy*, vol. 2, edited by D. Sobel, P. Vallentyne, and S. Wall, 98–127. Oxford: Oxford University Press.

Straumann, Benjamin. 2016. *Crisis and Constitutionalism: Roman Political Thought from the Fall of the Republic to the Age of Revolution*. Oxford: Oxford University Press.

Strauss, Barry S. 1987. *Athens after the Peloponnesian War: Class, Faction, and Policy, 403–386 BC*. Ithaca, NY: Cornell University Press.

Sullivan, Andy. 2019. "Southern U.S. States Have Closed 1,200 Polling Places in Recent Years: Rights Group." Reuters, September 10, 2019.

Sullivan, Kathleen M. 1997. "Political Money and Freedom of Speech." *UC Davis Law Review* 30:663–90.

Syme, Ronald. 2002. *The Roman Revolution*. Oxford: Oxford University Press.

Tackett, Timothy. 1996. *Becoming a Revolutionary: The Deputies of the French National Assembly and the Emergence of a Revolutionary Culture (1789–1790)*. Princeton, NJ: Princeton University Press.

———. 2015. *The Coming of the Terror in the French Revolution*. Cambridge, MA: Harvard University Press.

Taylor, Lily Ross. 1966. *Roman Voting Assemblies from the Hannibalic War to the Dictatorship of Caesar*. Ann Arbor: University of Michigan Press.

Teegarden, David. 2013. *Death to Tyrants! Ancient Greek Democracy and the Struggle against Tyranny*. Princeton, NJ: Princeton University Press.

Thommen, Lukas. 1995. "Les lieux de la plèbe et de ses tribuns dans la Rome républicaine." *Klio-Beiträge zur alten Geschichte* 77 (JG): 358–70.

Thompson, Dennis F. 1976. *John Stuart Mill and Representative Government*. Princeton, NJ: Princeton University Press.

Thucydides. 2009. *The Peloponnesian War*. Edited by P. J. Rhodes. Translated by Martin Hammond. Oxford World's Classics. Oxford: Oxford University Press.

Timm, Jane C. 2019. "North Carolina Judges Slam GOP Gerrymandering in Stinging Ruling, Reject District Maps: The Ruling Found State Legislative Boundaries Were So Partisan They Violated the State Constitution." *NBC News*, September 3, 2019.

Tocqueville, Alexis de. 2011. *Tocqueville: The Ancien Régime and the French Revolution*. Edited by J. Elster. Translated by A. Goldhammer. New York: Cambridge University Press.

Tuck, Richard. 2008. *Free Riding*. Cambridge, MA: Harvard University Press.

Tulis, Jeffrey K. 1987. *The Rhetorical Presidency.* Princeton, NJ: Princeton University Press.

Turgot, Anne-Robert-Jacques. 1913. "Éloge de Vincent de Gournay." In *Œuvres de Turgot et documents le concernant, avec biographie et notes,* vol. 1, edited by G. Schelle, 595–621. Paris: F. Alcan.

———. 1922. "Mémoires sur les municipalités." In *Œuvres de Turgot et documents le concernant, avec biographie et notes,* vol. 4, edited by G. Schelle, 566–620. Paris: F. Alcan.

Urbinati, Nadia. 1998. "Democracy and Populism." *Constellations* 5 (1): 110–24.

———. 2006. *Representative Democracy: Principles and Genealogy.* Chicago: University of Chicago Press.

———. 2014. *Democracy Disfigured: Opinion, Truth, and the People.* Cambridge, MA: Harvard University Press.

Vardi, Liana. 2012. *The Physiocrats and the World of the Enlightenment.* Cambridge: Cambridge University Press.

Viehoff, Daniel. 2014. "Democratic Equality and Political Authority." *Philosophy & Public Affairs* 42 (4): 337–75.

Waldron, Jeremy. 1989. "Rights in Conflict." *Ethics* 99 (3): 503–19.

———. 1999. *Law and Disagreement.* Oxford: Oxford University Press.

———. 2012. *The Harm in Hate Speech.* Cambridge, MA: Harvard University Press.

———. 2016. *Political Political Theory: Essays on Institutions.* Cambridge, MA: Harvard University Press.

Walton, Charles. 2015. "Clubs, Parties, Factions." In *The Oxford Handbook of the French Revolution,* edited by D. Andress, 362–81. Oxford: Oxford University Press.

Washington, George. 1796. "Farewell Address." National Archives. Accessed at the Avalon Project, Yale Law School.

———. 1797. "From George Washington to Jonathan Trumbull, Jr., 3 March 1797." National Archives. Accessed at Founders Online.

Wasserman, David. 2017. "The Congressional Map Has a Record-Setting Bias against Democrats." *FiveThirtyEight,* August 7, 2017.

Watson, Gary. 1975. "Free Agency." *Journal of Philosophy* 72 (8): 205–20.

Wedeen, Lisa. 1999. *Ambiguities of Domination: Politics, Rhetoric, and Symbols in Contemporary Syria.* Chicago: University of Chicago Press.

Whibley, Leonard. 1889. *Political Parties in Athens during the Peloponnesian War.* Cambridge: Cambridge University Press.

White, Jonathan, and Lea Ypi. 2016. *The Meaning of Partisanship.* Oxford: Oxford University Press.

Wiens, David. 2016. "Assessing Ideal Theories: Lessons from the Theory of Second Best." *Politics, Philosophy & Economics* 15 (2): 132–49.

Wilentz, Sean. 2016. *The Politicians and the Egalitarians: The Hidden History of American Politics.* New York: Norton.

Williams, David. 2004. *Condorcet and Modernity.* Cambridge: Cambridge University Press.

Wilson, Woodrow. 1908. *Constitutional Government in the United States.* New York: Columbia University Press.

Wolkenstein, Fabio. 2019. *Rethinking Party Reform.* Oxford: Oxford University Press.

Wood, Allen W. 2014. *The Free Development of Each: Studies on Freedom, Right, and Ethics in Classical German Philosophy.* Oxford: Oxford University Press.

Yakobson, Alexander. 1992. "Petitio et largitio: Popular participation in the Centuriate Assembly of the Late Republic." *Journal of Roman Studies* 82:32–52.

———. 1995. "Secret Ballot and Its Effects in the Late Roman Republic." *Hermes* 123 (H. 4): 426–42.

———. 1999. Elections and Electioneering in Rome: A Study in the Political System of the Late Republic. Vol. 128. Stuttgart: Franz Steiner Verlag.

Yang, Calvin. 2020. "Singapore GE2020: WP Chief Pritam Singh Says Its Goal Is Not to Needle the PAP, Acknowledges Hard Task of Creating Jobs." *Straits Times*, July 4, 2020. https://www.straitstimes.com/politics /singapore-ge2020-wp-chief-pritam-singh-says-its-goal-is-not-to-needle- the-pap-acknowledges.

Yew, Lee Kuan. 2005. "Spiegel Interview with Singapore's Lee Kuan Yew: 'It's Stupid to Be Afraid.'" *Der Spiegel*, August 8, 2005.

Ziblatt, Daniel. 2018. "Fully agree america was NOT a democracy pre 1965, let alone 1860." Twitter, January 29, 2018. https://twitter.com/dziblatt /status/957973270539718657.

Index